Education, Equality, and Justice
in the New Normal

Also available from Bloomsbury:

Echoes from Freire for a Critically Engaged Pedagogy, Peter Mayo
Educating for Peace and Human Rights: An Introduction, Maria Hantzopoulos
and Monisha Bajaj
On Critical Pedagogy, Henry A. Giroux
Pedagogy, Politics and Philosophy of Peace: Interrogating Peace and Peacemaking,
edited by Carmel Borg and Michael Grech
Politics and Pedagogy in the "Post-Truth" Era: Insurgent Philosophy and Praxis,
Derek R. Ford
*Postdigital Dialogues on Critical Pedagogy, Liberation Theology and Information
Technology,* Peter McLaren and Petar Jandric
Race, Class and Educational Reform: Critical International Dialogues, edited by
Antonia Darder, Cleveland Hayes II and Howard Ryan
Race, Education and Educational Leadership in England edited by Paul Miller
and Christine Callender
Race, Politics and Pandemic Pedagogy: Education in a Time of Crisis,
Henry A. Giroux
Reinventing Pedagogy of the Oppressed: Contemporary Critical Perspectives,
James D. Kirylo
The Student Guide to Freire's "Pedagogy of the Oppressed", Antonia Darder
*Transnational Perspectives on Democracy, Citizenship, Human Rights and Peace
Education* edited by Mary Drinkwater, Fazal Rizvi and Karen Edge

Education, Equality, and Justice in the New Normal

Global Responses to the Pandemic

Edited by
Inny Accioly and Donaldo Macedo

BLOOMSBURY ACADEMIC
LONDON • NEW YORK • OXFORD • NEW DELHI • SYDNEY

BLOOMSBURY ACADEMIC
Bloomsbury Publishing Plc
50 Bedford Square, London, WC1B 3DP, UK
1385 Broadway, New York, NY 10018, USA
29 Earlsfort Terrace, Dublin 2, Ireland

BLOOMSBURY, BLOOMSBURY ACADEMIC and the Diana logo are trademarks of
Bloomsbury Publishing Plc

First published in Great Britain 2022

Cover design: Charlotte James
Cover image: My little sister © Birungi Arnold

A catalogue record for this book is available from the British Library.

A catalogue record for this book is available from the Library of Congress.

Library of Congress Cataloging-in-Publication Data
Names: Accioly, Inny, editor. | Macedo, Donaldo P. (Donaldo Pereira), 1950- editor.
Title: Education, equality and justice in the new normal: global responses to the
pandemic / edited by Inny Accioly and Donaldo Macedo.
Description: London; New York, NY: Bloomsbury Academic, 2021. | Includes bibliographical
references. | Identifiers: LCCN 2021010177 (print) | LCCN 2021010178 (ebook) | ISBN
9781350225770 (paperback) | ISBN 9781350225763 (hardback) | ISBN 9781350225787
(ebook) | ISBN 9781350225794 (epub)
Subjects: LCSH: Educational equalization. | Social justice and education. | Discrimination in
education. | Privatization in education. | Social distancing (Public health) and education.
Classification: LCC LC213 .E376 2021 (print) | LCC LC213 (ebook) | DDC 379.2/6–dc23

LC record available at https://lccn.loc.gov/2021010177
LC ebook record available at https://lccn.loc.gov/2021010178

ISBN: HB: 978-1-3502-2576-3
PB: 978-1-3502-2577-0
ePDF: 978-1-3502-2578-7
eBook: 978-1-3502-2579-4

Typeset by Deanta Global Publishing Services, Chennai, India
Printed and bound in Great Britain

To find out more about our authors and books visit www.bloomsbury.com and
sign up for our newsletters.

TO

Paulo Freire
whose classic book, Pedagogy of the Oppressed,
challenges all conscientious beings to have the
courage to develop critical awareness so as to
denounce the barbarism of market forces that
subjugate millions of people to the violence of
hunger, to the indignities of homelessness, and to
asphyxiation caused either by the knee of a white
policeman or the pervasive denial of a ventilator.
Beyond a language of critique, the victims of systemic
racism, misogyny, and cruel market exploitation
require and also deserve a language of possibility
that translate into agency as subject of history
who can reimagine life with dignity, steeped in a
radical love that always births hope.

Contents

Illustrations

Figure

Table

Foreword

Antonia Darder

There is no return to normal, the new "normal" will have to be constructed on the ruins of our old lives, or we will find ourselves in a new barbarism whose signs are already clearly discernible.

—Slavoj Žižek, 2020[1]

Over the last year, we have been subjected to a surreal global landscape, which has effectively intensified human alienation. On an unprecedented scale, face masks, social distancing, and life as virtual existence demarcates the rhetorical and practical terrain of the "new normal." Everywhere we turn, the well-worn cliché of the new normal bombards our sensibilities, whether we are discussing conditions of education, health care, labor, or simply navigating everyday social life. Yet, there is nothing normal about living under the extreme antisocial conditions of lockdown, where one cannot comfort a loved one in hospital or even attend their funeral should they die. Or, where so many live in increasing precarity as they struggle to survive conditions for which the majority of the world's governments appeared utterly unprepared, despite global scientific warnings that a pandemic of this magnitude was not only possible, but imminent.

The "new normal," as a cliché or standardized code of expression, functions to distance us from reality, as Hannah Arendt[2] correctly suggests, and to obscure the old ruins that underlie current conditions worldwide. A microscopic lifeform has not created a "new normal." What we are facing today, simply put, is a massive amplification of conditions that so many around the world have been subjected to, at the hands of economic tyranny for centuries. By promoting the pretense that we are now entering into a new historical moment caused by the coronavirus, the architects of unparalleled economic inequalities and societal exclusions can not only abdicate themselves of responsibility for neoliberal atrocities, but also displace their responsibility for societal problems onto the victims of material exploitation and ruthless militarism. Throughout this pandemic, for example, conservative politicians in the United Sates, Brazil,

India, Hungary, and other nations have exploited the outbreak, scapegoating the most marginalized populations.[3] Meanwhile, neoconservative discourses of the "new normal" ignore neoliberalism's forty years of planetary plunder—plunder fueled by transnational corporate greed and state sanctioned indifference to the well-being of humanity and the environment.

Accordingly, mainstream media representations of the "new normal" have ushered the public into an illusory world of viral happenstance. Sensationalize stories related to the excruciating impact of Covid-19 are aired repeatedly by news anchors, with appropriate sentimental pretense, while news coverage of millions of people marching on the streets of Chile or the largest historical battle against neoliberal policies being waged by Indian farmers is systematically blocked from the airwaves. The mainstream media's efforts to veil people's struggles against their political and economic oppression illustrate how public discourses of the wealthy and powerful are arbitrarily marshaled, as Arendt argues, "against reality"[4] to conceal the deceptive entanglement of political economic forces responsible for the majority of human suffering. In direct contrast, those who publicly expose the deception and shenanigans of political figures and public institutions are deemed enemies of the state, as is the case of Wikileaks founder, Julian Assange; former US soldier Chelsea Manning; and former Central Intelligence Agency employee, Edward Snowden. Through legally sanctioned mechanisms, incontrovertible issues, and concerns about the political and economic actions of governments and transnational corporations remain hidden, while draconian policies are pushed through without critical analysis, democratic participation, or public debate.

In direct contrast, Accioly and Macedo's volume, *Education, Equality, and Justice in the New Normal,* openly interrogates critical questions related to schooling and society, questions that sit heavy on the minds and hearts of revolutionary educators, researchers, and activists the world over. At the center of their argument is the realization that ahistorical or apolitical examinations of the "new normal" will utterly fail to produce analyses or solutions capable of transforming global conditions of crisis. Also, well highlighted are the unchecked neoliberal excesses that set the political stage for the current crisis; a crisis whose catastrophic seeds were sown when the industrialized north set as its aim to subdue indigenous and racialized populations considered less human than themselves and to conquer the natural world. Their economic pursuits were carried out through an oppressive ideology of global conquest that "fetishized money and turned people into objects to be exploited."[5] This rule by capital

is at the root of the disastrous global conditions that predominate today—
longstanding conditions of Western imperialism

Contempt and a New Barbarism

*There are so many ways of being despicable it quite makes one's head spin. But
the way to be really despicable is to be contemptuous of other people's pain.*
                                                            —James Baldwin[6]

Over the last four decades, contemptuous policies of advanced capitalism have
led to unrelenting economic speculation and despicable extraction of natural
and human resources, leaving the majority of the world's population scrambling
for crumbs. In the midst of global traditions of empire building, human suffering
has for centuries been met by the contempt of the ruling class. Espousing a
neoliberal ethos, the contemporary builders of empires enlist bootstrap ideals
of individual responsibility, cut-throat competition, and the doctrine of "small
government" to promote the glories of privatization and defend their global
profiteering schemes. Even within the prayer halls of many traditional religious
institutions, fatalistic notions of poverty conserve a victim-blaming ideology,
which over the ages has absolved the barbarism of the ruling elite.

With cart blanche impunity, neoliberal advocates have sought to push
back hard-earned public health resources, educational spending, and labor
protections, while moving fiercely to privatize health care and education and
block the influence of trade union organizations. Ironically, this willful neglect
of the public welfare resulted in the woeful failure of conservative governments
to respond swiftly to the viral crisis. And, despite racialized allegations that
fault China, the global spread of Covid-19 has been largely due the disdain of
neoliberal pursuits, which have privileged the needs of capital over the needs
of people. Moreover, global financial policies and speculative initiatives of the
north are profoundly implicated in this unprecedented global health crisis, given
the role these have played in producing and perpetuating appalling levels of
poverty and environmental destruction worldwide.

For much of 2020, conservative governments and their economic advisers
along with business and corporate officials vacillated about the severity of the
virus, its global impact, and the actions to be taken. A culture of denial, which
for so long has hijacked debates about the welfare state and the environment,
contributed to the making of the viral crisis. In 2016, for example, Exercise

Cygnus, a government sponsored exercise, carried out to assess the readiness of the National Health Service (NHS) in the face of a viral respiratory pandemic, accurately predicted the chaos of the last year, including the huge shortage of ventilators. The report was never published and its recommendations were ignored.[7] Similarly, for Scientists at the Harvard School of Public Health,[8] the pandemic was not a surprise. In fact, they warned that many of the underlying causes of climate change were increasing the risk of global pandemics, of which Covid-19 will not be the last. Capital-led deforestation in the rainforests of the South America and Asia has been associated with climate warming and the loss of habitat, increasing the spread of harmful infection by animals that become displaced. High carbon producing livestock farms are also sources for spillover of life-threatening infections. True to scientific prediction, the coronavirus has resulted in over 100 million cases worldwide, with 2.3 million deaths[9] in one year, more deaths than all wars in the twentieth century combined or any other pandemic in history.[10]

As various contributors to this volume correctly argue, current disparities are the result of preexisting structural inequalities that have consistently perpetuated and reproduced conditions of impoverishment and anguish among subaltern populations. Conservative politicians in the United States, Brazil, India, Hungary, and other nations have exploited the fears generated by the pandemic to scapegoat the most marginalized populations.[11] Immigrants or refugees seeking safe harbor or adequate labor to ensure their families' safety and survival are portrayed as irresponsible viral spreaders, while the geopolitical circumstances of why people are forced to migrate are whitewashed in the media. Similarly, rather than to critically interrogate the underlying causes of the heightened crisis faced by Black and other racialized communities, mainstream television reporting on the pandemic exploited their grief as colonizing fodder for television audiences.

Yet, by and large, mainstream discourses of the "new normal" ignore the unprecedented demise of planetary safeguards during the last forty years. This is the product of transnational corporate greed and state sanctioned indifference to the destruction of the environment. Gross deficits in public health and environmental sanitation, consequences of neoliberal neglect,[12] have exacerbated the situation and made life more precarious for millions of people today. Chronic conditions of economic injustice have not only set off a global health crisis, along with its similar devastating impact on education and worker conditions, but also highlighted growing cleavages in political, economic, and racialized inequalities across societies. Globally, the gap between the rich and the poor continues to widen, with the racialized wealth gap today higher than it was in the 1960s[13] and global inequality between countries mirroring the 1800s.[14]

Extreme inequality is rampant. According to Oxfam[15,16] 8 men own more wealth than 3.6 billion people. The richest 1 percent have more than twice as much wealth as 6.9 billion people, while almost half of humanity survives on $5.50 a day. It is not surprising then that Black, Latino, Asian, Indigenous, and other racialized populations globally are facing overwhelming negative consequences associated with Covid-19 and its variants in our communities, where statistics show staggering disparities in infection rates and death rates of up to four times greater, compared to our white counterparts.[17] Moreover, for people with learning disabilities, who have always been considered problematic to capitalist accumulation, rates of death have been reported to be six times greater.[18]

In the wealthiest country, 30–40 million Americans today are facing the risks of the Covid-19 home eviction crisis,[19] a number bound to be worse in less affluent regions of the world. And, while predictions warn that evictions are likely to increase rates of homelessness,[20] city officials across the United States are demolishing homeless encampments in the midst of bitter cold weather.[21] Many from racialized communities continue to live in segregated overcrowded housing conditions or toil in crowded workplaces, which makes physical distancing and self-isolation difficult. Inadequate health care often leads to little access to vaccinations, if available. Late diagnosis also makes Black and other subaltern populations more susceptible to complications of coronavirus infection.[22] Not to mention, workers of color disproportionately hold essential jobs in health and social care, retail, public transport, and other sectors, putting them at higher risk of exposure.

One in ten people on the planet is severely undernourished. Food insecurity worldwide is increasing, as global food prices in 2020 reached a six-year high.[23] In the United States, the wealthiest country on the planet, 54 million people are currently facing food insecurity amid massive public health and economic crisis.[24] Not surprising, food insecurity has intensified since the elimination of federal assistance programs in the United States. The United Nations World Food Program predicts acute hunger may affect another 270 million people— an 82 percent increase since the start of the pandemic.[25] These deplorable levels of world hunger, when contrasted with the shocking levels of economic inequality noted earlier, reflect neoliberalism's contemptuous neglect for the most vulnerable, a disproportionate number who are women and children.

In education, over a billion children have been affected worldwide by the move to virtual learning, where racialized inequalities in digital access have widened the preexisting divide.[26] Many students living in poverty have limited or no access to internet services or to computers. In seventy-one countries worldwide, less than half the population has internet access. Despite this disparity, 73 percent of governments out of 127 reporting countries are employing online platforms to deliver education, while schools remain closed. In the majority of countries across Africa, less than a quarter of the population has internet access. Yet, students, already besieged by unrealistic norms of neoliberal accountability, are expected to learn virtually through even more disconnected forms of prescribed curricula, despite inadequate preparation, resources, or hands-on assistance. Teachers have also been found to be drastically unprepared to critically engage with the limitations of online teaching,[27] widening the already existing educational inequalities worldwide.

Similarly, the viral crisis has intensified the digital divide for small shop owners, particularly from subaltern communities of the Global South.[28] In countries of the Global North, people often assume everyone has high speed internet access and therefore, moving from doing business face to face to virtually, is simply a matter of a little training. However, when small shop owners in Latin America, for example, work face to face, the nearest access to internet is miles away, and they cannot afford a smart phone or computer; inequalities of technology are made profoundly evident. In stark contrast, the online transnational corporation, Amazon (owned by the wealthiest individual, Jeff Bezos, worth $113 billion[29]) has capitalized on the digital divide to become one of the few enterprises to boast its best year ever, with over $21 billion net income in 2020.[30] While most small shop owners have had to close down or are pessimistic that they can survive the crisis, they remain afraid that the crisis will further thwart their future economic survival. Relatedly, millions of freelance cultural workers and performing artists have been especially hard hit, given not only the existing fragility of their lives and livelihoods, but also the failure of governments to adequately comprehend the precarity of cultural labor or acknowledge performance work as legitimate work.[31]

Likewise, workers typified as low-skill, many who are women and/or of color, have also shouldered disproportionately the burden of the pandemic, losing jobs or being laid-off or furloughed with inadequate resources.[32] Current government failures have also resulted in an indirect attack on women, in that nearly half of all working women today labor in low-paying jobs. The share of workers who earn low wages is also higher among Black woman and other women of color than it is among white women. Transnationally, women have borne the brunt of the Covid-19 crisis, as they are the ones expected to do the extra work necessary to accommodate massive losses associated with government cuts to health care and education.

There is no question that these conditions reflect deep structural inequalities in the United States and other parts of the world, which have led to the disappearance of individual and collective rights for workers and subaltern populations, within a context of increasing precarity and uncertainty. And, even when oppositional national discourses by progressive politicians such as Bernie Sanders, Elizabeth Warner, or Jeremy Corbyn to champion refunding of education, health, and other public services, neoconservative responses worldwide echoed the Tory refrain, "There is no magic money tree"—that is, until they needed it for themselves.[33] Subsequently, in the midst of massive conditions of inequality, neoliberal governments funneled trillions of dollars to private corporations to preserve grossly unjust national economies—economies where mass poverty is not an aberration but a fundamental necessity. As such, workers were expected to pay (often with their lives) for a pandemic produced by the hand of capital. These signs of the new barbarism, as Žižek[34] suggests, not only highlight racialized, gendered, and working-class inequalities, but also make it undeniably evident that the greatest crisis to humanity is not Covid-19, but global capitalism.

A Crisis of Humanity

We truly face a crisis of humanity. Our very survival depends on us at the very least curbing the excesses of the out-of-control system of global capitalism, if not its outright overthrow.

—William I. Robinson[35]

With a deeply courageous and politically radical commitment, *Education, Equality, and Justice in the New Normal* not only calls out, in forthright measures, the undeniable betrayal of democracy, but also exposes the wretched global betrayal of humanity by the wealthy and powerful. Without mincing words, the contributors to this volume openly challenge the systematic dismantling of the welfare state, where the rule of the marketplace has ruthlessly trampled upon any formerly held social consensus of government responsibility to the people. In its place, the indiscriminate privatization of public institutions prevails, with education, health care, the environment, food and water resources, and even prisons converted into money-making ventures. In a variety of ways, the book speaks to how a neoliberal ideology of unchecked authoritarianism and financial gluttony continues to drive the global agenda of ruling elites, as neoliberal governments concern themselves with the health of the economy, over the health of people.

Bottomline here is that there is no fix for global capitalism. The "post-welfare state model of social order that celebrates unhindered markets as the most effective means of achieving economic growth and public welfare"[36] is unequivocally bankrupt to any vision of equality or justice before, during, or after the "new normal." The shameful mishandling of the coronavirus crisis has made this blatantly visible, particularly in the debacle surrounding lack of personal protection equipment for health-care workers and insufficient ventilators for patients suffering from Covid-19. Yet, the same market logic is driving the development and distribution of vaccinations. Rather than coming together in global solidarity as an international community concerned for the well-being of human life worldwide, competitive market reasoning persists among Covid-19 vaccine players who will split $100 billion in sales and $40 billion in profits.[37] For the pharmaceutical transnational Moderna, which charges the most per dose ($25–27), far from being the nightmare experienced by most, the pandemic has proven to be a corporate goldmine. And, as would be expected, wealthier countries readily secured the majority of vaccines available, while global populations most in need had considerably less access.[38] Beyond access, the cost of the vaccine to different countries is of concern. South Africa, the worse hit nation on the continent, for example, is being charged 2.5 times more than European countries for doses of the Oxford-AstraZeneca Covid-19 vaccine.[39] Thus, even with a potential treatment in sight, the world is bound to emerge from this dreadful chapter of history more unequal than ever,[40] unless people worldwide rise up collectively to oppose global policies and ways of life that ultimately promote our despair.

The Indisputable Power of Hope

Hope is essential to any political struggle for radical change when the overall social climate promotes disillusionment and despair.

—bell hooks (2008)[41]

The power of hope, as an essential ingredient for radical struggle, is summoned repeatedly across the pages of *Education, Equality, and Justice in the New Normal.* Despite various strident critiques of the historical and contemporary conditions faced worldwide, the authors of this book refuse to surrender their social agency or their faith in the people to transform the course of history. In the spirit of Freire, they recognize the power that a pedagogy of hope brings to the struggle for radical social change, whether struggles are in the classroom or in the streets. As hooks argues, hope is a necessary component if we are to radically counter, within schools or society, the forces of patriarchy, material oppression, and racism intensified under neoliberal rule. For the contributors here, education does not occur in a vacuum. It is a political endeavor for liberation, in which we critically unveil the conditions that shape the lives of teachers, students, and their communities and seek avenues for reinvention.

Moreover, the power of hope is even more essential to our political struggles against global economic tyranny, where stark inequalities are politically explosive and, to the extent that the system is unable and unwilling to reverse them, it turns to ever more violent forms of containment. Increasing state control over people's lives, therefore, is bound to reflect the global capitalist reality of the "new normal," particularly as governments more fiercely seek to impede the mass movement and protests of people on the streets. With this in mind, this book is a radical call to action, if we are even to dream of a more just and equal post-pandemic world. As such, Accioly and Macedo argue passionately for an education that is life-affirming, where students everywhere can experience the democratic conditions to develop their critical abilities as citizens of the world, who are prepared to freely engage their lived histories with self-determination, to embrace an abiding promise to global justice, and to commit to labor together as freedom fighters and loving architects of a truly just world.

The African revolutionary leader, Amilcar Cabral firmly believed that all political struggles for liberation commence with the courage to dream of a world that does not yet exist. It is this ardent spirit of hope and faith in the possibility of human beings to transform the world, which is profoundly reflected in images, stories, protests, and chants of three key examples, where millions of people last year put their lives on the line for a collective dream. People worldwide took to the streets in support of Black Lives Matter protests against the Minneapolis police killing of George Floyd, an unarmed Black man. The force of BLM protests not only intensified national debates in the United States, but also sparked much needed international debates about anti-Black racism. The far-reaching influence of the BLM movement underscored growing multinational resistance to state sanctioned racism, particularly against Black men and women around the world. In Bristol, for example, British protesters felled a statue commemorating Edward Colston, a seventeenth-century slave trader. This public defiance generated debates about racism and history, in a country where over 8 million people today identify as Black, Asian, minority, ethnic (BAME).

The violent US-backed overthrow of democratically elected President Allende in the 1970s brought into power Pinochet, one of the earliest proponents of neoliberalism. Along with a repressive state apparatus, the dictatorship swiftly put into place an extreme free market system of large-scale privatization. After years of unprecedented levels of austerity measures, state repression, and human rights violations, the people of Chile waged a mass struggle of resistance against the current government. Beginning in 2019, hundreds of thousands of people effectively launched a social uprising across sectors of the population in opposition of the Piñera government. At street protests, chanting "*El pueblo unido jamas sera vencido!,*"[42] the masses stood firm in their demand for not only changes to the national constitution, but the end of state repression. The people called for explicitly incorporating into the constitution social rights related to public education, health care, housing, employment, and prison reform, in an effort to end the brutal legacy of Pinochet's dictatorship. In October 2020, after a grueling year of national political struggle, 78 percent of the people of Chile democratically voted to approve the rewriting of the Chilean constitution.

Currently in India, farmers are continuing to wage one of the largest political strikes in the history of the world in response to neoliberal-inspired laws. On November 2020, 250 million people marched to Delhi to join a general strike in defiance of the Modi government's refusal to rescind initiatives aimed at a program of agrarian "modernization" that would result in the takeover of the nation's agricultural production by large transnational corporations, destroying the independent livelihood of small farmers, who comprise 56 percent of India's workforce. The farmer's astonishing level of solidarity and organizational commitment has been accomplished through their deep faith in the collective power of workers united, despite a lack of economic resources.

These constitute three inspiring and significant examples of contemporary political struggles in the flesh, which illustrate how the power of hope is absolutely indispensable to political struggle. Moreover, as we ponder on these examples, we can surmise that longstanding neoliberal assaults by racialized global capital against democratic efforts to build a humanizing and just social order is now generating a fierce global class war between the haves-and-have-nots. As the inhumane ideology of capital continues to fail people around the world, it is only a matter of time before the pendulum swings and the political struggles—of trade unionists, climate change activists, women in struggle, peace groups, and other revolutionary organizations around the world—will coalesces, with boots on ground, to fight against the inhumanity manufactured by global capitalism. Our human survival and the survival of the planet, indeed, depends on nothing less than a worldwide political movement to end the barbarism of capital rule. This demands not only the reinvention of a new meaning of education, but reimagining a life-affirming, just, and loving global existence—a world where life is exceedingly more important than the profit margins of the powerful. This exceptional volume represents a powerful step in that direction.

Contributors

Inny Accioly is Professor of Education at the Fluminense Federal University, Brazil. Her research interests focus on critical pedagogy in a multidisciplinary perspective that relates environmental education, grassroots movements, policy analysis, and international and comparative education. She is coeditor of *Commodifying Education: Theoretical and Methodological Aspects of Financialization of Education Policies* in Brazil (2016).

Iván Salinas Barrios is Assistant Professor at Departamento de Estudios Pedagógicos in Universidad de Chile, Chile. He is also Researcher at Fundación Nodo XXI, Chile. His research interests include teaching and learning, and teaching and teacher education.

Carmel Borg is Associate Professor at the University of Malta, Malta. A former dean of the Faculty of Education, he currently heads the Department of Arts, Open Communities and Adult Education. His research interests, as well as writings, focus on critical pedagogy, education for social justice, adult education, museum education, and curriculum development. He is the founding editor of the Malta Review of Educational Research (MRER) and the editor of the Education Research Monograph Series (ERMS).

Daniel Renaud Camargo is an artist, popular educator, and doctoral candidate in Community Psychosociology and Social Ecology at the Federal University of Rio de Janeiro, Brazil. He is a researcher in the Laboratory of Memories, Territories and Occupations (LABMEMS-UFRJ) and in the Research Group of Environmental Education Desde el Sur (GEASur). He has worked with traditional communities in Brazil for ten years.

Noam Chomsky is Laureate Professor in the Department of Linguistics at the University of Arizona, Tucson, USA, and Professor Emeritus at the Massachusetts Institute of Technology, USA, where he taught for more than half a century. His recent books include *Requiem for the American Dream: The 10 Principles of Concentration of Wealth & Power* (2017) and *Global Discontents: Conversations on the Rising Threats to Democracy, Who Rules the World?* (2018).

M. Beatriz Fernández is Assistant Professor in the Institute of Education and Center for Advanced Research in Education at Universidad de Chile, Chile.

Ourania Filippakou is Reader in Education and Director of Teaching and Learning at Brunel University London, UK. She holds a PhD from the UCL Institute of Education, University College London, UK, and her research is focused primarily on the politics of higher education. Her most recent book, coauthored with Ted Tapper, is *Creating the Future? The 1960s New English Universities* (2019). She is coeditor of the British Educational Research Journal.

Henry A. Giroux is Professor of Public Interest and the Paulo Freire Distinguished Scholar in Critical Pedagogy at McMaster University, Canada. His latest book is *Race, Politics, and Pandemic Pedagogy: Education in a Time of Crisis* (2021).

Amy Goodman is the host and executive producer of Democracy Now!, a national award-winning news program airing on 1,400 public television and radio stations worldwide. She has coauthored six New York Times bestsellers, including her latest book, *Democracy Now! Twenty Years Covering the Movements Changing America* (2016). Her many publications include *The Silence Majority: Stories of Uprisings, Resistance and Hope* (2012) and *Breaking the Sound Barrier* (2009), both written with Denis Moynihan, give voice to the many people standing up to corporate and government power.

Luiz Katu is a Potiguara chief who coordinates the Indigenous Peoples Articulation of the State of Rio Grande do Norte, Brazil. He led a movement to found indigenous schools in Rio Grande do Norte, where he teaches ethnohistory at the João Lino da Silva and the Alfredo Lima indigenous schools. Luiz Katu created the oldest traditional indigenous celebration in his state, the potato party in the Katu village. He also works with ethno-tourism.

Roberto Leher is Professor in the Faculty of Education and the Graduate Program in Education at the Federal University of Rio de Janeiro, Brazil. In 2014, he was elected Rector of the Federal University of Rio de Janeiro, Brazil, and held the position until 2018. He coordinates the Collective of Studies in Marxism and Education (COLEMARX) and is a collaborator in the Florestan Fernandes National School, which is coordinated by the Landless Workers Movement.

Andrea Lira is a feminist activist and doctoral candidate in Curriculum and Teaching at Teachers College, Columbia University, USA. She coordinates the Centro de Liderazgo en Educación at the Universidad de Magallanes, Chile.

Carlos Frederico B. Loureiro is Professor in the Faculty of Education and the Graduate Program in Education at the Federal University of Rio de Janeiro, Brazil. He coordinates the Research Laboratory in Education, Environment and Society (LIEAS) and has authored more than 300 publications, including books, chapters, and articles. He currently advises public agencies for environmental education policies.

Donaldo Macedo is Professor Emeritus and Distinguished Professor of Liberal Arts and Education at the University of Massachusetts Boston, USA. He is coauthor with Paulo Freire of *Literacy: Reading the World and the Word* (1987). His other publications include *Imposed Democracy: Dialogues with Noam Chomsky and Paulo Freire* (2012) and *Literacies of Power: What Americans Are Not Allowed to Know* (2006).

Sheila L. Macrine is Professor at the University of Massachusetts Dartmouth, USA. Her research has two arcs: first, she connects cultural, political, and institutional contexts of pedagogy related to the public sphere, democratic education, and social imagination; second, her empirical work involves embodied cognition, assessment, and the learning sciences. She has published numerous articles and published a number of books on critical pedagogy, including the second edition of her award-winning book *Critical Pedagogy in Uncertain Times: Hope and Possibilities*, and the forthcoming *Transnational Feminist Politics, Education, and Social Justice* (2021).

Stavros Malichudis is a reporter covering the refugee crisis in Greece for Solomon, an Athens-based investigative outlet, and international media. In 2019 he was a fellow of the Balkan Fellowship for Journalistic Excellence (BFJE).

Peter Mayo is Professor in the Department of Arts, Open Communities and Adult Education at the University of Malta, Malta. His research focuses on adult education, sociology of education, higher education, and museum education.

Mariateresa Muraca is a postdoctoral researcher at the Pará State University, Brazil, Professor at the Don Giorgio Pratesi University Institute, Italy, and Temporary Lecturer at the University of Verona, Italy, and at the Progetto Uomo

University Institute, Italy. She is the project manager in the Monte Sole Peace School for International Cooperation Projects in Gorongosa, Mozambique, and is scientific co-director of Educazione Aperta journal.

Iliana Papangeli is the managing director of Solomon, an Athens-based, non-profit, independent, investigative digital media outlet, with a focus on migration and refugee issues. She studied psychology and philosophy at the University of Ioannina, Greece, and completed a master's degree in social anthropology at the University of Aberdeen, UK. She is currently a PhD candidate in Social Anthropology at Panteion University, Greece, and is conducting her fieldwork on the island of Lesvos, exploring refugees' death and its particular presence in sharing physical and spectral environments with the living.

Celso Sánchez is poet, musician, environmental activist, and associate professor at the Federal University of the State of Rio de Janeiro, Brazil, in the School of Education, where he coordinates the Research Group of Environmental Education Desde el Sur (GEASur). He has worked with indigenous communities for more than twenty years.

Georgios Tsiakalos is Professor Emeritus of Pedagogy at the Aristotle University of Thessaloniki, Greece. His research and publications cover the fields of population genetics, critique of sociobiology, racism, social exclusion and poverty, education of minorities and immigrant, and educational reforms. He is an activist for the human and social rights of minorities, refugees, and the socially excluded; fighter against the far-right; and the founder of the "Pedagogues of Solidarity" initiative.

Paolo Vittoria is Professor of Pedagogy at the Federico II University of Naples, Italy. He also teaches Museum Didactics at the Accademia di Belle Arti of Naples and Philosophy of Education at the Don Giorgio Pratesi University Institute, Italy. He was a Professor at the Federal University of Rio de Janeiro, Brazil, from 2010 to 2017. He co-directs the *Educazione Aperta Journal* and collaborates with *Il Manifesto* newspaper.

Moving Beyond the Slow Death of Neoliberalism to a Life-Centered Education

An Introduction

Inny Accioly and Donaldo Macedo

The chapters in this volume invite policymakers, activists, educators, school administrators, and others to consider the role of education as central to the ever-increasing and complex social problems that have been exacerbated by the coronavirus pandemic crisis. We deeply believe that the coronavirus pandemic and its educational and societal ramifications cannot be comprehended through an amorphous approach that reduces the danger that we face worldwide to biology and medical threats alone. The editors and the contributing authors challenge readers instead to engage in critical analyses of how multiple countries address the economic, political, biological, and educational crises in which the coronavirus became the flashpoint that unveiled how capitalism, particularly through neoliberalism and its "*Godification*" of the market, had been exploiting and ravaging the planet to the degree that could only lead to its eventual unsustainability. That is, what became clear is that the market-centric response arising from this savage variant of capitalism has been unable to stop the spread of the virus, failing even to "grapple with a deadly pandemic of animal origin that has killed more than a million people, infected 63 million more [so far], and thrown millions more out of work."[1] Thus, in order to fully understand the architecture of the current pandemic and prevent future catastrophes, we need to move beyond the historical amnesia that offers selective views of reality, interpreted almost always from the dominant developed nations' perspectives and imposed through their rigid control of education and a compliant media. Under neoliberalism, these institutions are charged primarily with domesticating the mind of citizens rather than providing the necessary critical tools that would enable them to make the necessary linkages in order to develop a more comprehensive understanding of reality. The ability to make linkages would also enable individuals to answer Amy Goodman's question posed to Noam Chomsky in this volume: "How did the United States—the richest country in the world—become the worldwide epicenter of the coronavirus outbreak, with one person dying of COVID-19 every 47 seconds?" (Goodman and Chomsky 2021: this volume, p. 15).

What we cannot deny is that market solutions to social and health problems have not been able to effectively stop the coronavirus and its subsequent ravages—ravages that have had disastrous adverse impacts on nonwhite and lower-class populations and dependent economies. From Brazil to India and the United States, socially and economically disadvantaged ethnic groups have had a higher mortality rate due to the coronavirus contagion. African Americans and Latinx communities in the United States, especially those trapped in inner-city ghettos and lower-class whites who have been sentenced to generational cycles of poverty, experience both higher rates of contagion and death and less access to quality health care and education. This is due to the grave economic inequality birthed by policies that promote market deregulation, state welfare provisions for the business class, and the hollowing out of the social contract, and systemic racism.

The spread of human misery throughout the world has been not just triggered by the coronavirus contagion, but by policymakers worldwide who have embraced Milton Friedman's neoliberal edict that claims "the social responsibility of business is to increase its profits" (Friedman 1970). As this suggests, private enterprise's main preoccupation is not only to increase shareholder profits but also to hijack the state's social responsibility—its safeguarding of the public good—and in doing so enshrine a kind of leadership that abdicates any ethical and moral responsibility for the general public. Hence, neoliberalism of the type embraced by Margaret Thatcher and Ronald Reagan was imposed on the citizens of their respective countries and on dependent economies under the rubric of "free trade," which "cleverly hides, or seeks to cloud over, an intensified new edition of that fearful evil that is historical capitalism, even if the new edition is somewhat modified in the relation to the past versions" (Freire 1998: 114).

In other words, while we are not living in the Gilded Age of the Robber Barons such as the Rockefellers, Carnegie Mellon, and other members of the cabal whose private wealth increased in proportion to their unfettered and ruthless business practices, the absence of an ethical and moral compass in the neoliberal economic framework that has enabled the world's richest people, in some instances, to quintuple their fortune. This continued during a global pandemic, while the poor lower classes, and particularly nonwhites, scrambled to not go hungry or avoid eviction so as to adhere to policymakers' mandate to avoid the coronavirus contagion by sheltering in. Consider the obscene increase of personal wealth during the pandemic exemplified by Elon Musk, the owner of the Tesla car company and SpaceX enterprise, who "has quintupled his net worth since January [2020] . . . adding 132 billion to his wealth and vaulting him to the No.2 spot among the world's richest with a fortune of about $159 billion."[2] The real difference between the old Gilded Age and the New Gilded Age ushered in by neoliberalism is that the new billionaire class is more numerous and has exceedingly more political power. As blatantly stated by Elon Musk himself, when questioned about the United States' long history of exacting coups d'état in foreign democratic elections that are not in line with US foreign policy goals, he irreverently replied: "we will coup whoever we want. Deal with it."[3]

The Slow Death under Neoliberalism

The pandemic emerged in the midst of the slow death of the social contract which was brought on by neoliberal *laissez faire* approaches to government which, since the 1970s, have led inexorably to increasing deregulation, massive tax cuts for billionaires, and the pauperization of the lower classes. Hence, we need to situate the analysis of the current pandemic within a more comprehensive view of the intersecting factors that gave rise to the coronavirus pandemic in the first place, and how these factors interacted to produce the political context that has propelled the worldwide rise of the ultra-conservative right and its lethal racism (in Brazil, the United States, the United Kingdom, among other countries). The widening of the wealth inequality gap had, in fact, triggered a wave of street protests that preceded the pandemic, and notably a labor dispute in France that paralyzed the country. In most developed nations and developing countries such as Brazil, draconian cuts to education and health-care services, and divestment in housing, have led the world to unprecedented turmoil, particularly when austerity measures dictated by the world's oligarch class and their governing managers have been implemented. As Amy Goodman and Noam Chomsky make abundantly clear in their contribution to this volume, we must avoid the fragmentation of interconnected factors so as to comprehend the inevitable linkages between weak environmental policies, foreign policies, the imperative of profit maximization, and the pandemic. The making of linkages by policymakers, educators, and health-care workers is necessary to effectively address the coronavirus pandemic. Health-care policy cannot be conceived in a silo, as it is intertwined with other policies, including US foreign policy, as Chomsky points out in his answer to Goodman who asked what would happen if President Donald Trump were to be reelected:

> [i]t means that the policies of the past four years, which have been extremely destructive to the American population, to the world, will be continued and probably accelerated. What this is going to mean for health is bad enough. It will get worse. What this means for the environment or the threat of nuclear war, which no one is talking about but is extremely serious, is indescribable. (Goodman and Chomsky 2021: this volume, p. 15)

Chomsky's insightful analysis indicates that the future of humanity is not only linked to the coronavirus pandemic, but rests on the sustainability of the planet itself. For example, a "2015 study by Karesh and his colleagues found that land-use changes like deforestation, urban sprawl, and road building are the leading drivers of pathogen spillover from wildlife to humans."[4] The eruption of the coronavirus is not the first pandemic to be experienced within the last century (think of Ebola, Zika, yellow fever, among others), neither will it be the last one, unless policymakers worldwide radically shift paradigms from one in which "the social responsibility of business is to increase its profits" to one in which the political goal is to reverse the atrocities of neoliberal austerity measures and the shifting of wealth from the middle- and lower-class populace to the oligarch class, as Trump successfully did during his presidency.

Instead of expanding the economic inequality which has had a disastrous impact on both the health-care and the educational system, the paradigm reversal must also fight for the right to the basic elements necessary to sustain livelihood with dignity—a right that has been historically denied to a very large segment of world population, especially nonwhite lower-class communities, women, and LGBT people from countries that are considered underdeveloped as well as indigenous peoples. With respect to the latter, the negation of the right to survival is coupled with the erasure of their history, which can be understood also as an attack on biodiversity, since indigenous communities the world over play important roles in preserving diverse species and ecosystems. As pointed out by Katu, Sánchez, and Camargo in this volume, we are experiencing an "ecogenethnocide" (Katu, Sánchez and Camargo 2021).

Western policymakers need to comprehend that indigenous struggles for land and territory—which often go against the interests of agribusiness and mining—have aimed to prevent capitalist greed from leading humanity to the social, environmental, and climatic collapse we are experiencing now under the coronavirus pandemic. Take, for instance, the manifesto of the Yanomami and Ye'kwana peoples from Brazil:

> Hey, look at me. We see you. We tried to show you. You never bothered to learn our language. You were always looking down. We've been warning you since the beginning. The land is alive. This land can't be owned. This land is us, all of us. You wanted the stones, the gold, your shiny things, titles, flags, profits. You called that progress. We tried to teach you. But you've always been so greedy, too primitive, too savage to understand. Now you still bring curses over the Yanomami: illnesses. And once again, we are dying because of it and all indigenous land is being turned into ashes and mud. Five centuries. You never looked up to discover what we were holding in place: the sky itself. Your cities can see it. Your crops can see it. Your kids can see it. We can see it in your lungs. Take a deep breath, open your eyes and look up. Can you finally see it?[5]

According to the Yanomami tradition, "the falling sky" would be the image to describe the present time, and humanity is not free from suffering future successive pandemics. Scientific analyses of the dynamics of epidemics are cautioning against the wholesale commodification of nature, as they relate the increased occurrence of viruses to the global food production chain, the growing genetic monocultures of animals, and the profitability of multinational corporations, which carry out intensive exploitation of natural resources and land grabs extending into the last of primary forests worldwide. Simply put, "the functional diversity and complexity these huge tracts of land represent are being streamlined in such a way that previously boxed-in pathogens are spilling over into local livestock and human communities."[6]

Coupled with this alarming situation are larger population sizes and densities, the deprivation of the living conditions of the poor, overcrowded public transportation systems, the destruction of public health systems and their subsequent privatization, increasingly intensive workloads, and the ever-increasing defanging of labor rights. Such factors contribute to depressing the biological and the political immune response, and facilitate greater rates of transmission and mortality of the viruses, especially among the most marginalized, as the coronavirus has so abundantly demonstrated. Thus, we should not be at all surprised that the nonwhite lower-class populace throughout the world has suffered the most under the coronavirus contagion.

Even though there is a growing concern among scientists about global warming (now called euphemistically climate change), the neoliberal rationality that prioritizes profit over global sustainability continues its attempt to make people believe that the high technological advances so far achieved by humanity seem natural. This ideological naturalization process is always used for the benefit of the minority ruling class, while the rest of the world's population, particularly individuals concentrated in poor countries, are subjected to historical exploitation in order to satiate capitalism's unparalleled greed. Indeed, neoliberalism is not satisfied with extracting profit from labor alone, but justifies and accelerates a neocolonial framework designed to exploit, devalue, and dehumanize the majority of the oppressed worldwide. For this reason, it behooves those who consider themselves agents of change at this current global crossroads to engage in what Henry Giroux and Ourania Filippakou, in their chapter, call "coronavirus pedagogy"—an engagement that provides educators, activists, health-care workers, and others with the necessary critical tools to understand what the pandemic can teach us:

> The pandemic has made clear that market mechanisms cannot address the depth and scope of the current crisis. The failure of neoliberalism not only reveals a profound sense of despair and moral void at the heart of casino capitalism, but also makes clear that the spell of neoliberalism is broken and as such is in the midst of a legitimation crisis. The coronavirus pandemic has made clear that the neoliberal notion that all problems are a matter of individual responsibility and that each of us are defined exclusively by our self-interest has completely broken down, as the effects of neoliberalism's failure to deal with the pandemic unfold in shortages in crucial medical equipment, lack of testing, and failed public health services, largely due to austerity measures. (Giroux and Filippakou 2021: this volume, p. 31)

Rather than raising concerns that matter in times of the coronavirus pandemic, neoliberal apologists for market solutions go to extreme delusional lengths to make unreality seem normal. For example, the Brazilian President, Jair Bolsonaro, perversely argues that the lack of access to sanitation systems for millions of Brazilians should be viewed favorably to the degree that it strengthens their immunity to the coronavirus; allegedly, the poor and the homeless develop antibodies to every virus, so "they never catch anything. You see some bloke jumping into the sewage, he gets out, has a dive, right? And nothing happens to him."[7]

Far from slowing the neoliberal onslaught, growing awareness of the fact that 2 billion people now live in nations plagued by water problems, and the prediction that around two-thirds of the world could face water shortages in four years, fomented the greed of the stock market speculators who, in early December 2020, targeted agribusiness to introduce water as a traded commodity on Wall Street Market while most of the world was experiencing a second wave of the coronavirus pandemic.[8]

The terrifying implications of the neoliberal premise that still guides many body politics worldwide—the premise stated by President Ronald Reagan in his inaugural address in 1981 that "government is not the solution to our problem, government is the problem"[9]—were exposed by the pandemic and the failures of most states to protect their people. Even a key institution of neoliberalism, the International Monetary Fund (IMF), now recommends that, in 2021, economies should "resist tightening fiscal policy too early and instead ensure continued support for health care, individuals, and firms. In economies constrained in their ability to spend, a reprioritization of spending may be warranted to protect the most vulnerable."[10] However, it is not possible to say categorically that we are foreseeing the end of neoliberalism. What we can scientifically document is that the coronavirus pandemic has unveiled neoliberalism's total failure to support life on this planet. Even before its failure to address the coronavirus pandemic, market solutions were on the march as countries throughout the world installed far-right governments that would only guarantee protection for ruling-class interests—interests camouflaged in "the language of war [that] creates an echo chamber produced in both the highest circles of power and the right-wing cultural apparatuses that serve to turn trauma, exhaustion, and mourning into a fog of conspiracy theories, state repression, and a deepening abyss of darkness that serves the ends of those in power" (Giroux and Filippakou 2021: this volume, p. 31).

Falling right in line, the neoliberal ideology of the "new normal," the commonplace term used to describe our altered coexistence after the pandemic, induces acceptance of a future of fear in which there are no alternatives, generating fatalism, cynicism, and acquiescence. As pointed out by Leher in this volume, the term "new normal" is "polysemic," that is "the ideology of the 'new normal' denotes the confluence of many different perspectives for the future, all of which are pro-systemic" (Leher 2021: this volume, p. 39). The prospect within this formulation of the "new normal" is to expect greater exploitation of labor as "gig workers," which are estimated to represent in 2020 around 35 percent of the US workforce (57 million Americans), up from between 14 and 20 percent in 2014. According to a report in *Forbes*, "those figures are only expected to grow, with some predicting that freelance workers will make up more than half of the US workforce by 2023."[11] The scenario of mass dismissal of teachers during the pandemic also opened the doors for the gig economy in education, in general, and in higher education in particular. Mass dismissal was already reaching scandalous proportions in Brazilian private higher education institutions due to the expansion of distance learning—as addressed by Leher in his chapter—while in many US universities, non-tenure-track faculty members significantly outnumber tenure-track faculty, occupying contract positions that provide less job security and fewer benefits, more servitude, and virtually no academic freedom.

Due to the coronavirus pandemic, educational institutions worldwide migrated from face-to-face classes to remote learning, a term that encompasses both the delivery of school content through radio, television, and handouts, as well as through online educational platforms, software, and apps. The spread of pre-packaged education enables further corporate control over teaching and learning, raising important concerns about issues such as cultural imperialism and educator-deskilling which are discussed by Borg and Mayo in this volume. Besides this, the recrudescence of the opportunity gaps regarding access to food, housing, health care/insurance, financial relief measures, and devices and internet access put low-income students at a disadvantage relative to their better-off peers, as pointed out by Borg and Mayo (2021) who analyze the context in Malta. Generally speaking, remote learning has widened educational inequality in proportions that are not yet known. Notwithstanding the evidence, the hegemonic narrative of the "new normal" in education affirms the move to online classrooms:

> The Covid-19 pandemic must be seen as an "opportunity." Professors, unions, and students who had so far been resisting the mainstreaming of distance learning in basic and higher education will have to give in to reality. The time has finally come for the retirement of analog professors who insist on hindering the progress of the digital world in education. Once such corporative resistance is removed, governments shall be able to acquire the infrastructure required by the new digital world. (Leher 2021: this volume, 48)

In contrast to the market-driven use of technologies in education, Fernández, Barrios, and Lira (2021) discuss in this volume the important use of social media by Chilean teachers' organizations during the coronavirus outbreak. They mobilized social media to publicly address critical topics, such as police violence, education in the new Chilean constitution, and work overload of women in online teaching, and also to connect educators across Latin America in defense of public education against neoliberal policies. Right before the coronavirus outbreak, the October 2019 people's rebellion in Chile—when protesters marched against the unjust system that denied decent social security pensions, education, health, and housing—succeeded in approving the revocation of the constitution enacted under the Pinochet dictatorship in the 1980s.

Linked to these popular movements are the growing protests and demonstrations worldwide sparked by the cruel death of George Floyd, an unarmed Black man, by a white police officer in Minneapolis, USA, in May 2020, demonstrated that the slow asphyxiation inherent in the capitalist system, which "reaches, in its globalizing crusade, the maximum efficacy of evil nature" (Freire 1998: 114), is being challenged by those who daily struggle to be able to breathe. These uprisings serve as platforms to denounce the embedded racism, sexism, classism, homophobia, and other forms of discrimination which are rooted in capitalist forms of exploitation.

The rising level of *conscientization* reached through these protests and demonstrations makes it clear that, in the wake of the coronavirus pandemic, critical educators must refuse both a return to the old and an acceptance of the new neoliberal "normality" (which is the normalization of oppressive conditions). That is to say, normality forged by democratic forces sprung from below, as different agents from diverse sectors of the society engage in the co-creation of a humane normalcy, must, first and foremost, be based on principles of equity, social justice, and democracy.

Building the New World Through Life-Centered Education

Against a backdrop of the creation of a "new normal," which masks neoliberalism's stubborn violation of universal ethics under the rubric of progress, more than ever it is necessary to fight for the right to live—a right that, as we mentioned earlier, has been historically denied to a large part of the world's population, especially indigenous peoples, Black and mestizo communities, women, and LGBT people from countries which have relegated to the periphery of development.

We cannot talk about democracy as a force of progress so long as dominant policymakers celebrate the enhanced "free trade" and border crossing of goods enabled by the fall of the Berlin wall while, simultaneously, calling for new walls to be designed in order to keep the "wrong" people out—people who in most instances build those goods as part of a cheap workforce and constitute a mass of men and women without rights that can easily be exploited by the underground economy. This is the scenario presented by Vittoria and Muraca (2021) in this volume when they discuss the Italian government's interventions during the coronavirus pandemic to save the agriculture industries' interests by legalizing, but only for a limited period of time, clandestine immigrants who work in agriculture under very precarious conditions and without being assured any basic social rights, such as equal access to education.

That said, there is an urgent need to reestablish the direct relationship between the fight for the right to education and the fight for the right to survival. In other words, as Loureiro (2021) explains in this volume, it is important to develop educational processes in order to find ways to overcome social relations ruled by capital and construct policies that recognize and grant the right to education and to a healthy environment (considered both biodiversity and cultural diversity) as a common good.

For this purpose, we need to robustly embrace what Giroux and Filippakou (2021) call a "pandemic pedagogy" that points to the glaring contradictions that dominant institutions, from schools to media, have, with much efficacy, taught us not to see. The unveiling of these contradictions as a result of the pandemic is convincingly demonstrated in an illuminating chapter in this volume by Georgios Tsiakolos, Stavros Malichudis, and Iliana Papangeli. These authors correctly argue that

> Every time the [European] ban on refugees leaving the camps is announced, a message is sent to society: they are dangerous, but we have taken care to keep them away from you so you are not at risk. Thus, the narrative long adopted in official public discourse on the "danger" of refugees is further reinforced by an additional argument: they are not only supposedly dangerous to national security and the security of citizens, they are not only supposedly dangerous to national identity, now they are even dangerous transmitters of the virus. [...] The pandemic offers governments new opportunities for disenfranchisement. And if the policy concerns "foreigners" already suspected to be "dangerous," then the violation is easier to accept, even though it is an internationally forbidden denial of human rights. The acceptance of rights violations in "special cases" in order to protect "us" from supposed dangers is the beginning of acceptance of other violations that may undermine citizens' rights as well. (2021: this volume, p. 54)

Along the same lines, the Trump administration pursued a racist agenda to keep Latinx refugees from crossing the border into the United States by caging them in makeshift barbed-wire camps along the southwestern borders on the pretext of containing the coronavirus and preventing its transmission to law-abiding, God-fearing Americans. The historical hypocrisy of this policy is brilliantly deconstructed by Sheila Macrine in her chapter in this volume, in which she poignantly peels off, layer by layer, the evil that generates, shapes, and maintains a normalized hypocrisy that provides Americans with a false sense of security, even if it means the violation of human rights and support for pretenses that the United States has used and continues to use as justification to go to war—sometimes the very same wars dislodge and displace people who have no other option but to seek refuge anywhere and anyhow.

> Visions of people seeking asylum in holding pens and children in cages along the US/Mexico border haunt our collective memories. Yet, these are the very images that helped Trump and company to galvanize the racist sentiments that hastened his anti-immigration policies. Along with blatant and unapologetic xenophobic rhetoric, the Trump administration used the threat of the Covid-19 pandemic to "legally" expel refugee/asylum-seekers or stop them at the border. The unifying link among these tactics is the racially motivated fear-mongering related to alarms over potential violence (Chouhy & Madero-Hernandez 2019). Ultimately, the resultant anti-immigration policies, exacerbated by the pandemic, uncovered serious underlying fault-lines in our asylum policy and exposed the absence of humanitarian treatment by the United States. (Macrine 2021: this volume, p. 75)

This quotation calls our attention to what constitutes being recognized as fully human and that the pandemic has clearly demonstrated life with dignity was never a reality for the vast majority of the world's population. Now, under the "new normal" being crafted by the same architects of pandemics, for the vast majority of the "wretched of the earth," life is no longer a possibility, as they find themselves suffocated by the ever-constricting claws of a savage capitalist labor market.

Here the Marxist concept of alienation, which had its origin in the analysis of the production of wealth in capitalist societies, is useful. In this type of society, the means of production (land, machines, and, currently, technologies) are concentrated under the regime of private property (including intellectual property and patents, which hinder access to knowledge). Those who do not own the means of production become dependent on the sale of their labor to ensure their livelihood. Thus, the alienation of the workers is constituted by their disconnection from: (1) the object produced by their work; (2) the set of knowledge that makes up the different stages of the work process; (3) the fundamental characteristic of human beings that is their creativity to transform nature and to transform themselves in this process; (4) other human beings and nature.

This phenomenon observed by Marx in the nineteenth century had reached, in the second decade of the twenty-first century, highly destructive levels in which dehumanization is so accentuated that it often lead workers to actively seek paths that drive them to their own annihilation—annihilation made self-evident when, for example, they support presidents such as Trump in the United States and Bolsonaro in Brazil, among other right-wing politicians throughout the world who deny the severity of the coronavirus pandemic, by spreading lies about the lethality of the virus or denying the its very existence, or, in the case of Bolsonaro, cautioning against the dangerous side effects of the vaccine.[12]

Once alienated, we lose what differentiates humans from animals: our creative capacity to transcend the mere adaptation to the immediate and visible reality in order to glimpse a new future, thus transforming the course of history. Simply put, a pandemic pedagogy that makes the right to survival central to its aspirations, goals, and dreams must conduct critical analyses of the immediate reality, encourage the denunciation of the dehumanization that takes place in right-wing capitalist contexts, and nurture the imaginative capacity that aims and animates its transformation. Freire argued that animals adapt to their environment, while humans are capable of transforming their environment as historical agents who can, simultaneously, also reflect on the history that humans write so that they can later read what they had written. That is, humans should "rejoice in knowing that . . . [we are] 'conditioned' being[s], capable of going beyond [our] own conditioning" (Freire 1998: 115–16).

For those who courageously reject the pervasive seduction of the market, Freire asserted that the challenge rests on forging "human solidarity" and the critical awareness that "the place upon which a new rebellion should be built is not the ethics of the marketplace with its crass insensitivity to the voice of genuine humanity but the ethics of universal human aspiration" (Freire 1998: 116). This "ethics of human solidarity" must be an active solidarity in the "struggle for the enforcement of social rights and rights of existence of livelihoods which differ both from the interests of capital and from its civilizational standards. These same livelihoods nourish and educate us to face political struggle" (Loureiro 2021: this volume, p. 134).

In this respect, we have much to learn from the traditional peoples (artisanal fisherpeople, indigenous, and maroon populations, among others) whose productive activities involve little market interaction and enable practices of organic bonds with their land and territory. As Loureiro signals,

> Losing their vital ties to a territory which their culture produces and attributes
> meaning to is losing what they hold most sacred. Life for them has no price, and
> their territories cannot be exchanged in the form of commodities. [. . .] Their
> traditional character is marked by a way to read the present while considering

the past, which enables envisioning a future without significant losses in terms of customs, values, cultures and forms of coexistence which have historically been viable and decisive for the reproduction of certain social groups. It is then far from static: it is a movement of permanently interpreting what is realized, identifying what binds past, present and future. (Loureiro 2021: this volume, p. 135)

The reconfiguration of being in the world and with others within a conscientious and respectful harmony with nature can also take inspiration from the *buen vivir* practices, addressed by Katu, Sáchez, and Camargo (2021), which represents the political proposal of a substantial alternative to Western and capitalist development based on traditional indigenous values concerning nature and community. Such broad societal transformation can only be achieved through a reinvigorated education, one that is critical, democratic, equal, and accessible to all.

These are the principles that guide the analysis set out in this volume. With much conviction, we assume the importance of the defense of the public good; the importance of educators and teacher unions; the crucial role of environmental education; the need to guarantee cultural diversity, protect biodiversity, and strengthen ancestral cultures; and the fight for social and environmental justice. With these principles framing of their analyses, the authors represented in this book, from different national contexts, debate the current public proposals to combat the coronavirus pandemic disaster within theoretical lenses that take seriously and critically the neoliberal policies that, to a large extent, used the pandemic as catalyst for a perfect storm, unleashing worldwide unmatched human misery and despair. In particular, the authors engage the tensions and contradictions that fuel education debates concerning scenarios such as social distance, collective illness, growth of social and economic inequality, and privatizing reforms.

Consequently, this volume asserts that the affirmation of life with dignity— regardless of class, gender, race, sexual orientation, or ethnicity—needs to be the foundation of post-pandemic education, an education always guided by an ethical and moral compass. It also reaffirms that education must be, first and foremost, humane, and not predicated on the premise of a false utopianism designed by and serving the minority oligarch class. Freire refers to this as "the utopia of a minority" that aims "to create a society robotized by highly intelligent machines that can substitute men and women in a whole range of activities, [leaving] millions of Peters and Marys without anything to do" (Freire 1998: 117).

Thus, engaged educators after the pandemic must provide citizens of the world with tools that enable them to move beyond the platitudes offered by the oligarchy's conception of freedom, which reduces citizens to mere consumers of goods that they once made and, after being reduced to redundancy, they no longer even make. Critical citizens must understand how the evil forces of capitalism always prevent them from having any control over the means of production, as they remain straightjacketed to the mere sale of their labor. As insightfully captured by Freire:

> The freedom of commerce cannot be ethically higher than the freedom to be human. The freedom of commerce without limits is no more than the license to put profit above everything else. It becomes a privilege of the few, who in certain favorable conditions increase their own power at the expense of the greater part of humanity, even to the point of survival itself. A textile factory that is forced to close because it cannot compete with the price of labor in Asia, for example, not only brings down the factory owner (who may or may not be a transgressor of that universal ethical code of which I have spoken) but signals the expulsion of hundreds of workers from the process of production. And what about their families? I refuse, with all the conviction I can muster, to accept that our presence in history can be reduced to a deterministic adaption to our socio-historical condition. As I have said before, worldwide unemployment is not fatalistic inevitability. It is the result of the economic globalization and the scientific and technological advances that lack a form of ethics that serves the interests of all human beings and not just the unfettered greed of the power of the minority who control the world today. The application of technological advances, which requires the sacrifice of thousands of people, is one more example of how we can be transgressors of a universal human ethic in the name of the market, of pure profit. (Freire 1998: 116)

The coronavirus pandemic unveiled an obscene degree of inequality, intolerance, racism, and exploitation of workers, and also the contempt that the rulers have for people's dignity and lives. Against all this, defending public institutions, such as public schools and universities, public and free health care, social security, housing, and food for all, and recognizing the right to land, territory, and cultural identity are part of a major struggle in defense of all forms of life. Co-constructing a "new normal" that breaks the continuum of history—a history that consistently produced and reproduces genocides—is a challenge that must urgently be faced by educators and all progressive forces.

2

Chomsky on Trump's Disastrous Coronavirus Response, Bernie Sanders, and What Gives Him Hope[1]

Amy Goodman and Noam Chomsky

How did the United States—the richest country in the world—become the worldwide epicenter of the coronavirus outbreak, with one person dying of Covid-19 every forty-seven seconds?

Journalist Amy Goodman engaged in a dialogue with Noam Chomsky, the world-renowned political dissident, linguist, and author, discussing this unprecedented moment in history and its political implications. In the conversation, which took place in April 2020, Chomsky reflects on the significance of the Bernie Sanders campaign, calling it "an extraordinary success" that "completely shifted the arena of debate and discussion" in the United States. He also responds to President Trump's cuts to US support for the World Health Organization and the surge in coronavirus-related deaths in the United States to record highs, and discusses conditions in Gaza, the rise of authoritarianism around the world, and the progressive response.

Amy Goodman: In 2020, the United States became the worldwide epicenter of the coronavirus pandemic with about a third of the world's reported infections and a quarter of the global death toll, even though the US makes up less than 5 percent of the world's population. This unfolded even as the US Labor Department reported roughly 40 million Americans have filed for unemployment benefits since mid-March, and the scale of US job losses is set to rival the Great Depression.

I would like to discuss the political implications of this unprecedented moment, starting with what is happening in US politics right now. Today—April 8, 2020—Senator Bernie Sanders announced he was suspending his presidential campaign, making former Vice President Joe Biden the presumptive nominee to face Donald Trump in the November 2020 election. Professor Chomsky, what is happening right now in the context of the 2020 elections and what do you see happening in November?

Noam Chomsky: If Trump is reelected, it would be an indescribable disaster. It means that the policies of the past four years, which have been extremely destructive to the American population, to the world, will be continued and probably accelerated. What this would mean for health is bad enough. What this would mean for the environment or the threat of nuclear war, which no one is talking about but is extremely serious, is indescribable.

Suppose Biden is elected. I would anticipate it would be essentially a continuation of Obama—nothing very great, but at least not totally destructive— and there would be opportunities for an organized public to change what is being done, to impose pressures.

It's common to say now that the Sanders campaign failed. I think that's a mistake. I think it was an extraordinary success: it completely shifted the arena of debate and discussion. Issues that were unthinkable a couple years ago are now right in the middle of attention.

The worst crime Sanders committed, in the eyes of the establishment, was not the policy he was proposing; it was the fact that he was able to inspire popular movements, which had already been developing—Occupy, Black Lives Matter, many others—and turn them into an activist movement, which doesn't just show up every couple years to push a lever and then go home, but applies constant pressure, constant activism, and so on. That could affect a Biden administration. It could also—even if it's just a holding action—mean there's time to deal with the major crises.

Take Medicare for All or, the other major plank in Sanders's program, free college education. Across the whole mainstream spectrum, all the way to what's called the left in the mainstream, this is condemned as too radical for Americans. Just think what that means. The condemnation is an attack on American culture and society that you would expect from some hostile enemy. The detractors are saying it's too radical to say that we should rise to the level of comparable countries, which all have some form of national health care. Most of them have free higher education—the best-performing countries nationally, like Finland, free; Germany, free; right to our south, Mexico, a poor country, high-quality higher education, free. So, to say we should rise to the level of the rest of the world is considered too radical for Americans. It's an astonishing comment. As I say, it's a critique of America that you'd expect from some super hostile enemy.

That's the left of the spectrum. It tells you that we have really deep problems. It's not just Trump. He made it much worse, but the problems go much deeper, just like, say, the catastrophic ventilator shortage, which was based on good capitalist logic with the extra hammer blow of making the government ineffectual to deal with things. This is much deeper than Trump. And we have to face those facts. Some do. I'm sure you probably reported the setting of the Doomsday Clock in January?

Amy Goodman: Yes.

Noam Chomsky: Notice what happened. All through Trump's term, the minute hand of the Doomsday Clock, the best general assessment we have of the state of the world, moved closer to midnight—termination. In January 2020, it exceeded the highest point ever. The analysts gave up measuring minutes and moved to seconds: a hundred seconds to midnight, thanks to Donald Trump.

And the Republican Party, which is just monstrous, no longer qualifies as a political party. It simply sheepishly echoes everything the master says. Zero integrity. It's just amazing to watch. Trump's surrounded himself by a collection of sycophants who just repeat worshipfully everything he says. It's a real major attack on democracy, alongside the attack on "the survival of humanity," to quote a leaked JPMorgan Chase memo—raising the threat of nuclear war and dismantling the arms control system, which has, to some extent, protected us from total disaster. It's astonishing to watch.

The same JPMorgan Chase memo that I just quoted, about how the policies we're following are risking the survival of humanity, ended by arguing that the banks should cut back their fossil fuel support, in part because of the reputational consequences. Their reputation is being harmed. What does that mean? That means that activists are putting pressure on them, and they have to maintain some kind of reputation. Now, that's a good lesson.

And it works. We've seen some very striking examples. Take, say, the Green New Deal. A couple of years ago, that was an object of ridicule, if it was mentioned at all. Some form of Green New Deal is essential for the survival of humanity. Now it's part of the general agenda. Why? Activist engagement. Especially the Sunrise Movement, a group of young people, has acted significantly, up to the point of sitting in congressional offices. They received support from Alexandria Ocasio-Cortez and other young legislators who came into office as part of the Sanders-inspired popular wave—another great success. Ed Markey, senator from Massachusetts, joined in. Now it's a part of the legislative agenda. The next step is to force it through in some viable form. And there are very good ideas as to how to do that. Well, that's the way things can change.

With a Biden presidency, there would be, if not a strongly sympathetic administration, at least one that can be reached, can be pressured. And that's very important. The very good labor historian Erik Loomis—who has studied the efforts by working people to institute changes in the society, sometimes for themselves, sometimes for the society generally—made an interesting point: these efforts succeeded when there was a tolerant or sympathetic administration, not when there wasn't. That's one of many enormous differences between Trump, the sociopath, and Biden, who's kind of pretty empty—you can push him one way or another. This is the most crucial election in human history, literally. Another four years of Trump, and we're in deep trouble.

Amy Goodman: Can you talk about the enormity of this moment and the fact that the United States has become the epicenter of the pandemic in the world? What does this mean, the wealthiest country in the world?

Noam Chomsky: Well, countries have reacted to this in many ways, some very successfully, some more or less successfully. One is at the bottom of the barrel. That's us. The United States is the only major country that cannot even provide data to the World Health Organization, because it's so dysfunctional.

There's a background. Part of the background is the scandalous health-care system, which simply is not ready for anything that's out of the normal. It simply doesn't work. This is exacerbated by the strange collection of gangsters in Washington—it's almost as if they systematically took every step to make it as bad as possible. Through Trump's term, the last four years, he has been systematically cutting back on all of the health-related aspects of the government. Pentagon spending goes up. His wall goes up. But spending on anything that might benefit the general population goes down, particularly health.

Some of it is almost surreal. So, in October 2019, for example, with just exquisite timing, Trump canceled completely a USAID project—Predict, it was called—that was working in Third World countries, also in China, to try to detect new viruses that might turn into the anticipated pandemic. And in fact it was anticipated at least since the SARS epidemic in 2003. So we have a kind of combination of factors, some of them specific to the United States.

If we want to ensure or at least hope to avoid new pandemics, which are very likely to come and to be more serious than this one, in part because of the enormous rising threat of global warming, then we have to look at the sources of this one. And it's very important to think them through. So, to go back, pandemics have been predicted by scientists for years. The SARS epidemic was quite serious. It was contained—there was the beginning of development of vaccines. They never proceeded to the testing phase. It was clear at that time that something more was going to happen, and several epidemics did.

But it's not enough to know that. Somebody has to pick up the ball and run with it. Who can do it? Well, the drug companies are the obvious place, but they have no interest in it. They follow good capitalist logic: you look at market signals, and there's no profit to be made in preparing for a predicted and anticipated catastrophe. So they weren't interested.

At that point, another possibility is the government could step in. I'm old enough to remember the terror of polio was ended by a government-initiated and -funded project that finally led to the Salk vaccine, which was free, no intellectual property rights. Jonas Salk said it should be as free as the sun. That ended the polio terror, measles terror, others. But now the government couldn't step in, because there's another particular aspect of the modern era: the neoliberal plague. Remember Ronald Reagan's sunny smile and his little maxim about how government is the problem, not the solution. So the government can't intervene.

There were some efforts, nevertheless, to try to prepare for this. Right now in New York and other places, doctors and nurses are forced to make agonizing decisions about who to kill—not a nice decision to make—because they simply don't have equipment. And the main lack is ventilators. There's a huge shortage of ventilators. Well, the Obama administration did make an effort to try to prepare for this. And this dramatically reveals the kind of factors that are leading to catastrophe. They contracted with a small company that was producing high-quality, low-cost ventilators. The company was bought up by a larger one, Covidien, which makes fancy, expensive ventilators. And they shelved the project. Presumably, they didn't want competition with their own costly ones. Shortly after that, they turned to the government and said they wanted the contract ended. The reason was that it was not profitable enough, so therefore no ventilators.

We have the same thing in hospitals. Hospitals, under the neoliberal programs, are supposed to be efficient, meaning they should have no spare capacity, just enough beds to get by. And in fact, plenty of people, me included, can testify that even the best hospitals caused great pain and suffering to patients before this pandemic broke out, because of this just-on-time efficiency concept that has been guiding our privatized, for-profit health-care system. When anything hits out of the normal, it's just tough luck. And this runs across the system.

So we have a combination of capitalist logic, which is lethal but could be controlled, and an ineffectual government that can't control it under the neoliberal programs that say the government can't step in to pick up the ball when the private sector doesn't.

On top of that—now, this becomes specific to the United States—we have a freak show in Washington, a totally dysfunctional government, which is causing enormous problems. And it's not that nothing was known. A pandemic was anticipated all through Trump's term, even before. His reaction was to cut back preparation for it. Astonishingly, this continued even after the pandemic hit.

So, on February 10, 2020, when it was already serious, Trump released his budget for the coming year. The budget continues the defunding of the Center for Disease Control and other government institutions responsible for health. It increases funding for some things, like fossil fuel production, giving new subsidies to the fossil fuel industries. I mean, it's as if the country is simply—maybe not "as if"—the country is simply run by sociopaths.

And the result is that we cut back on the efforts to deal with the pandemic that was taking shape, and we increased the efforts to destroy the environment—efforts in which the United States, under Trump, is in the lead in racing to the abyss. Now, bear in mind that is a far more serious threat than the coronavirus. This pandemic is bad and serious, particularly in the United States, but we'll recover somehow, at severe cost. We're not going to recover from the melting of the polar ice sheets, which is leading to a well-known feedback effect—as they melt, there's less reflective surface, more absorption in the dark seas. The warming that's melting increases. That's just one of the factors that's leading to destruction, unless we do something about it.

And it's not a secret. The leaked memo I quoted from JPMorgan Chase, America's biggest bank, warned that, in their words, "the survival of humanity" is at risk if we continue on our present course, which included the funding of fossil fuel industries by the bank itself. Everyone who's got eyes open in the Trump administration is very well aware of this.

But the urgency of the pandemic has become convenient now. Trump is desperately seeking some scapegoat that he can blame for his astonishing failures and incompetence. The most recent one is the World Health Organization, along with the China bashing. Somebody else is responsible.

But the facts are very clear. China very quickly informed the World Health Organization last December that they were finding patients with pneumonia-like symptoms with unknown etiology. They didn't know what it was. About a week later, about January 7, they made public to the World Health Organization and to the general scientific community in the world that Chinese scientists had found out what the source was: a coronavirus resembling the SARS virus. They had identified the sequence, the genome. They were providing the information to the world.

US intelligence was well aware of it. They spent January and February of 2020 trying to get somebody in the White House to pay attention to the fact that there was a major pandemic. Just nobody would listen. Trump was off playing golf or maybe listening—likely checking his TV ratings. We have since learned that one very high-level official, very close to the administration, Peter Navarro, in late January had sent a very strong message to the White House saying this is a real danger. But even he couldn't break through.

Amy Goodman: Noam, you mention Peter Navarro, the trade representative, sending a memo—it came out in *The New York Times* in April 2020—in late January 2020 warning of the coronavirus, saying that, I think, something like up to a million people could die. And Trump took from that the need for setting a travel ban on China but not doing the corollary: ensuring that the United States had the proper tests and also had the PPE, the protective personal equipment, that doctors, nurses, and the custodial staff in hospitals needed to stay alive and to treat patients, in order to help them stay alive. And it came out the intelligence agencies were all warning Trump even before Navarro. Two years ago, when Trump disbanded his pandemic unit within the National Security Council, he said that when he's at the table in China talking about spending money on bombs or a wall, they're not saying, "Sir, you also have to look at what's happening here." And that pandemic unit was about not only how we deal with health care in the United States, but also ensuring, as the Center for Disease Control does and other agencies of the US government do, that scientists are sent out to other countries, like China, to investigate and to help other countries, because when it comes to a pandemic, we're all in this together. So, if you could talk about these early warnings and why testing and this personal protective equipment is so important?

Noam Chomsky: Well, remember that defunding health care continued even after the pandemic was already in force. Now, the budget proposal was astonishing. This is February 10, well into the pandemic. Trump cuts further the health-related components of the government, continuing the hit. They were still under the ax, just as they were throughout his term.

Actually, his actions were part of a very clever strategy. Whether this was consciously planned or just intuitive, I don't know. But the pattern of simply making one statement today, contradicting it tomorrow, coming out with something else the next day, was really brilliant. It means he's going to be vindicated. Whatever happens, he'll have said it. You shoot arrows at random, some of them are going to hit the target. And his technique with the Fox echo chamber and the worshipful base simply tuned to Fox, Limbaugh, etc., was that they're just going to pick whatever happened to be right, and say, "Look, our wonderful president, the greatest president we've ever had, our savior, knew it all along, and here was his statement." He can't miss.

It's very much like the technique of producing constant lies. The assiduous fact-checkers total them up. I think it's maybe at 20,000 lies by now. And he's laughing all the way. This is perfect. You tell constant lies, and what happens is the concept of truth just disappears.

Amy Goodman: There was Sean Hannity and Donald Trump right before him, on March 18 and 17, 2020, saying, "We have always taken the coronavirus pandemic seriously." But for weeks prior, members of the right-wing media, like Sean Hannity, Rush Limbaugh, Tomi Lahren, and others, as well as Republican members of Congress and the Trump administration, had been downplaying or mocking the coronavirus pandemic. This was shown in a three-minute video called "Saluting the Heroes of the Coronavirus Pandumbic" by *The Daily Show* with Trevor Noah, who was doing his show each night from home to protect against community spread. So, Noam Chomsky, world-renowned political dissident, well-known linguist, author, activist, as you listened to the Fox News—this is not just a television channel; these are the people that President Trump channels—and his senior advisers, as they continually played this down, do you hold President Trump responsible? Would you say he has blood on his hands?

Noam Chomsky: There's no question. Trump makes some crazy statement. It's then amplified by the Fox News echo chamber. The next day, he says the opposite. That's echoed; the echo chamber amplifies that. Notice that the tone of the reporting is interesting. It's all stated with perfect confidence, not what any sane, rational person would say, such as "We really don't know. There's a lot of uncertainty. This is the way things look today." There's nothing like that, only absolute confidence. No matter what the dear leader says, we amplify it. And it's an interesting dialogue. They amplify what he says. Sean Hannity can say, "This is the greatest move that was ever made in the history of the world." And the next morning, Trump tunes in to *Fox & Friends*, listens to whatever is said. That becomes his thought for the day. It's an interaction, Murdoch and Trump moving literally to try to destroy the country and destroy the world, because in the background—we should never forget—is a far greater threat that is coming closer and closer while Trump is leading the way to destruction.

He has some assistance. So, down in the southern part of the hemisphere, there's another madman, that is, Jair Bolsonaro, who's trying to vie with Trump to see who can be the worst criminal on the planet. Bolsonaro's telling the Brazilians, "It's nothing. It's just a cold. Brazilians don't get viruses. We're immune to them."

His health minister and other officials are trying to butt in and say, "Look, this is really serious." The governors, many of them, fortunately, are ignoring what he says. But Brazil is facing a terrible crisis. It's actually gotten to the point where in the favelas—these miserable slums in Rio where the government does nothing for the people—others have intervened to try to impose sensible restrictions, insofar as it's possible under those miserable conditions. Who? The crime gangs. The crime gangs that torture the population have moved in to try to impose health standards. The indigenous population is facing a virtual genocide, which won't bother Bolsonaro. He doesn't think they should be there anyway. Meanwhile, while all this is going on, scientific papers are coming out warning that in fifteen years the Amazon Basin is going to shift from being a net carbon sink to a net CO^2 emitter. That's devastating for Brazil—in fact, for the whole world.

So, we have the Colossus of the North, as it's called, in the hands of sociopaths, who are doing whatever they can to harm the country and the world. And the Colossus of the South, as it's been called, is in its own way doing the same thing. I'm able to follow this pretty closely because my wife Valeria is Brazilian and keeps me up to date with the news that's coming out in Brazil. And it's simply shocking to see.

But meanwhile, other countries are reacting sensibly. As soon as the news started coming out from China—and there was plenty of news right away, contrary to what is being claimed—the countries on the Chinese periphery—Taiwan, South Korea, Singapore—began to react quite effectively. Some of them have it basically under control. New Zealand has apparently quashed the coronavirus, maybe almost completely, with an immediate lockdown for a couple of weeks, and seems to have come close to ending it. You look into Europe, and most of Europe just dithered, but some countries, the better-organized countries, did act right away. It's very striking. It would be very useful for Americans to compare Trump's ravings with German Chancellor Angela Merkel's sober, factual account and talk to the German people, describing exactly what's happening and what has to be done.

Amy Goodman: Noam, I wanted to ask you, as you are sheltering at home in Tucson, Arizona, in the midst of this pandemic, to prevent community spread and to protect yourself and your family: What gives you hope?

Noam Chomsky: Well, I should say that I'm following a strict regimen, because my wife Valeria is taking charge, and I follow her orders. So Valeria and I are in isolation.

But what gives me hope is the actions that popular groups are taking all over the world, many of them. There are some things happening that are truly inspiring. Take the doctors and the nurses who are working overtime under extremely dangerous conditions, lacking—especially in the United States—even minimal support, being compelled to make these agonizing decisions about who to kill tomorrow. But they're doing it. It's just an inspiring tribute to the resources of the human spirit, a model of what can be done, along with the popular actions, the moves to create a Progressive International. These are all very positive signs.

Looking back in recent history, there have been times where things looked really hopeless and desperate. I can go back to my early childhood, the late 1930s, early 1940s. It looked as though the rise of the Nazi plague was inexorable, victory after victory. It looked like it couldn't be stopped. It was the most horrible development in human history. Well, turns out—I didn't know it at the time—that US planners were expecting that the post-war world would be divided between a US-controlled world and a German-controlled world, including all of Eurasia—a horrifying idea. Well, that horror was overcome. There have been other serious challenges that were overcome—with the civil rights movement, for example, when *young* Freedom Riders went out into Alabama to try to encourage black farmers to go to vote, despite the serious threat of being murdered, and being murdered themselves. These were some examples of what humans can do and have done. And we see many signs of it today, and that's the basis for hope.

Amy Goodman: If you can talk for a moment about what's happening globally on an issue that has been close to your heart for decades, and that is the Occupied Territories, Gaza, and the West Bank. What does the pandemic mean for a place like Gaza, called by the United Nations and people around the world a kind of "open-air prison" of almost two million people?

Noam Chomsky: It's almost impossible to think about. Gaza is two million people who are living in a prison, an open-air prison, under constant attack. Israel—which is the occupying power, recognized by everyone in the world except Israel—has been imposing very harsh sanctions ever since the Palestinians made the mistake of carrying out the first free election in the Arab world and electing the wrong people. The United States and Israel came down on them like a ton of bricks.

Israel's policy was explained by Dov Weissglas, the person in charge of the withdrawal of Israeli troops, the withdrawal of the settlers, and imposition of the new regime. He explained frankly, "We are putting the people of Gaza on a diet, just enough to keep them alive," meaning it wouldn't look good if they all die, but not offering anything more than that. So, a piece of chocolate or a toy for a child, that's out. Just enough to stay alive. And if you have a serious health problem, maybe you can apply to go to the hospital in East Jerusalem. Maybe after a couple of weeks, you'll be allowed to go. Maybe a child is allowed to go, but his mother is not allowed to come.

If the pandemic—there are now a couple of cases in Gaza—extends, it's a total disaster. International institutions have pointed out that by 2020 Gaza will probably become barely livable. About 95 percent of the water is totally polluted. The place is a disaster. And Trump has made sure that it will get worse. He withdrew funding from the support systems for Palestinians in Gaza and the West Bank—UNRWA, the United Nations Relief and Works Agency, killed the funding; Palestinian hospitals, killed the funding. And he had a reason. They weren't praising him enough. They weren't respectful of the god, so, therefore, we'll strangle them, even when they're barely surviving under a harsh and brutal regime.

Incidentally, this extends to Palestinians in Israel, as well. Human rights activists in Israel pointed out recently—there are articles about it in *Haaretz*—that Israel finally began to set up a few drive-by testing areas, but only in Jewish areas, not in the areas with Palestinian population. And to make sure that the intended results would follow, they announced it only in Hebrew, not in Arabic, so Palestinians wouldn't even know. Well, that's within Israel. In the Occupied Territories, it's far worse.

And the Trump hammer came in saying, "We're not even going to give you a penny, because you're not respectful enough of me." I don't know how to describe this kind of thing. I can't find words for it.

Amy Goodman: Noam Chomsky, what do you think is required in an international response to stop the rise of authoritarianism in response to this pandemic? For example, in the Philippines, the authoritarian leader and Trump ally, Duterte, talks about killing people; in India, the massive crackdown, without support of the 1.3 billion people of India, by Narendra Modi. President Trump was in India as the pandemic was taking off, never saying a word about it, packing a stadium with 100,000 people. There's Orbán in Hungary, who is now ruling by decree. What would it take to turn that around to be a progressive response?

Noam Chomsky: Well, actually, to the extent that you can find some coherent policy in the madness in the White House, one thing does emerge with considerable clarity—namely, an effort to construct an international of the most reactionary states and oppressive states, led by the gangster in the White House. Now, this is taking shape.

Since you mentioned India, Modi, who is a Hindu nationalist extremist, is systematically moving to destroy Indian secular democracy and to crush the

Muslim population. What's happening in Kashmir is horrifying. It was bad enough before; now it is getting much worse. Same with the huge Muslim population in India. The current lockdown is almost—you can almost describe it as genocidal. Modi gave, I think, a four-hour warning, saying "total lockdown." That's imposed on over a billion people. Some of them have nowhere to go. People in the informal economy, which is a huge number of people, are just cast out. "Go walk back to your village," which may be a thousand miles away. "Die on the roadside." This is a huge catastrophe in the making, right on top of the strong efforts to impose the ultra-right Hindutva doctrines that are at the core of Modi's thinking and background.

What's happening in South Asia generally is unthinkable. It's going to become unlivable pretty soon, if current climate policies persist. Last summer, the temperature in Rajasthan went up to 50 degrees Celsius. And it's increasing. There's hundreds of millions of people in India that don't have access to potable water. It's going to get much worse and could lead to a nuclear war between the two powers that basically rely on the same water resources, which are declining under global warming: Pakistan and India. I mean, the horror story that's developing is, again, indescribable. You can't find words for it. And some people are cheering about it, like Donald Trump and his friend Bolsonaro in Brazil, a couple of other sociopaths.

But how do you counter a reactionary international? By developing a Progressive International. And there are steps to that. They don't get much publicity, but—I think it's this coming December—there will be a formal announcement of what has been in process for some time. Yanis Varoufakis, the founder and leading figure in DiEM25, the progressive movement in Europe, and Bernie Sanders came out with a declaration calling for a Progressive International to combat and, we hope, overcome the reactionary international based in the White House.

Now, if you look at the level of states, this looks like an extremely unequal competition. But states are not the only things that exist. If you look at the level of people, it's not impossible. It's possible to construct a Progressive International based on people, ranging from the organized political groups that have been proliferating and have gotten a huge shot in the arm from the Sanders campaign, to self-help mutual aid and self-help organizations that are rising in communities all over the world, in the most impoverished areas of Brazil, for example. Even the astonishing fact that I mentioned, that the murderous crime gangs are taking responsibility for bringing some form of decent protection against the pandemic to the favelas in Rio—all of this is happening on the popular level. If it expands and develops, if people don't just give up in despair but work to change the world, as they've done in the past under much worse conditions—if they do that, there's a chance for a Progressive International.

And bear in mind that there are also striking cases of internationalism, progressive internationalism, at the state level. So, take a look at the European Union. The rich countries in Europe, like Germany, have recently given us a lesson in just what the union means. Germany is managing pretty well. They probably have the lowest death rate in the world, in a *Western* society. Right next door, northern Italy is suffering miserably. Is Germany giving them any aid? No. In fact, Germany even blocked the effort to develop euro bonds, general bonds in Europe which could be used to alleviate the suffering in the countries living under the worst conditions. But fortunately for Italy, it can look across the Atlantic for aid from a superpower in the Western Hemisphere, Cuba. Cuba is, once again, as before, exhibiting extraordinary internationalism, sending doctors to Italy. Germany won't do it, but Cuba can. China is providing material aid. So, these are steps toward progressive internationalism at the state level.

3

Militarization in a Time of Pandemic Crisis

Henry A. Giroux and Ourania Filippakou

We live at a time when the terrors of life suggest the world has descended into darkness. The Covid-19 crisis has created a dystopian nightmare which floods our screens and media with images of fear. Bodies, doorknobs, cardboard packages, plastic bags, and the breath we exhale and anything else that offers the virus a resting place is comparable to a bomb ready to explode resulting in massive suffering and untold deaths. We can no longer shake hands, embrace our friends, use public transportation, sit in a coffee shop, or walk down the street without experiencing real anxiety and fear. We are told by politicians, media pundits, and others that everyday life has taken on the character of a war zone.

The metaphor of war has a deep sense of urgency and has a long rhetorical history in times of crisis. Militarization has become a central feature of the pandemic age and points to the dominance of warlike values in society. More specifically, Michael Geyer defines it as the "contradictory and tense social process in which civil society organizes itself for the production of violence" (Geyer 1989: 9). Geyer was writing about the militarization of Europe between 1914 and 1945, but his description seems even more relevant today. This is clear in the way right-wing politicians such as Trump promote the increasing militarization of language, public spaces, and bodies. Terms such as "war footing," "mounting an assault," and "rallying the troops" have been normalized in the face of the pandemic crisis. At the same time, the language of war privileges the proliferation of surveillance capitalism, the defense of borders, and the suspension of civil liberties.

As the virus brings the engines of capitalism to a halt, the discourse of war takes on a new significance as a medical term that highlights the struggles to grapple with underfunded public health-care systems, the lack of resources for testing, the surge toward downward mobility, expanding unemployment, and the ongoing, heart-wrenching efforts to provide protective essentials for frontline and emergency workers. At the heart of this epic tragedy is an understated political struggle to reverse and amend decades of a war waged by neoliberal capitalism against the welfare state, essential social provisions, public goods, and the social contract. The failure of this oppressive death-dealing form of casino capitalism can be heard as Arundhati Roy observes:

> the stories of overwhelmed hospitals in the US, of underpaid, overworked nurses having to make masks out of garbage bin liners and old raincoats, risking everything to bring succor to the sick. About states being forced to bid against each other for ventilators, about doctors' dilemmas over which patient should get one and which left to die.[1]

The language of war is used by the mandarins of power to both address the indiscriminate viral pandemic that has brought capitalism to its knees and to reinforce and expand the political formations and global financial system that are incapable of dealing with the pandemic. Rather than using rage, emotion, and fear to sharpen our understanding of the conditions that abetted this global plague and what it might mean to address it and prevent it in the future, the ruling elite in a number of right-wing countries such as the United States and Brazil use the discourse of war either to remove such questions from public debate or to dismiss them as acts of bad faith in a time of crisis. Amartya Sen is right in arguing that "[o]vercoming a pandemic may look like fighting a war, but the real need is far from that."[2]

Instead the language of war creates an echo chamber produced in both the highest circles of power and the right-wing cultural apparatuses that serve to turn trauma, exhaustion, and mourning into a fog of conspiracy theories, state repression, and a deepening abyss of darkness that "serves the ends of those in power."[3] Edward Snowden is right in warning that governments will use the pandemic crisis to expand their attack on civil liberties, roll back constitutional rights, repress dissent, and create what he calls an "architecture of oppression." He writes:

> As authoritarianism spreads, as emergency laws proliferate, as we sacrifice our rights, we also sacrifice our capability to arrest the slide into a less liberal and less free world. Do you truly believe that when the first wave, this second wave, the 16th wave of the coronavirus is a long-forgotten memory, that these capabilities will not be kept? That these datasets will not be kept? No matter how it is being used, what is being built is the architecture of oppression.[4]

There is no doubt that the Covid-19 crisis will test the limits of democracy worldwide. Right-wing movements, neo-Nazis, authoritarian politicians, religious fundamentalists, and a host of other extremists are energized by what

Slavoj Žižek calls the "ideological viruses . . . [lying] dormant in our societies."[5] These include closing of borders, the quarantining of so-called enemies, the claim that undocumented immigrants spread the virus, the demand for increased police power, and the rush by religious fundamentalists to relegate women to the home to assume their "traditional" gendered role.

On the economic level and under the cover of fear, the United States in particular is transferring what Jonathan Cook refers to as:

> huge sums of public money to the biggest corporations. Politicians controlled by big business and media owned by big business are pushing through this corporate robbery without scrutiny—and for reasons that should be self-explanatory. They know our attention is too overwhelmed by the virus for us to assess intentionally mystifying arguments about the supposed economic benefits, about yet more illusory trickle-down.[6]

This constitutes a politics of "opportunistic authoritarianism" and is already in play in a number of countries that are using the cover of enforcing public health measures to enforce a range of anti-democratic policies and wave of repression. The pandemic has made clear that market mechanisms cannot address the depth and scope of the current crisis. The failure of neoliberalism not only reveals a profound sense of despair and moral void at the heart of casino capitalism, but also makes clear that the spell of neoliberalism is broken and as such is in the midst of a legitimation crisis. The coronavirus pandemic has made clear that (1) the neoliberal notion that all problems are a matter of individual responsibility and (2) that each of us defined exclusively by our self-interests has completely broken. That is, the effects of neoliberalism's failure to deal with the pandemic unfold in shortages in crucial medical equipment, lack of testing, and failed public health services, largely due to imposed austerity measures.

One consequence of the failed neoliberal state is an uptake in levels of oppression in order to prevent the emergence of massive protests movements and radical forms of collective resistance. The suspension of civil rights, repression of dissent, upending of constitutional liberties, and the massive use of state surveillance in the service of anti-democratic ends has become normalized. Many of the countries driven by austerity policies and a culture of cruelty are using the pandemic crisis as a way of shaping their modes of governance by drawing from what activist Ejeris Dixon calls elements of a "fascist emergency playbook." These include:

> Use the emergency to restrict civil liberties—particularly rights regarding movement, protest, freedom of the press, a right to a trial and freedom to gather.

> Use the emergency to suspend governmental institutions, consolidate power, reduce institutional checks and balances, and reduce access to elections and other forms of participatory governance. Promote a sense of fear and individual helplessness, particularly in relationship to the state, to reduce outcry and to create a culture where people consent to the power of the fascist state; Replace democratic institutions with autocratic institutions using the emergency as justification. Create scapegoats for the emergency, such as immigrants, people of color, disabled people, ethnic and religious minorities, to distract public attention away from the failures of the state and the loss of civil liberties.[7]

The evidence for the spread of this ideological virus and its apparatuses and polices of repression are no longer simply dormant fears of those fearful of the rise of authoritarian movements and modes of governance. For instance, Viktor Orbán, Hungary's prime minister, passed a bill that gave him "sweeping emergency powers for an indefinite period of time. . . . The measures were invoked as part of the government's response to the global pandemic."[8] What is becoming obvious is that the pandemic crisis produces mass anxiety that enables governments to turn a medical crisis into a political opportunity for leaders across the globe to push through dictatorial powers with little resistance.

For instance, as Selam Gebrekidan observes: "In Britain, ministers have what a critic called 'eye-watering' power to detain people and close borders. Israel's prime minister has shut down courts and begun an intrusive surveillance of citizens. Chile has sent the military to public squares once occupied by protesters. Bolivia has postponed elections."[9] In the Philippines, President Rodrigo Duterte, who has flagrantly violated civil rights in the past, was given emergency powers by the congress. Under the cloak of invoking public health measures because of the threat posed by the coronavirus plague, China has broken up protests in Hong Kong and arrested many of its leaders. In the United States, Trump's Justice Department has asked Congress "for the ability to ask chief judges to detain people indefinitely without trial during emergencies—part of a push for new powers that comes as the coronavirus spreads through the United States."[10]

In the United States, Trump blames the media for spreading fake news about the virus, attacks reporters who ask critical questions, packs the courts with federal sycophants, dehumanizes undocumented immigrants by labeling them as carriers of the virus, and claims that he has "total authority" to reopen the economy, however dangerous the policy, in the face of the coronavirus pandemic. In this instance, Trump markets fear to endorse elements of white supremacy, ultra-nationalism, and social cleansing while unleashing the mobilizing passions of fascism. He supports voter suppression and has publicly stated that making it easier to vote for many Americans such as Blacks and other minorities of color would mean "you would never have a Republican elected in this country again."[11] In the midst of economic hardships and widespread suffering due to the raging pandemic, Trump has tapped into a combination of fear and a cathartic cruelty while emboldening a savage lawlessness aimed at the most vulnerable populations. How else to explain his calling the coronavirus the "Chinese virus," regardless of the violence it enables by right wingers against Asian Americans, or his call to reopen the economy hastily knowing that thousands could die as a result, mostly the elderly, poor, and other vulnerable.

Militarizing the Media and the Politics of Pandemic Pedagogy

In the age of the pandemic, culture has been militarized. Donald Trump and the right-wing media in the United States have both politicized and weaponized the coronavirus pandemic. They have weaponized it by using a state of emergency to promote Trump's political attacks on critics, the press, journalists, and politicians who have questioned his bungling response to the pandemic crisis. They have politicized it by introducing a series of policies under the rubric of a state of exception that diverts bailout money to the ruling elite, militarizes public space, increases the power of the police, wages attacks on undocumented immigrants as a public health threat, and promotes voter suppression. In addition Trump has further strengthened the surveillance state, fired public servants for participating in the impeachment process, and initially claimed that the virus was a hoax perpetuated by the media and Democrats who were trying to undermine Trump's re-election.

Trump's language of dehumanization coupled with his appalling ignorance and toxic incompetence appears as a perfect fit for the media spectacle that he has made a central feature of his presidency. Trump's "anti-intellectualism has been simmering in the United States for decades and has now fully boiled over" and when incorporated as a central feature of the right-wing social media becomes "a tremendously successful tool of hegemonic control, manipulation, and false consciousness."[12] Trump's apocalyptic rhetoric appears to match the tenor of the moment as there is a surge in right-wing extremism, anti-Semitism, explosive racism, and a culture of lies, immediacy, and cruelty. What we are witnessing as the pandemic intensifies in the United States, and in some other countries across the globe, is the increasing threat of authoritarian regimes that both use the media to normalize their actions and wage war against dissidents and others struggling to preserve democratic ideas and principles.

Given his experience in the realms of Reality TV and celebrity culture, Trump is driven by mutually reinforcing registers of spectacular fits of self-promotion, joy in producing troves of Orwellian doublespeak, and the ratings his media coverage receives. One of the insults he throws out at reporters in his coronavirus briefings is that their networks have low ratings as if that is a measure of the relevance of the question being asked. Unlike any other president, Trump has used the mainstream media and social media to mobilize his followers, attack his enemies, and produce a twitter universe of misinformation, lies, and civic illiteracy. He has championed the right-wing media by both echoing their positions on a number of issues and using them to air his own. The conservative media such as Fox News has been enormously complicitous in justifying Trump's call for the Justice Department to dig up dirt on his political rivals, including the impeachable offense of extorting the Ukrainian government through the promise to withhold military aid if they did not launch an investigation into his political rival, Joe Biden. Moreover, they have supported his instigation of armed rebellions via his tweets urging his followers to liberate Minnesota, Michigan, and Virginia by refusing to comply with stay-at-home orders and social distancing restrictions. Ironically, he urges antisocial distancing protests that violate his own federal guidelines.

Trump has used the police powers of the state, especially the Immigration and Customs Enforcement (ICE) to round up children and separate them from their parents at the border. Placing loyalty above expertise, he surrounds himself with incompetent sycophants, and makes policy decisions from his gut, often in opposition to the advice of public health experts. All of this is echoed and supported by the conservative and right-wing ecosystem, especially Fox News, Breitbart News, and what appears to be a legion of right-wing commentators such as Rush Limbaugh, who falsely claimed the virus is a common cold, and Laura Ingraham, who deceitfully compared Covid-19 to the flu. Fox News not only produced conspiracy theories such as the claim the virus was the product of the "deep state" and was being used by Democrats to prevent Trump from being reelected, it also produced misinformation about the virus and represented what seventy-four journalism professors and leading journalists described as "a danger to public health." Like most authoritarians, Trump does everything to control the truth by flooding the media with lies, denouncing scientific evidence, and critical judgment as fake news. The latter is a direct attack on the free press, critical journalists, and the notion that the search for the truth is crucial to any valid and shared notion of citizenship.

The crisis of politics is now matched by a mainstream and corporate-controlled digital media and screen culture that revels in political theater, embraces ignorance, fractured narratives, and racial hysteria (cf. Butsch 2019). In addition, it authorizes and produces a culture of sensationalism designed to increase ratings and profits at the expense of truth. As a disimagination machine and form of pandemic pedagogy, it undermines a complex rendering of social problems and suppresses a culture of dissent and informed judgments. This pandemic pedagogy functions so as to shape human agency, desire, and modes of identification both in the logic of consumerism while privileging a hyper form of masculinity and legitimating a friend/enemy distinction. We live in an age in which theater and the spectacle of performance empty politics of any moral substance and contribute to the revival of an updated version of fascist politics. Thoughtlessness has become a national ideal as the corporate-controlled media mirror the Trump administration demand that reality be echoed rather than be analyzed, interrogated, and critically comprehended. Politics is now leaden with bombast, words strung together to shock, numb the mind, and images overwrought with self-serving sense of riotousness and anger. Trump shamelessly reinforces such a politics by showing propaganda videos at presidential news conferences.

What is distinct about this historical period, especially under the Trump regime, is what Susan Sontag has called a form of aesthetic fascism with its contempt of "all that is reflective, critical, and pluralistic."[13] One distinctive element of the current moment is the rise of what we call hard and soft disimagination machines. The hard disimagination machines, such as Fox News, conservative talk radio, and Breitbart media, function as overt and unapologetic propaganda machines that trade in nativism, misrepresentations, and racist hysteria, all wrapped in the cloak of a regressive view of patriotism.

As Joel Bleifuss points out, Fox News, in particular, is

> blatant in its contempt for the truth, and engages nightly in the "ritual of burying the truth" in "memory holes" and spinning a new version of reality [that keeps] the spirit of 1984 . . . alive and well . . . . This, the most-watched cable news network, functions in its fealty to Trump like a real-world Ministry of Truth from George Orwell's 1984, where bureaucrats "rectify" the historical record to conform to Big Brother's decrees.[14]

Trump's fascist politics and fantasies of racial purity could not succeed without the disimagination machines, pedagogical apparatuses, and the practitioners needed to make his "vision not merely real but grotesquely normal."[15] What Trump makes clear is that the weaponization of language into a discourse of racism and hate is deeply indebted to a politics of forgetting and is a crucial tool in the battle to undermine historical consciousness and memory itself.

The soft disimagination machines or liberal mainstream media such as NBC Nightly News, MSNBC, and the established press function largely to cater to Trump's Twitter universe, celebrity culture, and the cut-throat ethos of the market, all the while isolating social issues, individualizing social problems, and making the workings of power superficially visible. This is obvious in their mainstream's continuous coverage of his daily press briefings, which as Oscar Zambrano puts it, "is like watching a disease in progress that is infecting us all: a parallel to coronavirus" (Zambrano 2020). Unfortunately, high ratings are more important than refusing to participate in Trump disinformation spectacles. Politics as a spectacle saturates the senses with noise, cheap melodrama, lies, and buffoonery. This is not to suggest that the spectacle that now shapes politics as pure theater is meant merely to entertain and distract.

On the contrary, the current spectacle, most recently evident in the midst of the coronavirus crisis functions as a war machine, functioning largely to nurture the notion of war as a permanent social relation, the primary organizing principle of society, and politics merely one of its means or guises. War has now become the operative and defining feature of language and the matrix for all relations of power.

The militarization of the media, and culture itself, now functions as a form of social and historical amnesia. That is, in both form and content it separates the past from a politics that in its current form has turned deadly in its attack on the values and institutions crucial to a functioning democracy. In this instance, echoes of a fascist past remain hidden, invisible beneath the histrionic shouting and disinformation campaigns that rail against alleged "enemies of the state" and "fake news," which is a euphemism for dissent, holding power accountable, and an oppositional media. A flair for the overly dramatic eliminates the distinction between fact and fiction, lies and the truth.

Under such circumstances, the spectacle of militarization functions as part of a culture of distraction, division, and fragmentation, all the while refusing to pose the question of how the United States shares elements of a fascist politics that connects it to a number of other authoritarian countries such as Brazil, Turkey, Hungary, and Poland. All of these countries in the midst of the pandemic have embraced a form of fascist aesthetics and politics that combines a cruel culture of neoliberal austerity with the discourses of hate, nativism, and state repression. The militarization of culture and the media in its current forms can only appeal to the state of exception, death, and war. Under such circumstances, the relationship between civil liberties and democracy, politics and death, and justice and injustice is lost. War should be a source of alarm, not pride, and its linguistic repositories should be actively demilitarized.

Conclusion

Under the Trump regime, historical amnesia is used as a weapon of (mis) education, politics, and power and is waged primarily through the militarization and weaponization of the media. This constitutes a form of pandemic pedagogy—a pedagogical virus that erodes the modes of agency, values, and civic institutions central to a robust democracy. The notion that the past is a burden that must be forgotten is a center piece of authoritarian regimes, one that allows public memory to wither and the threads of fascism to become normalized. While some critics eschew the comparison of Trump with the Nazi era, it is crucial to recognize the alarming signs in this administration that echo a fascist politics of the past. As Jonathan Freedland points out, "the signs are there, if only we can bear to look."[16] Rejecting the Trump-Nazi comparison makes it easier to believe that we have nothing to learn from history and to take comfort in the assumption that it cannot happen once again. Democracy cannot survive if it ignores the lessons of the past, reduces education to mass conformity, celebrates civic illiteracy, and makes consumerism the only obligation of citizenship. Max Horkheimer added a more specific register to the relationship between fascism and capitalism in his comment: "If you don't want to talk about capitalism then you had better keep quiet about fascism."[17]

The lessons to be learned from the pandemic crisis have to exceed making visible the lies, misinformation, and corruption at the heart of the Trump regime. Such an approach fails to address the most serious crimes of Trump. Moreover, it fails to examine a number of political threads that together constitute elements common to a global crisis in the age of the pandemic. The global response to the pandemic crisis by a number of authoritarian states when viewed as part of a broader crisis of democracy needs to be analyzed by connecting ideological, economic, and cultural threads that weave through often isolated issues such as white nationalism, the rise of a Republican Party dominated by right-wing extremists, the collapse of the two party system, and the ascent of a corporate-controlled media as a disimagination machine and the proliferation of corrosive systems of power and dehumanization.

Crucial to any politics of resistance is the necessity to take seriously the notion that education is central to politics itself, and that social problems have to be critically understood before people can act as a force for empowerment and liberation. This suggests analyzing Trump's use of politics as a militarized spectacle not in isolation from the larger social totality—as simply one of incompetence, for instance— but as part of a more comprehensive political project in which updated forms of authoritarianism and contemporary versions of fascism are being mobilized and gaining traction both in the United States and across the globe. Federico Mayor, the former director general of UNESCO, once stated that "You cannot expect anything from uneducated citizens except unstable democracy." In the current historical moment and age of Trump, it might be more appropriate to say that what can be expected from a society in which ignorance is a virtue and civic literacy and education are viewed as a liability, one cannot expect anything but fascism.

The pandemic crisis should be a rallying cry to create massive collective resistance against both the Republican and Democratic parties and the naked brutality of the political and economic system they have supported since the 1970s. That is, the criminogenic response to the crisis on the part of the Trump administration should become a call to arms, if not a model on a global level, for a massive protest movement that moves beyond the ritual of trying Trump and other authoritarian politicians for an abuse of power. Instead, such a movement should become a call to put on trial a capitalist system while fighting for structural and ideological reforms that will usher in a radical and socialist democracy worthy of the struggle.

What is crucial to remember is no democracy can survive without an informed citizenry. Moreover, solidarity among individuals cannot be assumed and must be fought for as part of a wider struggle to break down the walls of ideological and material repression that isolate, depoliticize, and pit individuals and groups against each other. Community and a robust public sphere cannot be built on the bonds of shared fears, isolation, and oppression. Authoritarian governments will work to contain both any semblance of democratic politics and any attempts at large-scale transformations of society. Power lies in more than understanding and the ability to disrupt, it also lies in a vision of a future that does not imitate the present and the courage to collectively struggle to bring a radical democratic socialist vision into fruition.

The "New Normal" in Education Is Ultra-Neoliberal

In Defense of the Strategy that Breaks with the Time Continuum

Roberto Leher

This chapter seeks to enable reflection about the connections between the multivariate crises which fracture the effectiveness of the ideologies that reinforce the neoliberal accumulation system; the worsening of the crisis due to the pandemic; and, in Brazil's particular case, the future expectations of ultra-neoliberalism in line with the neofascist ideology. Polysemic, the ideology of the "new normal," denotes the confluence of many different perspectives for the future, all of which are pro-systemic. In this scope, education is being deeply reconfigured. Projections suggest a shrinkage in public educational assets, with the use of information and communication technologies (ICT), the expropriation of faculty members' intellectual role, the replacement of scientific knowledge by operational skills that are relevant to the market, a new scale of commodification and an intensification of "cultural disputes" against some values from the Enlightenment and the French Revolution. (Leher 2020a).

The Ideology of the "New Normal"

The #LeadTheNewNormal campaign, supported by the United Nations Secretary General, sends a message that revolves around "resilience" (United Nations 2020), the capacity to adapt, mainly among the younger generation. Before the pandemic, the ideology of the "new normal" was examined in 2008 by Wysong and Perrucci (2017) in the United States' structural crisis context. When facing the significant job losses and the devastation of the workers' income, the corporate press and think tanks from the dominant sectors brought the ideology to light again.

> Deep Inequality clarifies the origin and development of an ideology known as the "new normal," which is an elite-driven rhetoric of explaining and justifying economic hardships and challenges experienced in the last decade by the 80 per cent of Americans who occupy the bottom of the stratification hierarchy. Meanwhile, the top 1 per cent (the wealthiest Americans) and their minions in the next 19 per cent (executives, senior management, and highly-credentialed professionals) continue to capture nearly all of the benefits of economic growth experienced in the last decade, while the other 80 per cent (salaried professionals, wage workers, the self-employed, and the economic underclass) continues to struggle to stay afloat. (Muschert 2019)

The essence of this ideology is building an image for the future in which there is no alternative: workers can only get used to and settle for the profound and lasting downturn in their living conditions.

> The discussion draws heavily on key statements about the new normal derived from corporate media, political discourse, and public relations organizations (whether private or public sector), all of which come to clarify that the new normal is structurally inevitable, that there is no option but to adjust, and that such economic struggle is often the result of individual failures. (Muschert 2019)

Everyone who is following the pandemic from a scientific point of view knows that this is a truly dangerous and highly lethal reality which has interrupted commodity flows in the world's economy and, what is often discussed but not clearly explained, has aggravated preexisting social and economic issues. As revealed by the International Labor Organization's indicators (Organización Internacional del Trabajo 2020), in Latin America the period from 2014 to 2019 was the one with the lowest growth since 1950 (0.4%) and, with Covid-19, unemployment exploded and many activities of self-survival were made impossible, generalizing discouragement. The pandemic has thrown many millions of people into poverty due to a lack of occupation capable of ensuring minimum living conditions, which demands worldwide public measures to alleviate poverty at different scales. Due to the cost to the state, the alleviation of the misery of the millions of people discouraged by the pandemic is now used to justify the deepening of ultra-neoliberal policies, with a general loss of social rights. The "new normal" promotes adjustments and changes in neoliberalism, always in line with the "natural" "exits" to the crisis advocated by the mainstream: the generalization of another scale of labor exploitation, more expropriation of social rights, and a new order of magnitude of plundering of natural resources—all of which promoted as virtues. In this case, it is an "exit from the crisis" through the right, which has important particularities in Brazil's case.

The "New Normal" and the Paths to Neofascist Policies

Since the early 1990s, a period of consolidation of the neoliberal accumulation system (Saad Filho and Moraes 2018), the hegemonic ideology has been supported by the bourgeois class fractions under financial dominance. During this period there was an alternation in the government with different emphases: Fernando H. Cardoso resorted to the Washington Consensus' agenda; Lula da Silva and Dilma Rousseff had a stronger social agenda and a greater state presence in subsidized financing of so-called national champions, large contractors, and commodity giants. The impeachment of President Dilma Rousseff in 2016 (Miguel 2019) indicated an inflection in this zigzag. The autocratic solution triggered a right-wing offensive, making neoliberalism even more deeply averse to social policies and labor rights, hence the term "ultra-neoliberalism."

After Jair Bolsonaro's inauguration (January 2019), ultra-neoliberalism started to be hybridized with neofascist proposals (Mattos 2020), giving new contours to the bourgeois autocracy. This new situation had the direct or indirect support of the bloc in power (Poulantzas 1981), generating convergences and divergences between its private apparatuses of hegemony (Fontes 2020). Divergences have been particularly accentuated in the educational and environmental fields. Despite frictions, all the private apparatuses of hegemony have an agreement with the capital agenda: the shrinkage of the state's primary expenditures—therefore, funds for social care and investments—in favor of the world of finance and the deconstruction of the remains of the Federal Constitution's social rights.

The election of Jair Bolsonaro sparked a process with its own dynamism. The president does not hide his demagogic-Bonapartist pretensions (Gramsci 2007: 248). Therefore, he tries to present his government as if it was detached from the ruling bloc (to present himself to his electorate as "anti-system") although his actions are mainly facing "up." One of the Brazilian peculiarities stems from the fact that the bloc in power does not have its own political expression in the form of an organic party to represent its interests, with hegemonic strength. In the post-coup electoral process, the bloc was represented by a group of establishment parties which, although fragmented, had decisive support from members of the judiciary and from mainstream media, attaining the removal of Lula da Silva from 2018 elections, despite the polls indicating him as the electorate's favorite, with about 35 percent of the nominations. Since the bloc did not agree on a single candidate with popular support, it joined forces in the second round in favor of the right wing, sustained by various religious denominations, business associations, rent-sector operators, wholesale sectors, the radical petty bourgeoisie, military organizations, police forces, and for the political lumpen proletariat (militias). In summary, "Bolsonarism" found its Bolsonaro.

Bolsonaro's election unlocked the conciliation between ultra-neoliberalism and neo-fascism. Therefore, in Brazil, the "new normal" ideology is a heterogeneous set of thought dispositions. The extreme right adds to ultra-neoliberalism the social Darwinism and the characterization of internal enemies to be fought through the doctrine of "cultural wars" and even through open threats. Appeals to hatred toward the other, to chauvinistic nationalism, to racist expressions, to conspiracy theories, and to negationism indicate dangerous approaches to fascist ideology. Underlying the glamor of new technologies, the "new normal" can only be viable as an autocracy.

The "State of Exception" Evidenced by the Pandemic

Given the ideologies that seek to reestablish the predominance of a conception of normality that aims to hide neoliberal debris, structural racism and irrationalist offense against education, science, and culture, it is inspiring to rescue a proposition of Walter Benjamin on history: the "state of exception."

> The tradition of the oppressed teaches us that the "state of exception" in which we live is actually the general rule. We need to build a concept of history which corresponds to this truth. Only then will we realize that our task is to create a real state of exception; then our position will be stronger in the battle against fascism. The latter benefits from the circumstance that its opponents face him in the name of progress, considered as a historical norm. The astonishment caused by the fact that these episodes "are still" possible in the 20th century is not philosophical astonishment. It does not generate any knowledge, except the knowledge that the conception of history from which such astonishment emanates is unsustainable. (Benjamin 1987: 226)

The "state of exception" expresses an evolutionist conception of time:

> There is a painting by Klee called *Angelus Novus*. It represents an angel who seems to want to get away from something he is staring at. His eyes are wide

open, his mouth dilated, his wings spread. The angel in history must look like that. His face is turned to the past. Where we see a chain of events, he sees a unique catastrophe, which accumulates ruin upon ruin and disperses them at our feet. He would like to stop to wake the dead and collect the fragments. But a storm blows from paradise and catches on his wings so hard that he can no longer close them. This storm drives him irresistibly into the future, to which he turns his back, while the heap of ruins grows to the sky. This storm is what we call progress. (Benjamin 1987: 226)

For decades, neoliberal ideology, the fetish of free market, and the globalization of commodity and capital flows have been retreading the ideology of progress. The driving force of progress rests on a certain notion of time, and neoliberalism precisely spreads the belief that the future is foreshadowed forever: a future that does not even include the notions of history and society as in Francis Fukuyama's elaboration of the end of history (Bosoer 2020). The neoliberal accumulation system would be the peak of a capitalism that no longer has competing forces that could confront it ("there is no alternative"). This conception is considered, for its innovative qualities—the creative destruction—the supreme degree of civilization. In the current stage of dependent capitalism, the "social" margin of neoliberalism is increasingly residual, with autocracy standing out, as signaled, as the way to contain the resistance to the rubble of "progress."

Struggles and Resistance Challenge "New Normal" Foundations

Neoliberal ideologies and all traditions that refuse history, including certain idealistic postmodernisms, try to prevent looking at—and, above all, acting upon—the rubble (history), forbidding any remnant of potential alternatives to combat the determinants that cause them. However, many struggles in the most remote territories have shown, albeit in a fragmented and partial way, the unique catastrophe that is growing due to the current pattern of capital accumulation. Struggles in urban spaces, in the fields, in the forests, make it explicit that there are resistances and flashes of alternatives to the referred pattern of accumulation. Only the outbreak of social struggles that make explicit the determinants of the "state of exception" can reveal and combat what the "new normal" intends to trivialize.

In the last years of the dictatorship which ruled Brazil from 1964 to 1985, the number of strikes grew exponentially: from less than 100 in 1981 to 4,000 in 1989. During Collor's presidential term (1990–1992), strikes were reduced to an important 2,000 in 1991. Although it was a period of intense conflict, the average annual strike rate in the decade from 1992 to 2002 was 490. During Lula's presidency (from 2003 to 2010), the annual average was only 300 strikes, which, in general, were shorter (Ferraz 2018). It is a low number, considering the pension reform approved during his government with profound impacts on public servants. After 2013, there was an abrupt increase in the number of yearly strikes, going from 554 in 2011 to 877 in 2012 and 2,050 in 2013 (an increase of 133.8%). This level remained high until 2016 (2,093 strikes). After the coup, despite deeply regressive measures, the number of strikes fell again: 1,566 in 2017, 1,453 in 2018, and 1,118 in 2019 (Departamento Intersindical de Estatística e Estudos Socioeconômicos 2020). Other social conflicts continued to be important, such as the strike of delivery app drivers—ignited after the pandemic started—and the anti-racist struggles against police violence in favelas, which has been victimizing the Black youth. Precarious workers and the peripheries move.

Understanding rural conflicts is mandatory for the interpretation of dependent capitalism. According to the historical series collected by the Brazilian Pastoral Land Commission (Comissão Pastoral da Terra—CPT 2020), an organization linked to the National Confederation of Brazilian Bishops of the Catholic Church, the conflicts went from 1,186 in 2010 to 1,217 in 2015 and 1,536 in 2016. After the coup, they remained high: 1,431 in 2017, 1,498 in 2018, and, in the first year of Bolsonaro's term, 1,833 in 2019. In the past nine years, 411 people have been killed in these conflicts.

Despite the rise of urban struggles (2013–2016), the high conflictuosity of rural areas and, as of 2016, the successful general strike against the pension reform proposed by Temer's government in 2017, which was joined by approximately 40 million workers, these struggles failed to consolidate wide coalitions, greater journeys, or large national mobilizations. There have been no substantial struggles against the 2016 coup, Temer passed Constitutional Amendment no. 95/2016, which freezes and restricts social spending for twenty years, as well as a labor counter-reform. These events denote an evident lack of summoning capacities from the main trade union centrals, left-wing parties, and from the coordination of social movements such as the Popular Brazil Front (Frente Brasil Popular)—managed by the Workers' Party (Partido dos Trabalhadores—PT) and the Brazilian Landless Workers' Movement (Movimento dos Trabalhadores Rurais Sem Terra—MST)—and the Fearless People Front (Frente Povo Sem Medo)—linked to the Homeless Workers' Movement (Movimento dos Trabalhadores

Sem Teto—MTST), which is closer to the Socialism and Freedom Party (Partido Socialismo e Liberdade—PSOL).

The unfolding of the multitudinous and massive demonstrations of 2013 allows us to conclude that the interregnum between the struggles from 2003 to 2012 had an impact on the formation of class-consciousness. The bureaucratization of the Unified Workers' Central (Central Única dos Trabalhadores—CUT), its uncritical readjustment to "Lulism," and, above all, the scarcity of its pedagogical polarization with corporate private apparatuses of hegemony and with right-wing initiatives present in the religious field, in sports, in culture, and so on resulted in new forms of deep socialization—for which internet platforms were crucial—which formed common sense under the strong influence of the right-wing (Gramsci 2007: 54, 56, 194–197). This process expresses a situation similar to the transformism to which Gramsci refers (Boothman 2017).

The left disregards the fact that the extreme right and its think tanks (e.g., Atlas Network, Mises Institute, Instituto Millenium, Liberal Institute) opened gaps in the protests of 2013 and in its developments, such as the massive right-wing demonstrations of 2015 and 2016. Such disregard reveals the left's concerning detachment from the daily life of precarious workers who live in extreme deprivation in slums and territories of poverty. Meanwhile, economic agents' federations and confederations, as well as many of their private apparatuses of hegemony and parties, revealed an evident consensus among the elite concerning the need to "pause" democracy so as to rearrange the interests of capital (Miguel 2019: 20). These federations were led by the Industrial Federation of the State of São Paulo (Federação das Indústrias do Estado de São Paulo—FIESP), and relied on support from the Brazilian Social Democracy Party (Partido da Social Democracia Brasileira—PSDB) and the Democrats (Democratas—DEM) party.

The Ideology of the New Normal in Education

The ideology of the "new normal" entered the education field in merciless and overwhelming fashion. The "normal" to be hidden is, according to a teacher from a multinational education corporation, cruel. In Brazil, 2,230 (88.2%) out of the 2,537 existing higher education institutions are private.[1] Most of them (1,303 or 58%) are for-profit and belong to corporations controlled by financial organizations which have education as a mere part of their investment portfolio. Many of these companies trade their shares in the stock market.

The commodification of higher education in Brazil has no parallel around the world. Its magnitude can not only be verified in the fact that private institutions in Brazil hold 75.4 percent of "clients" (i.e., students) or in their near monopoly over education: the twelve largest groups account for 44 percent of all enrollments. The extent to which higher education is commodified is also present in its adherence to a time scale strongly compressed by the stock market dynamics and its profitability imperatives. The financial nature of these investments requires the realization of short- and medium-term profits, which is not simple in the education sector.

Brazil counts with a large young population—19.6 percent are twenty-five to thirty-four years old—and scarce access to higher education—represented by a 37.4 percent gross rate and a 25.7 percent net rate. Its higher education market, however, is very limited due to two inseparably connected factors: income inequality and a small number of students who finish high school—which is a prerequisite to higher education. In 2018, 13.5 million places were offered in Brazil, 6.3 percent of which by public institutions, whereas fewer than 2 million students finished high school that same year.

Corporations themselves recognize the role of public funds in raising their high profit rates through two main ways. The Students Financing Fund (Fundo de Financiamento Estudantil—FIES) provided support to 140,000 students in 2020, grew to comprehend 1,300,000 in 2015, dropped to 821,000 students in 2018 and finally reached 85,000 in 2019. Its costs, implicit subsidies included, amounted to slightly over 1 billion Brazilian reais in 2010, 24.3 billion in 2015, 34.4 billion in 2016, 30.2 billion in 2017, and 17.5 billion in 2018. Meanwhile, between 2015 and 2018, public funding for operational and capital expenditures of Brazil's sixty-three federal universities did not exceed 8 billion Brazilian reais per year.

The acquisition of places by the government through tax exemptions by the University for All program (Programa Universidade Para Todos—ProUni) rose from 312,000 contracts in 2009 to 575,000 in 2018. That process involved an increase in the supply of distance-learning courses, which is fundamentally a form of corporate response to decaying profit rates due to shrinking state investment. Table 4.1 is self-explanatory.

The process of course expansion through distance learning gained momentum in 2014. In 2018, 53 percent of all places were offered through distance learning—and 99 percent of them by private institutions. Despite the absence of a systematic survey, it is possible to state that this mode of teaching increased during the pandemic. Two common beliefs about this expansion

Table 4.1 For-profit Private Organizations in Higher Education (2012, 2016, 2018)

	2012	2016	2018
In-classroom learning	1,894,775	2,336,393	2,606,476
Distance learning	659,629	1,050,088	1,635,555

Source: Based on Inep data (Brasil 2013, 2017, 2019).

must be challenged, the first of which affirms that, because they operate in the financial and stock markets, these corporations emphasize academic rigor. They are focused on cost reduction. The second belief proposes that this expansion occurred under close state control, which is questioned by a report issued by the Brazilian General Accounting Office (Tribunal de Contas da União 2017).

The use of distance learning to cut costs by these companies has led to mass faculty layoffs. In the absence of a systematic survey, one may affirm to be sure that in slightly over a year more than 5,000 professors were dismissed, out of a total 180,000 working for private institutions. The distance-learning boom in for-profit private educational organizations during the pandemic caused the dismissal of 1,600 professors only in São Paulo—many of whom were given notice through texting apps. Professors on part-time contracts, who correspond to 30 percent of private institutions' faculties, saw their working hours drop to the point of earning US$100 for a month for a complex work, which requires a postgraduate degree. A professor who qualified the company's corporate strategies as "cruel" (Domenici 2020a) had been working exclusively for the same company for eight years and had their working hours reduced from twenty-four to six per week.

During the pandemic, the same corporation that dismissed and drastically reduced its faculty's working hours started using robots to correct student assignments, causing a new wave of layoffs (Domenici 2020b). The market interests of these educational corporations merge with those of giants from the information and communications technologies (ICT) sector, of corporate associations, and of foundations connected to corporations to outline a new future scenario for education in Brazil.

Public institutions are also suffering the influence of corporations and their commercial interests. Under the umbrella of the sector's leaders, the pandemic may be paving the way to the entrance of megacorporations into the infrastructure used to expand distance-learning or hybrid courses.

Naomi Klein acutely understood such movement:

> [The governor of New York, Andrew] Cuomo had announced a similar partnership with the Bill and Melinda Gates Foundation to develop "a smarter education system." Calling Gates a "visionary," Cuomo said the pandemic has created "a moment in history when we can actually incorporate and advance [Gates's] ideas . . . all these buildings, all these physical classrooms—why with all the technology you have?" he asked, apparently rhetorically. (Klein 2020a)

The narrative is well known: the Covid-19 pandemic must be seen as an opportunity. Professors, unions, and students who had so far been resisting the mainstreaming of distance learning in basic and higher education will have to give in to reality. The time has finally come for the retirement of analog professors who insist on hindering the progress of the digital world in education. Once such corporative resistance is removed, governments shall be able to acquire the infrastructure required by the new digital world. This shall be the "new normal" in education.

According to Klein (2020a), Google's former CEO Eric Schmidt admits that "We should also accelerate the trend toward remote learning, which is being tested today as never before." The philanthropy expressed in claims such as "we are all together in the pandemic" as well as in "generous" initiatives such as the "free" supply of platforms conceals the fact that corporations are using public institutions as room for low-cost tests and thus gaining strategic business knowledge.

Besides, Klein (2020a) insists, information, big data, business, and the ideology of security walk hand in hand. The Snowden affair, Giuliano Empoli's (2019) book *Les Ingénieurs du chaos*, and movies such as *The Social Dilemma* and *The Great Hack* about the operations of Cambridge Analytica demonstrate that algorithms target not only tangible commodities, but also the political market, and always in favor of the right wing.

The algorithms of big platforms aim at increasing (1) the time users spend on them, through mechanisms which are incompatible with ethics and involve psychological manipulation; (2) commercial and ideological interaction; (3) the collection of data from users—the actual business of these corporations, which monetize information from users. Based on big data, algorithms forge user profiles that erase the real subjects, limiting users to strongly manipulated "communities." Political consequences are evident: a racial supremacist will be inserted in "communities" in line with his beliefs, which are "protected" from scientific interaction, which indicate political candidates and partisan books, naturalizing and reinforcing racism.

In Brazil, the government collects files about teachers who protest against neofascist threats (Valente 2020); deans elected by academic communities are ignored by the president, who appoints his own favorites while officially igniting the dismissal of left-wing professors (Leher 2020b). This same government intends to put an end to the job stability of professors at public universities, making it easier to discharge them due to theoretical and political disagreement.

Under the mantle of the "new normal," governments have found a way to nearly apolitically overcome resistance to educational reforms which restrict thinking to acquiring "certain" competences, in line with neoliberal reforms (Goldstein, Macrine and Chesky 2011). Most corporate private apparatuses of hegemony announce schools in the future being managed by their complex network of operators, and plan the spread of charter schools, of remuneration for teachers being based on tasks and performance, of teaching competences associated with the algorithms of technological artifacts, and so on. Dispossessing teachers of their knowledge under autocratic circumstances, however, has further consequences.

According to the Organization for Economic Co-operation and Development (OECD 2019), the education under the "new normal" is understood as part of an ecosystem in which the authority of educators is watered down and shared with other decision-makers, such as parents, employers, students, and the community. Several networks enable these agents to share responsibilities whereas students become the organizers of their own learning process—"learning to learn." One may not overlook the irony contained in the fact that the "new normal" for education in the midst of the "digital revolution" of the twenty-first century resorts to the same principles preached by the New School (Escola Nova) movement of the early twentieth century (Duarte 2001).[2] The notion of learning how to learn resonates with the extreme right wing's expectations, since it deprives teachers of their role as intellectuals and organizers. More than a few religious cults and militia groups want to increase the subordination of schools to what they call "community"—namely, "the chosen ones" or the "we" opposing the "others." The term is used to denote the parts of "the community" which the right identifies as the guardians of Brazilian families' Christian values—as interpreted by neo-charismatic leaders.

The new normal manipulates fear and instability to offer the comfort of resignation in the midst of a social order that is the harbinger of continuous catastrophe:

> The idea of new normal steeped in the politics of emergency is, according to Robbins (2008), rooted in a form of neoliberal globalization in which the elite reinforce and institutionalize insecurity and anxiety—social, economic, and cultural—as central to the evolutions of the new normal. Robbins (2008,

p. 344) connected the discourse of fear to the new normal, noting that the criminalization and militarization of schools serve as clear illustrations of the march to global neoliberalism because schools serve as a primary site for where young people learn to live within the new normal: The function of regimenting-gone-wild in public schools—since, in its systemically violent undermining of basic human and pedagogical relationships, it clearly fails to satisfy its stated intentions of producing safe school environments—might be to teach kids how to learn to live (in fear) with neoliberal globalization in the future. (Goldstein, Macrine and Chesky 2011: 117)

One may summarize this ideology as a way to depoliticize and weaken the nexuses between the kind of education that challenges reactionary common senses and the development of consciousness, both of which are embedded in anti-systemic struggle. It is thus a pedagogy that naturalizes autocracy, hypercommodification, and the dispossession of educators' knowledge as a way to dismantle resistance against the destruction of what is left of social and labor rights. In Brazil, such ideology celebrates ideas of "cultural war" against democratic and libertarian traditions while restraining the common, the public, and the emancipation of humankind.

Conclusion

Capital as a class is informing several changes, such as new forms of remote work and working from home, as well as the expansion of self-entrepreneurship via digital platforms (uberization) (Ramonet 2020). As observed by Naomi Klein (2020b), the substitution of in-classroom education by virtual instruction may set a new standard for human relations deprived of effective face-to-face contact. Individualism is a part of the "new normal." Big corporations spreading these ideas, such as Google, Amazon, Facebook, Apple, and Microsoft, happen to be the ones making the most profit during the pandemic. The sharp confrontations between empires concerning global control over 5G and big data technologies exemplify that fact.

The "new normal" envisages a future in which a considerable part of existing school apparatuses will be deactivated in favor of massifying distance learning. This is not at all about utopias, but rather about a process currently in progress in higher education in Brazil. Schools and universities which will take the temporary role of hubs for the new reality tend to be institutions under the influence of corporations and their private apparatuses of hegemony. Therefore, corporations must be challenged.

> In order to democratize the internet, it is necessary to transform its forms of property and organization. [. . .] The internet can never be democratic while it belongs to private companies operating it to obtain profit. Ensuring that everyone has the resources required for a self-determined life and opportunities to participate in the decisions that affect them [. . .] requires us to develop cooperatively and publicly owned digital structures, both in terms of internet "cables" and so-called platforms. (Tarnoff 2020)

The "new normal" is incompatible with the common public school. Autocracy is implicit in a future scenario which bans social policies focused on the world of labor and committed to overcoming social inequality. In the "new normal," the bloc in power joins the strategists and the soldiers of the "cultural war": their common goal is to remove from the array of future possibilities the public, common, and secular school committed to educating insubmissive citizens.

Even extreme situations contain the germs of contradictions. For over thirty years education workers and students have acted as collective subjects in an outstanding resistance to neoliberalism. New lessons are being learnt in the struggle against the current ultra-neoliberalism in its neofascist face. The differential moment still to fully blossom happens when these struggles take root as another hegemony able to overcome the capitalist order being presently renovated as the "new normal." Resorting once again to Benjamin, workers are responsible for radically revealing the "state of exception" in order to overcome it. Such an immense historic challenge requires strong national-popular will to act for the transformation of reactionary common senses, always in internationalist fashion, in the active interweaving of new alliances between the dispossessed to build a new, libertarian, and anti-capitalist historic bloc.

Note

The chapter was translated from Portuguese to English by Jun Shimada.

Xenophobic Europe

Racist Policy toward Refugees

Georgios Tsiakalos with Stavros Malichudis and Iliana Papangeli

In June 2020, refugee families, most arriving in Athens from the Moria camp on the island of Lesvos, were unable to find housing and remained homeless for days, sleeping in Athens' Victoria Square. June 1, 2020, marked the implementation of the Greek law which terminates the provision of shelter for 11,237 refugees and beneficiaries via the Emergency Support and Accommodation System (ESTIA) housing program.

"They arrived at Victoria Square, as others had come before them about five years ago. Back then we had said we were caught off guard. Now what do we say? I was there today," wrote Georgios Tsiakalos, Professor Emeritus of Pedagogy at the Aristotle University of Thessaloniki, who has dedicated himself to defending the rights of asylum seekers arriving in Greece. Since 2015, he has been traveling around the country and commenting publicly on what has become known as the "refugee crisis," highlighting cases of human rights violations while, at the same time, opening his home to people in need.

We had an extensive conversation with Tsiakalos[1] about the reality of the refugees abandoned in Victoria Square and the thousands of asylum seekers who remain trapped in Greece (when they are seeking asylum in other European countries); the discriminatory policies of the European Union at the expense of mobile populations; "early deportations," a term Tsiakalos uses to describe the EU asylum system, which aims to prevent the arrival of refugee populations on the continent; and how anti-coronavirus measures affect different social classes and categories of citizens.

Malichudis and Papangeli: To begin with, we would like to talk about the coronavirus pandemic. In Athens, no safety measures were taken by the state in the refugee centers, and no help was provided to the homeless refugees

to deal with coronavirus. How do you interpret the actions of the Greek government to call on citizens to follow protection rules, but not to provide any protection to one of the most vulnerable groups in Greece?

Tsiakalos: If I had to answer with just one sentence, I would say: for the governments of European countries, the lives of those seeking asylum and protection in Europe do not matter. This is particularly true of those coming from Africa and countries by US military intervention and its allies. Before the coronavirus pandemic, we saw tens of thousands of dead in the Mediterranean; why expect different behavior toward them in the time of the pandemic? Let's look at what happened in Greece: in March, social distancing measures were mandated for all citizens of the country. They were the right measures to protect health. However, the term "social distancing" has a different meaning for citizens than it has for the refugees on the Greek islands who are forced to live in camps. Not only was avoiding close contact between the people in the camp impossible, but the government imposed a ban on anyone leaving the camp so that they would not come into any contact with citizens. And it is characteristic that the measures were lifted for citizens in the middle of May, yet they have been renewed every fourteen days for the refugee centers. In fact, the refugees are held in overcrowded conditions in tight spaces and without the provision of masks.

Malichudis and Papangeli: Who does such a policy banning refugees from leaving camps serve?

Tsiakalos: Every time the ban on refugees leaving the camps is announced, a message is sent to society: they are dangerous, but we have taken care to keep them away from you so you are not at risk. Thus the narrative long been adopted in official public discourse on the "danger" of refugees is further reinforced by an additional argument: they are not only supposedly dangerous to national security and the security of citizens, they are not only supposedly dangerous to national identity, now they are even dangerous transmitters of the virus. All refugee policies have served the general political choice of creating a sense of danger from outsiders, justifying government measures needed to protect us, even if they violate human rights. The pandemic offers governments new opportunities for disenfranchisement. And if the policy concerns "foreigners," already suspected to be "dangerous," then the violation is easier to accept, even though it is an internationally forbidden denial of human rights.

The acceptance of rights violations in "special cases" in order to protect "us" from supposed dangers is the beginning of acceptance of other violations that may undermine citizens' rights as well.

Malichudis and Papangeli: Is this a phenomenon that occurs only in Greece or also in other European countries?

Tsiakalos: Unfortunately, the pandemic has given other countries the opportunity to prevent even the arrival of those who can rightfully enter the country. The case of family reunification is typical. Several thousand refugees had the right to move from Greece and Italy to European countries where their families live, and their right was officially recognized by those countries. But as soon as the pandemic broke out, they were banned from traveling indefinitely to prevent the virus from spreading. One might accept this as an overly strict but necessary measure, if we did not witness a different treatment of refugees and citizens.

For example, Germany completely stopped the arrival of refugees, for whom it had already given its approval, but organized a huge operation repatriating German tourists from almost all countries of the world. Within 5 weeks more than 240,000 were repatriated from 62 countries. In addition, tens of thousands of seasonal workers from other countries were brought in, because they were considered necessary for harvesting asparagus. These workers traditionally live together in communes, which then resulted in the rapid emergence and spread of the virus. Refugees were required to stay in dire conditions in the camps and were not permitted to go and live with their families. The seasonal workers were recruited, left their families for financial reasons, were transferred under the responsibility of the employers and with the help of the German state to Germany, but in terms of their stay there they were treated the same as the refugees in the camps. I believe that the three cases I have mentioned (mass repatriation of German tourists, general refusal of refugees who were formally allowed to be reunited with their families, recruitment and lodging of seasonal workers) show with clarity the different regard the state has for different categories of people and the different way with which the state treated them in relation to the virus. This is for those who rushed to say that we are all equal against the virus. The truth is that the virus does not discriminate but a political system based on exploitation, inequality, and discrimination works to exacerbate the effects of the virus on groups already impacted by entrenched social inequality. Disenfranchised refugees and exploited seasonal workers are treated with the same disregard during the pandemic. But whereas refugees are systematically and always associated with supposedly imminent dangers, seasonal workers are essential to the economy. Even if their health and lives are at stake, the workers are not viewed as a political problem that requires restriction.

Malichudis and Papangeli: In the first months of the pandemic you had a special TV show called "Glimpses of Pandemic Society," aimed to do three things: (a) raise awareness of the need for strict adherence to the rules aimed at preventing the spread of the virus, (b) highlight the lack of measures taken by the government to handle the consequences of the pandemic for the unemployed, the poor, immigrants, the homeless, and other categories of the socially excluded, and (c) critique how the government used the pandemic to impose measures that infringe on basic civil rights. Why is intervention needed in these three areas? Give us some examples.

Tsiakalos: The pandemic has strongly exposed many problems directly related to politics: from health-care structures to the existence of widespread irrational beliefs that have already taken root in politics. This is why we are obliged to defend the survival and human dignity of all through word and active solidarity, on the one hand, to defend rational thought on the other, as its destruction paves the way for manipulation of citizens and the rise of anti-democratic forces. Let us recall Georg Lukacs's choice of title for one of his most important works *The Destruction of Reason*, where (Chapter VII. "Social Darwinism," racial theory and fascism) he describes the path to Nazism and the subsequent Nazi crimes.[2]

In my shows, first of all, I presented the scientific data, which showed the need to take measures to protect against the virus. This information was necessary for the protection of everyone, but also because, as in other countries, there were many in Greece who were oriented toward the views of conspiracy theorists and politicians such as Donald Trump, Jair Messias Bolsonaro, Boris Johnson and other neoliberals or fascists. And this is particularly dangerous both from a health and political point of view.

Of course, it was also necessary to deal with the fact that the results of the pandemic were not equally severe for all social classes and categories. In Greece we had a strict quarantine system at home and a traffic ban limiting all but necessary outings which required prior notification of the police. But how can day laborers survive who suddenly have no money to buy what they need? And how can the children of poor families, immigrants, and refugees participate in education when education is transformed into home schooling exclusively through communication technologies that are nonexistent in their homes? In such cases, there was a need to organize practical solidarity, even in violation of strict travel measures but with strict observance of sanitary protection rules. And it was organized. Many teachers prepared traditional learning materials for their lesson and delivered them to children at their homes. And in many cases, they also provided the families with the essentials necessary for their survival when they discovered them lacking. For this purpose, informal support networks were created. The same went for the social kitchens of solidarity activists who used to serve mainly the needs of the homeless and refugees but were being asked to do the same for many more impoverished families. They succeeded and became an example for the leaderships of some municipalities.

The pandemic, alongside the restrictions by the governments, brought the absolute exclusion from education of one group of children: the children of the refugee families staying in the camps. Since 2015, governments had already implemented a policy of apartheid with respect to the education of children of refugees: they would go to school in the afternoon, at a time when the Greek children have already left, and would be taught a reduced curriculum both in terms of hours and quality. Even this limited access to education was met with opposition by fascist groups, with attacks on children and teachers. But the vast majority of teachers and citizens who stood against the fascists demanded the government allow full participation in normal classes for refugee children living outside the camps. Regarding the children living inside camps, the governments did not back down and instituted educational apartheid. With the arrival of the pandemic and the ban on refugees leaving the camps, these children were left without even this minimal education.

I could give many examples, but I think it suffices to say that the society of solidarity in practice is the one that effectively resists both the political as well as the health dangers posed by the pandemic.

Malichudis and Papangeli: We have not forgotten that the main purpose of our discussion is refugees but we want to ask one last question about the pandemic. How do you see the concerns of academics and intellectuals about the pandemic and refugees?

Tsiakalos: The pandemic response was associated with two terms "quarantine at home" and "social distancing." But these measures do not mean the same thing to people of different social classes and categories. Many see the imposed constraints as harsh and vague and as deepening their struggle for survival; others see it as an opportunity to reflect on priorities in their lives and society at large. Most academics and intellectuals belong to the second category, and their output on what is happening in this pandemic society and what they think can and should change after this experience was truly vast. They were widely hosted in the media, where the philosophers took the lead, with the main question being essentially the same: "how does the hierarchy of values change or should change after the experience of the pandemic?" I do not wish nor is it possible within this discussion to analyze and evaluate the concerns and proposals that have been made. For brevity, I will borrow the first half of Marx's eleventh thesis on Feuerbach: "The philosophers have only interpreted the world, in various ways." But this merely preserves the system whereas Marx insisted, that "the point is to change it." We must change the economic and political system in the direction of a "human society or social humanity," as the tenth thesis describes the desired and striven for society of the future.

I believe everything connected with the birth of the phenomenon of mass asylum and the treatment of refugees by European countries is rooted in acceptance of state of exception. "The threshold that separates humanity from barbarism has been crossed," says Giorgio Agamben,[3] noting that "the state of exception" is even stronger in the pandemic. Slavoj Žižek says: "One thing is sure: isolation alone, building new walls and further quarantines, will not do the job. Full unconditional solidarity and a globally coordinated response are needed, a new form of what was once called Communism."[4] To turn to the question about intellectuals, the eternal question remains: how will such changes come about? Who loses and who gains from the proposed changes? And thus who hinders them and who has an interest in seeing them realized?

Malichudis and Papangeli: The issue of refugees in our country, and in Europe, is at a critical juncture. In Greece, the "decongestion of the islands" led to the "occupation" of Victoria Square by people coming from the islands. In other words, thousands of people who received asylum in Greece have now been forced into homelessness. In Europe, Germany has promised to solve the issue during Germany's presidency of the Council of the European Union (July through December 2020), and so has the EU Commission. You've been closely following developments for years. Could you explain where we're at currently?

Tsiakalos: We're at the most worrying turning point for Greece and for Europe since the so-called refugee crisis began. For the first time, the governments of European countries are questioning the basic principles, values, and international treaties that have characterized societies since the post–Second World War era. And, unfortunately, we see Greece at the forefront of these developments.

From the very first day, I was with the homeless families sleeping in Victoria Square. There was a total of forty-eight people, eight families, many young children, one of them a fourteen-day-old infant. The next day another thirty to thirty-five people arrived. Some said that "the refugees have occupied the square," but the correct wording is the refugees "were abandoned on the streets" by the services that forced them to leave Moria promising that they would be housed in apartments in Athens. In other words, the government sent an "international" message that it was finally transferring refugees from the islands to mainland Greece, but what the government did not do was take into consideration the most basic measures for housing of these refugees. I don't know if this is due to a lack of coordination between the services, or if it was done on purpose, as part of the government agenda to show that the problem is supposedly no longer manageable.

Malichudis and Papangeli: What exactly do you believe was the Greek government intention?
Tsiakalos: The current government's refugee policy has gone through two phases. In the beginning, when the current government came to power, it stated that the problems could be easily dealt with, as long as there was a willingness for change. First, its policy aimed to reduce the time it took to process asylum applications, and then also to undertake immediate deportation of those who are not granted asylum. Secondly, the policy aimed at the immediate decongestion of the islands by transferring refugees to various locations on the mainland. The government quickly realized that the processing time could not be reduced as much as it had anticipated, nor was the deportation process as easy as it had imagined. In terms of decongestion on the islands, Mr. Koumoutsakos, the relevant minister, began the process of transferring refugees to the mainland. However, while the negative reactions to the arrivals of refugees on the mainland were minimal, this policy was abandoned suddenly and without explanation. Instead of tackling the issue with appropriate measures, the refugees began to be seen as "invaders." In this case, presenting the refugee issue as a threat and not as a humanitarian challenge is a conscious political choice, not only of the Greek government, but also of the governments of many other European countries, as well as the EU itself. In this context, the image of homeless refugees in a square is used by governments to establish the view that the problem is no longer manageable and beyond the governments to control, thereby working to generate and fuel negative reactions from locals. Thus, even the reemergence of the neo-Nazi party, Golden Dawn, and others like them, under the guise of "outraged citizens," acquires elements of legitimacy.

Malichudis and Papangeli: What are some immediate solutions that would help the refugees?
Tsiakalos: The previous Greek government had already begun to close the housing centers in mainland Greece and to create new ones on the islands. We

know that the proposal for the refugees to remain on the islands and suffer came from McKinsey,[5] the private consulting firm which was commissioned by the EU to develop a proposal on tackling the refugee crisis—for a fee of 1 million euros. There were tragic consequences as a result of this policy agenda. For the current government, decongestion of the islands must resume as a primary undertaking, and this must be done in conjunction with a comprehensive housing program on the mainland. For this purpose, a program such as the ESTIA program is suitable—the renting of apartments and tourist units that are empty due to the pandemic, and, if necessary, modernizing some of the existing housing centers. It would be more beneficial if empty apartments that are owned by municipalities were used for this purpose. The City of Athens has a lot of apartments which came into its possession by EFKA (Social Security Fund). Instead, the government decided to set up three new reception centers on leased land on the islands of Samos, Leros, and Kos, although they claim they are interested in decongestion of the islands. The funding that was calculated and approved for this was €132,680,000. If this money, or at least a part of it, was given to the municipalities to renovate and equip the empty apartments and buildings they own, then these dwellings could be used both now and later, not only by refugees but also by Greek families in need. This can be implemented immediately, offering a solution to the pressing issues. But obviously it's a political decision not to implement any of these solutions. The housing problem also stems from another government act: many refugees remain here under Greece's responsibility, although they have been accepted by other countries. It concerns those refugees for which, under the Dublin III Regulation, another country is responsible. And these cases number in the several thousand.

Malichudis and Papangeli: Do you mean that these refugees have already been accepted by another country and yet Greece forces them to remain here?
Tsiakalos: We oblige them to stay here, at least for longer than necessary. The Dublin III Regulation stipulates that the asylum application submitted in Greece by the members of the same family is transferred and decided upon in the country where another family member had previously applied for asylum. This is usually called "family reunification"; at its core this policy makes it easier for asylum authorities to process requests by combining information from all family members. In these cases, the asylum application is made in Greece, then it is transferred electronically to the other country, which must respond within two months. If they get a positive response, the refugee family can leave immediately. But from 2015 until now, Greece has systematically delayed all these processes. According to the data from the Greek Asylum Service, in February 2020 3,229

refugees had been accepted by other countries but had not been transferred yet. Allow me to point out that once the other country has accepted the request, then it cannot do anything to prevent the transfer unless a period of six months has elapsed.

The delay does not only happen after the acceptance by the other country: it also happens in all previous phases. There are thousands of cases that fall under the Dublin Regulation but have been given a set time to apply for asylum by the end of 2021 or later. Although these applications will not be judged in Greece and will be transferred to another country, the applicants are detained in our country for more than two years, artificially increasing the number of Greek refugees.

Malichudis and Papangeli: What is the basis for the detainment of refugees granted asylum by other countries? The Greek governments says it does not want Greece to have many refugees; it would be logical to facilitate the fastest possible transfer to other countries.

Tsiakalos: Many people in our country find it difficult to believe that this is happening systematically; when they accept this fact, they seek to find the cause in the bureaucracy or blackmail by other countries, with the Greek government caving due to our deep economic crisis. The fact is, it is an implementation of the official policy of the European Union called "deterrence policy," which means taking measures to deter those who in the future would seek to come to Europe. A few years ago, a prominent member of the ruling party described this policy: "They have to do worse here than in their own countries. Hell must be like paradise in relation to what they will endure here." Of course, this policy does not have the effect the government is seeking and for a simple reason. There are hundreds of thousands of legal immigrants and refugees in Europe living apart from their families. In all countries there are laws that provide the right for visas to be issued to family members for the purpose of family reunification. However, since 2016, the relevant national laws have been poorly implemented or in practice suspended. Germany is a prime example: in 2016, it completely suspended enforcement of family reunification for two years and then decided that the number of people to be issued the relevant visa could not exceed 1,000 per month. Therefore, it will take ten to fifteen years for applicants to be able to make use of this right granted to them by law. This is the reason thousands of women with babies and young children choose the perilous voyage across the sea and endure all this suffering. The deterrence policy does not deter anyone, because the decision to immigrate specifically for this category of people is a singular opportunity to protect their family, an institution that is otherwise praised by most conservative politicians.

Malichudis and Papangeli: Germany currently holds the EU presidency, and Horst Seehofer, the minister responsible for refugee claims in Germany, plays a key role in setting the policy agenda for the refugee crisis. It has been widely recognized that initiatives should be taken to agree on a common policy to deal with the problems, thus alleviating the burden that so far Greece, Italy, and Spain have been shouldering. What's your assessment?

Tsiakalos: The sense that such efforts will be made has already been weakened by Horst Seehofer himself, who said that if there are solutions, they will be given during the next term of the Portuguese EU presidency. However, it is certain that we will see intense activity toward the acceptance of a common policy, which will be in complete contradiction with the values and principles that we have seen enshrined in refugee policy until now. Let me state it more clearly: leaders of European countries have no problem with the number of immigrants and refugees; they have a problem exclusively with immigrants and refugees coming from the war-torn and impoverished regions of Asia and Africa. Ironically, the conflicts in Asia (Afghanistan, Iraq, Syria) are a result of unsolicited US and European intervention, and the conflicts and poverty in Africa are a result of the long-term US and EU economic infiltration, which has led to financial decline along with political and military interventions that have keep corrupt leaders in power. For the victims of this foreign policy, who are forced to seek protection far from their homelands, Europe believes the international treaties and laws that it has created should not apply. In the first case—the refugees from Asia—it's a refusal to accept responsibility for the catastrophic military interventions against their citizens. The intervention in Iraq was carried out because Iraq allegedly had chemical weapons that threatened the West. It turned out to be a lie, but the country was destroyed, it became a haven for jihadist gangs; the political situation never normalized, people are in danger and had to flee to save themselves. By refusing to grant asylum and protection to these people, the countries whose intervention brought disaster are sending a message to their citizens that the military operation has succeeded, was therefore justified, and there is absolute security in Iraq. The same is true of Afghanistan, where the Taliban is now being called upon by the United States and Europe to join the government, even if its very presence was an excuse for military intervention in the first place and it has established a regime of terror throughout most of the country. Only Europe's attitude toward the refugees from Syria is different, and this is due to the fact that its declared enemy, Bashar al-Assad, is still in power. In the second case, of refugees from Africa, we're dealing with a classic case of racist policy based on people's skin color.

Malichudis and Papangeli: You say that Europe has an issue only with immigrants and refugees from Asia and Africa, and not with the large number of immigrants and refugees in general. What is this view based on?
Tsiakalos: On indisputable data, which is accessible to all. Europe, due to the low birth rate of the last decades, needs a large number of immigrants to be able to address problems with the economy, and especially of its insurance systems. The problem here is more acute than in any other part of the world. At the same time, Europe has the material potential to absorb a large number of immigrants very quickly. Given the above, it pursues a policy of attracting and accepting immigrants, but excluding the categories of people I mentioned earlier. Let me give an example. In 2017, the number of refugees who crossed the Aegean and the Mediterranean was 171,000. This number was considered particularly high and led to measures to reduce it. These measures have had huge financial costs as they involve ships, weapons, personnel. And the measures have also resulted in the death of thousands of people in the waters of the Mediterranean. But in the same year, 662,000 immigrants from Ukraine and 193,000 from China, essentially from Hong Kong, passed through and received a residence permit. A simple comparison of numbers answers the question of whether Europe "can handle" more immigrants and refugees. We see that anti-refugee rhetoric is based on a blatant lie, which aims to persuade and intimidate those who don't know the truth.

I will add one more point: the number of immigrants and refugees from Eastern Europe has been high since 2016, as Poland, in need of labor, has accepted irregular immigrants from its eastern borders. As a rule, Poland did not offer asylum and protection, but they did grant residence and work permits. At the same time, while Poland treated them and used them as immigrants, Poland insisted on describing them as refugees and thus justified its refusal to participate in the distribution of refugees coming from the Aegean and the Mediterranean, saying that it had already accepted more refugees than Greece, Italy, and Spain as a whole. Of course, it was an absurd claim, but unfortunately it was also reinforced by those in our country who similarly blurred the term "immigrants" and "refugees," and insisted on calling people from Syria, Afghanistan, Iraq, and other war-torn countries "immigrants," even "clandestine immigrants" rather than refugees seeking protection.

Malichudis and Papangeli: These are relatively unknown facts to most people. Can you tell us how the EU reacted to this situation?

Tsiakalos: The EU's reaction demonstrates the fact that certain measures apply to migration and asylum on Europe's eastern borders, and other rules apply to migration on the southern borders. In a recent paper, Chiara Loschi and Alessandra Russo (2020)[6] compare the different ways the EU has handled (irregular) migration at the two gateways, Ukraine and Libya. Their answer is clear: European policy is not the same across all borders; its policy depends on the policy adopted and defended by the countries directly involved. If Poland is not hostile to the Ukrainians, the Belarusians, etc., then the whole of Europe opens its borders. Thus, under pressure from Poland, the EU, in May 2017, tackled the problem of irregular migration by removing Ukraine from the list of countries requiring Schengen visas. The "irregulars" or "clandestine immigrants," as they would be called by some in our country, became legal overnight and were no longer a "threat." They can travel freely to any EU country, and that country decides whether it will allow them to stay or not.

However, while Greece agreed that Ukrainians were no longer a threat to Europe and made it easier for Poland, Greece did not make the same request on behalf of the people passing through our country. Who benefits from this position and political behavior? It's up to each of us to examine. What the example of Ukraine clearly shows, however, is that Europe has no problem accepting large numbers of immigrants and refugees. It also reveals that there are no, by definition, enemies and friends among immigrants/refugees. The EU defines which groups are "friends" and "enemies" on paper, and, whenever it wants, it turns enemies into friends and keeps others on the list of dangerous and unwanted. From there on, the EU behaves accordingly toward that group of people.

Malichudis and Papangeli: What does "behave accordingly" mean?

Tsiakalos: Again, I will use the example of the refugees from Afghanistan.

Germany is deporting well-integrated Afghans, whom its employers say are essential to running their businesses. The same goes for well-integrated nurses from Afghanistan who are being deported, while the German health minister is traveling to Mexico to attract 40,000 nurses, who will receive language courses, travel expenses, a residence permit, and a job.

So, you see that this is a political choice that is implemented despite the opposition of local employers and against the interests of the economy. Do you think that this happens by chance and for no reason? Certainly not. It serves a purpose: it aims to influence popular opinion that Afghans are not in danger in their own country, even if international organizations consider Afghanistan to be the most dangerous region in the world. At the same time, it sends the message that the security of European countries are at stake, thus, legitimizing emergency measures of patrolling and the militarization in the Mediterranean, all of which would not be possible, and accepted by society if it wasn't for the threat of the alleged "refugee-enemy."

Malichudis and Papangeli: Are there similar examples that support your view that racist policies have been enacted against refugees from Africa?
Tsiakalos: Official United Nations figures show that of the ten countries with the highest numbers of displaced persons due to war and persecution, five are in sub-Saharan Africa, four in Asia (Syria, Afghanistan, Iraq, Myanmar), and one in Latin America (Venezuela, where leaving the country is related to food shortages, and not to war or armed civil conflicts). Immigrants and refugees from sub-Saharan Africa mainly use the Mediterranean route (to Italy and Spain) to reach Europe, and then the Aegean route (to Greece). These are the most dangerous routes in the world. According to official figures, from 2014 to 2019 more than 19,000 people lost their lives. Of those who try to get to Italy, it is estimated that one in six loses their lives. In addition to those who lose their lives in the Mediterranean, there is a greater number of people who lose their lives in the Sahara or in the slave markets of Libya. What is the actual number of refugees, which makes Europe consider them the greatest threat and which justifies spending hundreds of millions of dollars a year to prevent them from coming? In 2018, 58,525 people made it to Spain and 23,037 to Italy. In 2019 the numbers were 25,731 and 11,471 respectively. Asked to comment on the confirmation of The European Border and Coast Guard Agency (FRONTEX) that the number of illegal entries at Europe's southern borders has fallen sharply, Fabrice Leggeri, director of FRONTEX stated: "Of course the numbers are lower now, but the migratory pressure on Europe remains huge." That is, even though the arrivals from sub-Saharan Africa have decreased, Europe will continue to state that there remains a huge danger. And it will continue a policy that can rightly be called, "Black lives don't matter in the Mediterranean" in stark contrast to the movement in the US that insists "Black Lives Matter."

Malichudis and Papangeli: So is it "Black Lives Don't Matter" in Europe?
Tsiakalos: Is there any doubt? The fact that these are "Black lives" that motivates the director of FRONTEX to make statements about "huge immigration pressure" is made clear by another group of immigrants and refugees that

provoke no such response. In 2018 and 2019, 35,568 and 91,765 people, respectively, sought asylum and protection in Spain, coming from five Latin American countries. They came by plane, as these countries do not require a Schengen visa. In this case we have a significant increase in arrivals, but this is neither in the news nor is an issue for Europe. It is also not in the news that in Spain the request for protection of 39,715 citizens of Venezuela was approved for humanitarian reasons (with only 205 rejections). During the same period, the largest number of similar approvals for citizens of sub-Saharan Africa was thirty-five who were Nigerian citizens (with eighty-two rejections). Another typical example would be the recent announcement[7] on push-backs at Spain-Morocco border by the European Center for Constitutional and Human Rights (ECCHR), one of the most authoritative legal networks, in collaboration with the research agency Forensic Architecture, at the University of London. According to the announcement, Black citizens of sub-Saharan Africa do not have access to legal routes to Spain and, therefore, to international protection. And this is precisely the result of the racist policies applied at the Spanish-Moroccan border. The organization's Deputy Director, Christina Varvia, has argued that Europe continues to systematically discriminate against Black immigrants and refugees.

To avoid any misunderstanding, when I compare the difference in how the Ukrainians and Latin Americans who wish to come to Europe and ask for protection versus the Afghans, Iraqis, and people from Africa, I do not believe the former should receive the negative treatment experienced by the latter. On the contrary, I believe all people in need should have the possibility to submit their petition without first putting their life in danger. Through the comparison I wish to highlight the hypocrisy of those saying Europe can bear no further immigrants, and also the flagrantly negative stance taken toward the victims of military interventions of the US and their European allies, and the openly racist policies toward people from Africa.

Malichudis and Papangeli: Of course, in Europe people don't say that they have a problem with people of color when it comes to immigrants and refugees; instead they talk about "different religions" and "different cultures," that allegedly makes integration difficult.

Tsiakalos: Yes, that is what's being said, so let me add some information on this subject. The majority of people in sub-Saharan Africa are Christians, mostly Catholics—there are almost as many Catholics in that region (235 million) as there are in Europe (285 million). Immigrants and refugees from the region speak the languages of the former colonial countries, English or

French. Therefore, they objectively face fewer integration problems than all the other groups. Their only particular problem is combating the racism of many Europeans and especially European governments. So I wonder: if Muslims and other non-Christian immigrants and refugees are a problem for Catholic Poland, what is the problem with Catholics of Africa? Do the words of Pope John Paul II who was Polish count for anything? Europe is doing something different today, with Poland leading the way with this inhumane policy. Poland, the homeland of Pope John Paul II, who in his exhortation on September 14, 1995,[8] described the values and cultures of African societies in the most positive words and with absolute respect. So, since neither religion, nor culture, nor ignorance of European languages is a problem for even conservative Europeans, do I need to say more to explain the roots of the EU's hypocritical and inhumane policy toward people from Africa?

Malichudis and Papangeli: What do you expect from the initiatives of the German presidency of the EU to resolve the refugee issue?
Tsiakalos: I don't expect a solution, because European governments, while decisively participating in creating conditions that give rise to mass migration in the world, are trying to keep away refugees from the countries I mentioned earlier. In public discourse in Europe, mainly issued by governments, it is presented that countries like Germany, with a population of 82 million and a GDP of 3.5 trillion (per capita of 42,000), considers hosting 1.1 million refugees, an unbearable burden, whereas Uganda, with a population of 40 million and a GDP of 24 billion (per capita 634), can evidently host 1.4 million refugees. UN figures show that impoverished countries, such as Ethiopia, Sudan, or Bangladesh, have received 27 percent of refugees, and a total of 85 percent with other developing countries. The political decision to prevent the arrival of refugees in Europe leads to a series of measures, the most important of which is the so-called externalization of asylum, that is, to countries outside Europe. In essence, the "Fortress of Europe" using threats and few gifts turns many poor countries into ditches and embankments.

It is an ineffective medium- and long-term policy, costing thousands of lives, undermining the core values of our civilization and democratic political system, strengthening dictatorships in Africa and the Middle East, breeding and reproducing large-scale corruption, and at the same time strengthening the neo-Nazi, far-right groups in Europe. In this context, the countries of Europe in the south, mainly Greece, become hostages of blackmail through the utilization of immigration from neighboring countries. For example, Turkey has an agreement with Europe not to allow any immigrants to leave Turkey for Greece and Bulgaria, even when they have legal papers. Exit is only allowed to other neighboring countries. This agreement precludes the possibility of someone coming to Greece legally and seeking asylum and is one of the many forms of externalization of asylum. But in March 2020, the Turkish president Recep Tayyip Erdogan opened one border station at Greek-Turkish border in Evros for immigrants who wanted to leave the country. This was something new with the apparent aim of the Turkish president being to blackmail the EU and secure concessions on a range of issues. The result was that Greece closed its borders and responded to the efforts of the refugees with tear gas. "Greece under attack" was the slogan used at the time to describe the situation—a term suggestive of the 9/11 terrorist attacks. The operation to prevent the approach of refugees or irregular entry involved the police, the army, the militia, forces from various European countries and the Greek far-right. This veritable battlefield did not lack neo-Nazis from across Europe, who came to take part in the war of white Europe against the "barbaric East." We recall that similar events took place in 2016 on the Greek-North Macedonia border, but at that time North Macedonia suddenly closed its borders and erected a rudimentary fence. When some refugees in a symbolic move tried to remove a small part of the fence a few meters long, the police of North Macedonia responded by using tear gas and rubber bullets against the refugees who were on Greek soil. Greece back then strongly protested against the behavior of its neighboring country. Today such behaviors are taken for granted for the whole of Europe and for our country.

Malichudis and Papangeli: Can you further explain this policy of "externalization of asylum?"

Tsiakalos: From early on, European policy aimed to keep immigrants and refugees from the Middle East and Africa away from Western and Northern Europe. Until 2001, people from all over the world who wanted to seek asylum and protection in Europe could take a plane to any airport and apply there on arrival. As a rule, they would choose one of the wealthier EU countries, mainly Germany, France, the United Kingdom, Sweden, the Netherlands, and Belgium. Also, those from North Africa would come via sea on ships. These were legal trips, as long as they had a valid passport from their country and the right to enter the country of destination was verified by the police authorities at the airport or port, as was always the case until then. In 2001, the EU decided that this check should be carried out by airlines and shipping companies before departure, and that those who do not have a Schengen visa (for countries which require them) should be excluded from boarding. Fines for airlines and shipping companies that do not comply are devastating and threaten their very existence. This is a transfer of control to private entities outside the EU. The countries of Southern Europe agreed to this decision, without taking into account that for thousands of prospective immigrants and refugees from Africa and the Middle East the only routes were now from the Evros River (Greek-Turkish border) and the Mediterranean to be labeled "irregular entries." Thus, wealthy EU countries "got rid of" dealing with the arrival of people in need of asylum.

Malichudis and Papangeli: On the subject of "Europe and refugees," we know a lot about Turkey's role and the impact on Greece, but little is known about what's happening in African countries, with the possible exception of Libya. Currently, what's happening in Libya?

Tsiakalos: For Libya, it is known that Europe equips and finances organizations that, if their members happened to be in Europe, would very well be described as "terrorists," "mobsters," "slave traders." What has been well-documented countless times are accounts of the murder, rape, torture, arrest, and sale, as slaves, of people from sub-Saharan Africa, and the blackmailing of families for ransom, so that their captured family member is not executed. All this is known to EU leaders. Also well-documented is the cooperation of the so-called Libyan port authorities, funded by the EU, with specific traffickers. So, in reality, migration is not hindered; rather, control and trafficking remain in the same hands (with the blessing of the EU), resulting in the rampant growth of corruption, the effective legalization of the slave trade in North Africa, and the murder of Black people multiplying. But for Europe, the doctrine "no matter the cost, this policy will be followed consistently" is still in place. It was a policy launched immediately after the 2001 decision on air and sea transport.

Malichudis and Papangeli: What exactly happened when these international agreements were created?

Tsiakalos: At that time, Europe began and to this day continues to make bilateral agreements to "fight illegal immigration" with more than twenty African countries, always paying local leaders, regardless of the means those leaders use to prevent "illegal immigration." One can say: where there is a dictatorship, there is certainly also cooperation and agreement with the EU. The agreements concern prohibiting the exit of citizens who want to leave their country, or third-country nationals who are in a state legally and wish to leave for the North. In essence, this means imposing a regime of human rights abuses on free movement. Ironically, it is a violation of the right that the West demanded to be recognized by the countries of Eastern Europe until the collapse of their regimes in 1989. The same right is now denied to African citizens and prevents Africa from creating a space for the free movement of its citizens. It all started systematically at the 2002 EU Summit of Heads of State, in Seville, with the decision to make relations with African countries conditional on their willingness to accept the implementation of a European policy to "combat illegal immigration." For the first time, they proposed sanctions against countries that did not cooperate, with the then prime minister of Spain (José Maria Aznar) and the chancellor of Germany (Gerhard Schröder) insisting on the policy, despite most other countries still being opposed. The French Interior Minister Nicolas Sarkozy opposed the German chancellor, saying that "it is not possible to send a message that rich countries punish the poor." But just a year later, Britain's Tony Blair presented a framework for rewarding those who cooperate and punishing those who refuse. He called his initiative "A New Vision." His proposals included setting up reception centers for asylum seekers in non-EU countries, including Albania, Croatia, and Ukraine. He withdrew it shortly before the European Council meeting in Thessaloniki, in 2003, but nevertheless decisions were made there and the foundations for the policy were laid, resulting in the inhumane consequences we see today. That was and is the "new vision" of Europe.

Malichudis and Papangeli: What does this policy mean in practice?
Tsiakalos: I'll give you the example of a key state, Niger, that has been called "Europe's Migration Laboratory"[9] by Daniel Howden and Giacomo Zandonini. The state agreed to block the exit to the Sahara, and has also agreed to take back all African nationals who had crossed Niger on their way to Europe, where their asylum applications were rejected, leading to their deportation. Each month, thousands of West African migrants cross Agadez, the last major city before the border on their way to the Mediterranean. There are many services to prevent them from crossing, as well as a mission of the International Organization for Migration (IOM), which tries to persuade them to return to their home countries, providing them with financial assistance. But one can learn through Wikipedia that the most important part of this city's economy is the transportation of migrants to the North, as it benefits not only traffickers but also local businesses, police, truck owners, drivers, and others. All the data show that the number of migrants and refugees is not decreasing, but the cost of human life is increasing. The most important reason for the large increase in deaths is the fact that the

authorized military units set up camp in the few oases where there is water, so that the refugees are forced to cross the Sahara bypassing the traditional caravan routes and thus face losing their lives. I must say that in these areas there are also EU military forces present, mainly from Italy, France, and Germany. And let me add that who benefits from the money spent on implementing this policy are not the citizens of those countries. The ones who benefit the most are the European arms and special equipment companies which provide privatized border security.

Malichudis and Papangeli: In your speeches in the past you have talked many times about similar phenomena of border militarization in Greece. Can you explain?

Tsiakalos: Greece was the country where all the technologies and practices that are now widely used to combat what is called "irregular migration" were tested. The first impregnable fence on the European continent was built on its border with Turkey using the North Atlantic Treaty Organization (NATO) wire. A complete border monitoring system was installed here, consisting of thermal cameras, carbon dioxide detectors, and heartbeat detectors for people hidden in trucks. But in recent years we have entered a new phase: the exploitation of the "refugee risk" for the development of military forces in our region by all countries involved in the wars in the Middle East and Africa. At the request of Greece, Turkey, and Germany, NATO agreed, in February 2016, to offer assistance for the refugee and migrant crisis in the Aegean Sea. Since then, six NATO ships have been in the Aegean with the exclusive mission of "contributing to international efforts to stem illegal trafficking and illegal migration in the Aegean Sea, through intelligence, surveillance and reconnaissance in the Aegean Sea and at the Turkish-Syrian border." It is understood that "tackling the refugee crisis" is a project of general militarization of the region, which presents a growing danger to those uprooted from their homelands due to wars and poverty.

Malichudis and Papangeli: Indeed, we seem to be getting used to the idea of war. In a recent interview, well-known Spanish philosopher and author Josep Ramoneda sharply criticized the military references in public discourse that European leaders have used to explain their decisions to contain the pandemic.[10] Do you think that this rhetoric contributes to the growing acceptance of militarization?

Tsiakalos: Of course it contributes, either out of ignorance or deliberately. In Greece, the connection of the coronavirus pandemic with refugees and militarization becomes deliberate and overt. Immediately after the incidents in Evros that we talked about, the minister of defense stated that Turkey continues its attacks against Greece by sending refugees infected with coronavirus. The first measure that is already being implemented is the construction of a steel wall, five-meters tall, with a length of 38 kilometers on the border with Turkey, and the strengthening of deterrence measures in the Aegean. Do not be surprised by the ease with which refugees and coronavirus can be linked to justify increased national security. For the military-industrial complex there is no hesitation in presenting a poor woman with her baby coming in a boat from Turkey as a threat to the security of the nation.

Malichudis and Papangeli: In summarizing our discussion, we have early deportations, an EU that continues to discriminate against Black people in Africa, a Greek government that seeks political gains to the detriment of refugees rather than finding real solutions. Does this boil down to only pessimistic conclusions about the progress of what has been termed the "refugee crisis"?

Tsiakalos: The situation is at a critical point. And it's critical not only for the people who need support, but also for the European countries. How much longer will citizens have to accept the inconceivable spending on security systems to face a nonexistent risk, when at the same time governments reduce spending on health and education, which already receives a smaller budget? To this day, fear-mongering is used to intimidate society, but I think this tactic has an expiration date. How quickly it will end depends on many factors, most importantly is of course the mobilization of citizens and organizations, which are already resisting these policies. And it is varied. Who would have imagined a few years ago that the Protestant Church in Germany would resist government policy with an unparalleled vigor, chartering ships to save refugees from drowning in the Mediterranean? We are experiencing an unprecedented disobedience movement in the Mediterranean, without governments having the power to subdue it. Every show of strength on the part of governments only fortifies the solidarity movement.

Malichudis and Papangeli: Yes, but even political parties that associate themselves with the Left are rooted in the logic of risk aversion, with perhaps a few exceptions.

Tsiakalos: The example of the Protestant Church, which exactly due to its active solidarity with refugees, after decades of steady loss in membership, is gaining members, shows what I think will happen when political parties realize that it makes sense, even as an electoral gain, to have a refugee policy that, along with having a moral foundation, will reveal the impasse and ineffectiveness of the European policy so far, its economic consequences and the dangers it poses to democracy and prosperity. The "refugee crisis" has indeed changed the political landscape in Europe by fueling far-right ideologies, generating far-right and Nazi parties and thus influencing traditional parties. But this trend is not inevitable. As you know, I systematically monitor and record official policies and their barbaric effects. But I also systematically and closely monitor the actions of people, organizations, and institutions that defend humanity and civilization with words and deeds. My optimism stems from the comparison of the potentials on both sides of the conflict: the resistance of the people to the onslaught of barbarism is enormous and capable of protecting human civilization. I have no doubt about the result. The only question is—until resistance against brutality prevails—how many more victims will we mourn on the altar of an economic and political system of exploitation and inequality, those sacrificed by the ruling priests for whom human dignity and human life do not matter?

Coronavirus Pandemic and the "Refoulement" of Refugees and Asylum Seekers

Sheila L. Macrine

Visions of people seeking asylum in holding pens, and children in cages along the US/Mexico border haunts our collective memories. Yet, these are the very images that helped Trump and company to galvanize the racist sentiments that hastened his anti-immigration policies. Along with blatant and unapologetic xenophobic rhetoric, the Trump administration used the threat of the Covid-19 pandemic to "legally" expel refugee/asylum seekers or stop them at the border. The unifying link among these tactics is the racially motivated fear-mongering related to alarm over potential violence (Chouhy and Madero-Hernandez 2019). Ultimately, the resultant anti-immigration policies, exacerbated by the pandemic, revealed serious underlying fault-lines in our asylum policy and exposed the absence of humanitarian treatment by the United States. In response, this chapter takes a critical look at the already harrowing and precarious lives of the Latin American refugee/asylum seekers, intensified by Trump's anti-immigration policies and coronavirus. The brutality of these policies is shown here to be examples of state-sponsored *biopolitical* racism and reveal how the "invisible" coronavirus has made the systemic racial/ethnic/gender inequities of our asylum system more "visible" (Santos 2016). The chapter concludes that an engagement with Freirean (1970, 1973, 1994) approaches can cultivate critical responses to this accelerated age of despair. It is argued that critical pedagogic action (Darder 2017; Freire 1994; Freire and Macedo 1998; Macrine 2016, 2020) can empower refugee/asylum seekers with knowledge about human rights violations by giving rise to transformative learning: to challenge current policies, to develop legal recourse, to demand ethical behavior, to encourage policy and advocacy efforts, to create accessible legal services, as well as, to enable and extend opportunities for citizens and non-citizens to engage in social justice for change.

Autocracy and Refugees/Asylum Seekers

In 2016, the United States elected an autocratic president—propelled by unprecedented assaults on asylum and immigration policies, along with calls for border-walls along the US-Mexican divide. In the fall of 2020, the United States completed one of the most consequential and contentious presidential elections in our lifetimes: Trump vs. Biden. Fortuitously, history was made with the greatest voter turn-out to elect Joe Biden as the 46th president and Senator Kamala Harris as the first woman and woman of color to serve as vice president. Yet, the legacy of the Trump administration shamelessly leaves in its wake: a climate of conspicuous racism, xenophobia, a rise in the white supremacy, the growth of alt-right-wing populism, and the emergence of neo-fascism (Giroux 2019). Sadly, Trump's brazen reign has created serious political and enduring ideological divisions within United States that have fermented distrust among our global allies, while contributing to the rise in conservatism and fundamentalism. Some of his most pernicious polarizing tactics consisted of mobilizing voters through the normalization of racist discourse, the refusal to condemn white supremacists, the bombardment of post-truth messages by right-wing media, and the exploitation existing grievances (McCoy et al. 2018).

Trump's barefaced xenophobic policies specifically restricted to persons from Latin America and Muslim countries.[1] During both Trump campaigns of 2016 and 2020, his platforms aggressively regularized overt racism (for his base) making previous "invisible" racial discrimination more "visible" (Santos 2016). Even, weeks before the 2020 election, he continued to cut the "already rock-bottom refugee admissions even deeper for the upcoming 2021 year that virtually sealed-off a pathway for the persecuted and obliterated the once-robust American reputation as a sanctuary for the oppressed" (Kanno-Youngs and Shear 2020: 2).

The result was that Trump and company successfully closed the United States from refugee/asylum seekers that helped to electrify his base throughout his presidency. His use of racially coded language that highlighted issues of crime and welfare appealed not only to his base, but to the US poor and working classes already anxious about their own security. Clearly, Trump's rhetoric was crafted to flagrantly alarm voters that refugees would take their jobs, social services, and cost the government money—a blatant charge that has been refuted in many studies (Kanno-Youngs and Shear 2020).

Post-truth, Big lies, and the Weaponization of Racism

Trump's assault on truth, referred to as post-truth, consisted of falsehoods, misleading claims and outright lies with over 20,000 false and misleading claims.[2] Indeed, the Coronavirus spawned a whole new crop of Trump falsehoods including: injecting people with disinfectants and exposing patients' bodies to UV light as a so-called cure. Macedo (2006) offered a prescient term "stupification" to describe perspectives on such "big lies" within the larger social and political context. Indeed, Trump's assault on the truth demonstrates a clear example of how the stupification of the masses can exist even given the wholesale belief in known-untruths by his base. Tragically, the consequences of Trump's verifiably false language and misinformation campaigns have caused significant damage to democracy and to the American polity (Pfiffner 2018). Trump's post-truth can be categorized into four types: (1) trivial lies; (2) exaggerations and self-aggrandizing lies; (3) lies to deceive the public; and (4) egregious lies (Pfiffner 2018: 1). These egregious false statements were injured that the democratic process, undermined enlightenment epistemology, and corroded the premises of liberal democracy (Pfiffner 2018).

Never shy about his open hostility toward refugee/asylum seekers, he flaunted his antagonism with twisted speech to handily weaponized racial-discontent tapping into fears, beliefs, ideas, and anxieties already present within his party, and his base (Sides, Tesler, and Vavreck 2018). Called the "great disruptor," Trump used discursive means and protectionist language to fuel fear that helped fulfill his 2016-election refrain to "Build that wall!" In addition, his persuasive speech triggered a lopsided sense of patriotism—echoed throughout both of his presidential election campaigns with the mantra: "Make American Great Again." These rhetorical devices not only transfixed his base but also stoked fear, hatred, and anger driving a wedge in US society (Saramo 2017: 9). These "in-plain-sight" messages reinforced a national xenophobia narrative that framed refugee/asylum seekers and immigrants, particularly those of color, as parasitic and dangerous to the American way of life.

Trump and Inhumane Treatment at the Border

As conflicts around the world have increasingly gone unresolved, the number of refugee/asylum seekers has steadily grown into a global crisis. According to UNHCR,[3] the numbers worldwide have grown from 10 million per year a decade ago to over 20.4 million per year in 2020. It goes without saying that a great deal of political and media rhetoric whipped-up fear about refugees and asylum seekers has produced a conservative-vacuum nurturing calls for hardline nationalistic fixes, paranoid protectionism, and neo-fascism (Giroux 2019).

Considered a nation of immigrants, the United States has a long history of welcoming immigrants, asylum seekers, and refugees. Yet, this position has dramatically shifted in recent years. This erosion of United States' commitment to and leadership within the international refugee system cannot be ignored. For example, in 2019, the UNHCR reported that the South American refugees fleeing poverty, political unrest, gang violence, natural disasters, or other serious circumstances denotes the worst displacement crisis in the Americas in recent history, second only to the Syrian crisis.[4]

In response to the crisis, rather than responding in a humanitarian way, Trump called for border-walls. His rationale followed three prominent racially motivated arguments: (1) the link between migration, criminals, and terrorism, (2) the allegation that immigrants drain a nation's resources, and (3) the claim that immigration threatens a society's cultural achievements and genetic purity.[5] For example, Trump claimed his proposed southern border-wall was to protect United States citizenry by stopping the flow of refugees/asylum seekers from South America. These notions helped him to continue to issue construction contracts for the border-wall even during the pandemic (Slowey 2020). The notion of "protectionism," embedded in Donald Trump's 2016 presidential campaign, is extremely perilous and reflects moves by some countries toward an authoritarian one-party-rule. Giroux (2019) argues that the turn toward neo-fascism and protectionisms is evidenced in some European countries that call for "genetic purity" in response to the refugee crisis (Macrine and Edling 2021). An example is Hungary which adopted an "illiberal democracy" of draconian policies and reforms (including border-walls) that is eroding the traditions of democracy and liberalism. Like Trump, Orbán used persuasive language to wage propaganda campaigns for protectionism and neo-nationalism by exploiting fear-mongering and insinuating violent assaults from foreigners, Muslims, and other dark-skinned immigrants. This is not new; authoritarian leaders have historically used fear and border-walls to spread fear, increase isolationism, and closed-mindedness for centuries.[6]

After taking office in January 2017, Trump derided the United States' asylum system as a "big-fat-con-job" and accused asylum seekers of exaggerating the violence they were fleeing (Nelson and Habbach 2019). Trump politicized the plight of refugee/asylum seekers with more and more restrictive immigration/

asylum policies (Chouhy and Arelys Madero-Hernandez 2019). One such policy, the Migrant Protection Protocols of 2019, restricted access to asylum, which violated the Geneva Convention, and obliterated the once-robust American reputation as a sanctuary for the oppressed (Kanno-Young and Shear 2020). Sadly, the refugee crisis continued to be used to ferment fear, as evidenced in Trump referring to Latin American refugee/asylum seekers as "*Murderers, Rapists, and Bad Hombres*" emphasis in original (Bad Men) (Chouhy and Madero-Hernandez 2019).

Coronavirus: Making the "Invisible" Visible

In fact, almost 80 million people across the globe are forcibly displaced, prompting Filippo Grandi[7], the UN High Commissioner for Refugees, to claim that we are "witnessing a changed reality in that forced displacement nowadays is not only vastly more widespread but is simply no longer a short-term and temporary phenomenon"[8] Unfortunately, the already deeply precarious lives of refugees/asylum seekers are among the most threatened due to the pandemic. The International Rescue Committee (IRC) reports that thirty-four conflict-affected countries could reach up to 1 billion coronavirus infections and 3.2 million deaths.[9]

This vulnerability to the coronavirus has revealed underlying fault-lines in societies around the world in dealing with the refugee crisis (Simet 2020). These rifts have exposed heightened frailties and oppressions of the most vulnerable refugee/asylum seekers consisting of over 65 percent women and children (Spathopoulou 2020). According to Schalatek (2020), "the invisible coronavirus has made visible the many inequities, injustices, persistent gender inequality, and sexism." By the second half of 2020, the Covid19 pandemic all halted the international movement and mobility of refugee/asylum seekers. Handily, the Trump administration used the coronavirus to advance xenophobic disinformation campaigns to advance their right-wing political agendas and to justify the border-walls (deCook 2020). With unabashedly racist rants on Twitter (March 2020), Trump claimed that his border-wall was needed "more than ever"—mirroring racist responses in many host countries in Europe.

While Latin American refugee/asylum seekers are among the most threatened by the coronavirus, people are still fleeing violence and persecution seeking safety and asylum despite the threat of the pandemic. Compounding these hazards, once they arrive in the United States, they are jammed into substandard-housing where they cannot practice social distancing, charity shelters, and tent cities, that house up to 2,000 or more people.

One of these encampments is located in Brownsville, Texas, called the Matamoros, which has little or no access to health care. Children are crammed into cages with no access to showers or hot meals and serious overcrowding and prolonged detention for adults, some with standing-room-only conditions with no room to lie down or even sit.[10] Inhumane conditions such as these make freedom seekers even more vulnerable to the spread of coronavirus. Laura Rivera (2020) from The Southern Poverty Law Center (SPLC) writing about the Trump administration's reckless response to the pandemic and Covid-19 adds that,

> This administration has chosen racism and xenophobia over a science-based approach in its gravely misguided response to the COVID-19 pandemic . . . [the] administration officials are weaponizing its immigration detention, enforcement and court apparatus to further terrorize immigrants and force legal advocates to risk exposure to the virus. (2020: 1)

Accordingly, coronavirus has unmasked our failure to treat migrants with human decency and dignity. Even as refugee/asylum seekers continue to experience multi-layered victimizations, the coronavirus has been used to further persecute and legitimize the continuation of the "us-vs-them" mentality. Being stigmatized by race, ethnicity, sexual orientation, and social class, solidifies and confirms their feelings of insecurity and invisibility and forces them to accept unfair treatment. Recently, author and activist Arundhati Roy (2020) charged that the poor were already the "unknowns" before the coronavirus pandemic, and they'll be the "unknowns" long after it if we don't begin to cure our world of poverty and inequality. Prophetically, she warns that,

> The tragedy is immediate, real, epic and unfolding before our eyes. It isn't new . . . [but] now, in the era of the virus, a poor person's sickness can affect a wealthy society's health. . . . It will feed the increasing capacity and desire of the ruling-classes to socially distance and self-segregate from the classes who move on foot and by boat—particularly the proletariat of the Global South, compressed in more confined spaces and cast as biohazardous. (Roy 2020: 1)

Refoulement and Coronavirus

The "linchpin" to justify these severe actions was Trump's directive to the Center for Disease Control (CDC (2020) to issue an order for the immediate deportation of non-citizens without valid documents, by citing an obscure quarantine law, called "Refoulement." This law identifies vulnerable individuals as "dangers" to the public health, spreaders of disease, or security threats (Lauterpacht and Bethlehem 2003). It also justifies the unlawful return of those seeking a haven to countries where they are subjected to serious human rights abuses and persecution. Trump used this "novel policy" to systematically and rapidly expel and forcibly returned refugees/asylum seekers, which violates both United States and international laws and treaties designed to protect people-at-risk of persecution, torture, and trafficking (Arenilla 2015; Lakhani 2020).

The "Refoulement" principle defies the responding principle to protect those from persecution called "Non-refoulement" which was established in Article 33 of the 1951 Convention of Relating to the Status of Refugees, and ratified in the 1967 Protocol—Status of Refugees. That said, the international law very clearly states that the principle of non-refoulement is absolute and must be applicable at all times, including during war times, internal political instability, and any other major public emergency—including a pandemic (UN 2018). Therefore, the principle of "Non-refoulement" has utmost importance for safeguarding human rights because it goes beyond the right to seek asylum by stating that asylum seekers have a right to life and right to freedom from torture. The UN Human Rights Committee stated that during any public emergency that threatens a nation, we must guarantee the "non-derogable" right to life; the freedom from torture, cruel, inhuman, and degrading treatment or punishment; and the freedom from medical or scientific experimentation without consent. Further noting that these rights cannot be suspended regardless of the type or severity of the public emergency (UNHRC 2001). Even the US federal law states that, regardless of immigration status, "[a]ny alien who is physically present in the United States or who arrives in the United States" shall be afforded the right to seek asylum.

Likewise, Article 14 of the Universal Declaration of Human Rights protects the right to seek asylum as a fundamental human right. Consequently, we need to be ever-vigilant and advocate for "Non-refoulement" as the cornerstone of any new refugee law or policy. That is because the principle of non-refoulement guarantees that no one should be returned to a country where they would face torture, cruel, inhuman, or degrading treatment or punishment and other irreparable harm (Hathaway 2005). Interestingly, these protections are already in place because the human rights law delineated in the Convention against Torture[11] mandates that the United States must not send anyone to a state where there are substantial grounds for believing that such a person would be in danger of being tortured.

State-Sponsored *Biopolitical Racism*

It is argued here that "Refoulement" is an example of state-sponsored "biopolitical racism." The term "biopolitics" was coined by Foucault (1978) to describe how governments regulate populations through "biopower"—the subjugation of bodies and the control of populations. He added that biopolitical "state racism" creates an "external enemy" from which society must be defended, and therefore gives the sovereign-state the ability to exercise the ultimate power in the name of protecting its citizens (1978: 255).

This tactic of creating and "external enemy" is evidenced in the actions by the architect behind Trump's draconian immigration policies, right-wing Stephen Miller, who "targeted refugees, asylum seekers and their children, engineering an 'ethical crisis' for a nation that once saw itself as the conscience of the world. Miller rallied support . . . by courting the white rage that found violent expression in tragedies from El Paso to Charlottesville" (Guerrero 2020: 20).

Under the Trump administration, such state-sponsored "biopolitical racism" has both redrawn and exposed the boundaries between those who are considered "valuable" (to be included) and "not valuable" (Mavelli 2017). The hidden existence of the once invisible "us and them" ideology has become even more visible and widened under Trump's policies highlighting deep-seated divides. These transparent fissures actual transcend traditional accounts of racism (Mavelle 2017). Boaventura de Sousa Santos (2016) astutely describes an "invisible thread" called an "abyssal line" that forms a dividing line between the valued/un(under)valued, recognized/un(under)recognized, the visible/invisible. This articulated differentiation helps us to understand the gaps among groups and individuals that occupy opposite sides of this line.

Moreover, Trump's brutal state-sponsored biopolitical racist and xenophobic policies have acted like a "silver-bullet" in his three-year push to end asylum protections for most seekers from Central America. For example, reports show that US Immigration and Customs Enforcement (ICE) agents carried out more than 105,000 rapid expulsions through the end of July 2020. These efforts were conducted under the public health order of "Refoulement" (as described earlier) that essentially closed the border to refugee/asylum seekers (including families and unaccompanied children) during the coronavirus pandemic (Rose and Falk 2020). In fact, the Trump administration's sweeping new regulations seek to permanently limit asylum protections for those arriving at the southern border. As a result, most refugees are turned away with no access to due process, often without any explanation.[12] Such racist acts function as biopolitical metrics (Mason 2009) that work to adjudicate whether or not a life is deemed eligible for basic human rights (Dillon and Neal 2008). By combining these new forms of "biopolitical racism" with traditional outward forms of racism are reminiscent of some of the worst eugenically based atrocities of the twentieth century where "neo-racism [was used] as the internal means in defense of a society against its abnormal individuals. . . . Nazism graft[ed] this new racism onto the ethnic racism that was endemic in the nineteenth century" (Foucault 2003: 317).

The Rights of the Child and Coronavirus

One of the most disturbing and egregious aspect of the "refoulement" implementation is the treatment of unaccompanied children as "kids in cages."[13] Refoulement violates Article 22 of the Convention on the Rights of the Child, which emphasizes that the rights of unaccompanied minors arriving at the border and seeking asylum must be respected at all times (Ataiants et al. 2018). While the international protection of children, as asylum seekers, is almost universally accepted as the norm. It is worth pointing out that the current US immigration policies fall miserably short, and remains the only country in the world that has not ratified the Convention on the Rights of the Child (UNTS 1990). Regrettably, the Trump administration and its enforcement agencies have been indifferent to the suffering and death of refugee/asylum seekers both at the border and in the cages set up across the country. Unfortunately, the coronavirus pandemic has accelerated this cruel indifference, and unless we act swiftly and change course, "more will die than could be prevented. These deaths will be on government hands" (Rivera 2020: 1).

This crisis is so dangerous, that Oxfam (2020) warns that by the end of 2020 approximately 12,000 people per day will die from hunger linked to coronavirus, and even more will die from the disease itself. Examining the extraordinary journey of refugee/asylum seekers faced with poverty, hunger, lack of health care, trauma, and loss has shown that women and children as the most vulnerable to both violence and coronavirus (Hayward 2007). Hopelessly victimized in numerous ways, the number of children living in multidimensional poverty— without access to education, health, housing, nutrition, sanitation, or water—has soared exponentially to over 1.2 billion due to the coronavirus pandemic according to UNICEF[14] and Save the Children.[15]

Responding, the World Health Organization (WHO) declared the coronavirus pandemic a public health emergency of international dimensions and authorized the use of emergency measures. But they declare that it is absolutely crucial that any emergency measures taken must be consistent with international law and human rights (2005). Indeed, they added that all countries have the right to manage risks at their borders, but cautioned that fighting a crisis by infringing the rule of law and human rights only plants seeds for bigger crises (Zheng 2020).

The Shadow Pandemic: Women and Indigenous Refugees

The United Nations entity, UN Women, launched the "Shadow Pandemic" public awareness campaign dedicated to gender-equality and the empowerment of women focusing on the global increase in domestic violence amid the coronavirus health crisis.[16] This group makes recommendations to all sectors of society, from governments to international organizations, and to civil society organizations in order to prevent and respond to violence against women and girls, at the onset, during this global health crisis.

Further, the UN Refugee Agency warns that refugee/asylum seekers, women and children, including displaced Indigenous peoples, are at higher risk due to the spread of the coronavirus throughout Latin America. It poses a grave health crisis that threatens Indigenous peoples who already experience poor access to health care, have significantly higher rates of communicable and non-communicable diseases, at the same time lack access to sanitation, clean water, soap, disinfectant, and other essential services.[17] While the rate of coronavirus infections has dramatically increased worldwide, the high virus mortality among certain vulnerable groups, and those with underlying health conditions, increases. Yet, there have been few comprehensive studies that focused solely on the plight of Indigenous refugee/asylum seekers and their rate of infection. Further obfuscating things is the lack of relevant coronavirus, and other infectious disease, prevention and mitigation information available in many indigenous languages.

Needless to say, the plight of the refugee/asylum seekers, in search of safety and better lives, is fraught with threats due to violence based on race, ethnicity, religion, gender, sexual orientation, including well-documented human rights violations, rape, torture, and sex-trafficking. Violence, and domestic violence, exacerbated by the pandemic has resulted in higher negative health outcomes.

Since the pandemic outbreak, Refugee International[18] noted that the most vulnerable victims (women, children, and LGBTQ+) have experienced appalling acts of gender-based violence.[19] In other words, the coronavirus pandemic creates an additive risk factor in an already harrowing voyage. Refugee women, girls, and those in the LGBTQ+ communities have also experienced severe risks to ongoing and systematic rape, as well as, other forms of sexual and gender-based violence—coupled with extreme vulnerability to the virus. They are already at risk at every stage from the treacherous journey, to reception in host countries, to the shrinking options, and non-durable solutions in host countries including language and cultural differences.

While, it is a given that countries have the right to take measures to manage their borders, they must take actions to protect those arriving at their borders. This can be accomplished by adopting a holistic responsibility-sharing model that advocates for social justice solutions (Freire 1970) that can mitigate policy reforms in combating brazen racial injustices and to dismantle the rising anti-immigration sentiments rooted in white supremacy.

Conclusion

In sum, this chapter took a critical look at the traumatic experiences of Latin American refugee/asylum seekers complicated by the racist tightening of US immigration policies, and accelerated by the Covid-19 crisis. Sadly, the unholy legacy of the Trump administration has emboldened conspicuous xenophobia aimed at ending asylum, as we know it, by activating an obscure principle called "refoulement." This amounts to a form of state-sponsored "biopolitical racism" that blatantly violates both American law and International Human Rights standards.[20] Therefore, exposing such illegal-actions and multi-layered oppressions faced by refugee/asylum seekers can help to make visible the "invisibilization" of refugees/asylum seekers (Santos 2016). By drawing a line from the state-sponsored "biopolitical racism" to our broken US immigration system unmasks the intolerant rationalities of the Trump administration. As discussed earlier, Sousa Santos (2016) offers an epistemological basis for a "decolonial ascendance" to inform and help us go beyond the divisive line of "us and them" to achieve a good life for all.

Another key to combating state-sponsored "biopolitical racism" is through participatory pedagogies such as the successful awareness-raising methods for both the oppressed and the oppressors initiated by Paulo Freire (1970). These approaches can provide promising mechanisms for reaching disenfranchised refugee/asylum seekers in host communities and for empowering US citizens to honor our history and humanistic traditions as a nation of immigrants. Guided by an engagement with Freire's (1970, 1973, 1994) critical hope and critical pedagogic action can help to alleviate the horrors of the refugee/asylum seekers and celebrate their extraordinary courage and contributions, while motivating US citizens to challenge current immigration laws. These critical approaches link the ideas, hope, and action necessary to combat such oppressions, to find tolerance, common purpose, and common ground, and at the same time press for social justice reforms (Freire 1994; Giroux, 2020; Macedo and Bartolomé 1999; Macrine 2020).

In the end, the final impact of the pandemic, and the timing and effectiveness of vaccines is still utterly uncertain. It is equally uncertain how the balance between current forms of immigration law and the existing international refugee protections and human rights standards can be resolved in the near and longer-term future. This is an important goal in reforming the US immigration system—and a key aspect of restoring the rule of law. But we know that something needs to be done and quickly to grant safety to the extraordinary bravery of these freedom seekers. Poignantly, the UN High Commissioner for Refugees-Antonio Guterres (2005) stated that "every refugee's story is different and their anguish personal, [but] they all share a common thread of uncommon courage—the courage not only to survive, but to persevere and rebuild their shattered lives."

Neoliberal Recrudescence versus Radical Transformation of the Reality in Italy

What and Why Must We Learn from the Coronavirus Pandemic?

Paolo Vittoria and Mariateresa Muraca

Introduction

On February 24, when the World Health Organization (WHO) still had not announced the existence of a pandemic and the new coronavirus appeared to be mainly a problem for the Chinese, the first recorded cases of SARS-CoV-2 urged the Italian government to take containment measures in the two regions concerned: Lombardy and Veneto. The provisions included closing schools and universities, suspending local transport and public office activities, companies, and retail businesses—except for those operating in essential services—as well as isolation with the consequent prohibition of entering or leaving the most virus-stricken municipalities. As the first Western country to be infected by the virus, Italy had been taken by surprise: for this reason, the following weeks saw attempts to justify the confusion and contradictions that characterized the initial phase of the virus crisis and which are still ongoing today. Some of this tension regards the relationship between:

Health and Economy

Unlike other places in the world, Italy immediately made considerable efforts to safeguard the health of its citizens as a primary asset. It is an essential principle on which the structure of our country's social state has historically been based, even though the cuts imposed by neoliberal policies in recent decades have put it under severe strain—as the initial months of the pandemic tragically proved. On the other hand, there was also strong pressure aimed at subjecting political decisions to the interests of profit, particularly expressed by the Italian industry confederation (Confindustria). In fact, even in full lockdown, many companies managed to avoid the restrictions and were, moreover, the principal advocates of reopening without, however, always making efforts to ensure the health of their employees. This scenario included events that involved several politicians from the areas considered as "more productive," who attempted to adopt the necessary containment measures, minimizing the seriousness of the impact of Covid-19. The most renowned of these events was probably the "Milan doesn't stop" campaign, launched on February 27 by Mayor Beppe Sala from the Democratic Party and which was followed by similar initiatives in other cities. The most serious, however, was failing to set up a "red zone" in the two municipalities of Nembro and Alzano Lombardo, in the province of Bergamo, whose populations were wracked by the epidemic. This fact is currently undergoing legal inquiry.

Safety and Freedom

In the public debate, the democratic nature of the Italian system has often been asserted in opposition to the political decisions that were more distinctly coercive to countries like China. For many reasons, however, one part of public opinion stood back from forms of control thought to restrict individual freedom and the right of association, especially when it concerned individual behavior or access to personal information. In other respects, the citizens themselves often took control into their own hands by whistle-blowing on their own neighbors in the name of acritical and unconditioned respect of the laws in force. Therefore, in the vein of Giorgio Agamben (2020), some analysts, discerning the conditions for setting up a state of exception, highlighted the risk of authoritarian tendencies caused by exploiting fear.

Sense of Community and Fear of Others

In a number of places, the social distancing imposed by the spread of the new coronavirus has been seen to spark forms of solidarity and unexpected closeness. For example, the spontaneous moments which, at the onset of the pandemic, saw neighbors on their balconies, united by the sound of music as well as many other initiatives that sprang up so that vulnerable people were not left alone. More profoundly, Ida Dominijanni (2020) writes about a generalized experience of a shift in subjectivity, able to modify individual and social subconscious, provoked by feeling like the intentional bearer of help for others but also the potential carrier of infection. On the other hand, the threat of illness was a powerful element on which to raise and strengthen highly exclusionary barriers. The many shipwrecks that continued to occur in the Mediterranean during the lockdown period and in the following months revealed an incapacity to extend the boundaries of the sense of community to really and truly include everyone.

Expert Knowledge and Individual Responsibility

The novel nature of the infectious agent at the onset of the pandemic posed the distressful problem of the lack of useful knowledge for understanding and foreseeing its impact. Consequently, in a short time, the epidemic became an infodemic where the viewpoints of institutions and experts—who became television stars overnight—have continued to pursue, oppose, and repudiate each other. Our thoughts have literally been colonized by the only topic deemed possible to talk about. This circumstance is also an opportunity: it offers us the chance to abandon, once and for all, the modern illusion of an internally compact science with solid certainties; to recognize that all knowledge is situated and is the result of a shared and always inconclusive study path; to feel that we cannot entirely delegate experts with our responsibility to know and decide. Will we be able to seize this opportunity? For now, the dominating direction appears to be more inclined to create new factions and oppositions (negationists, no-vax, conspiracy theorists, scientists), in order to pursue a glimmer of safety, but the games are still open.

These are the main axes that have characterized the Italian climate since the beginning of the pandemic and which have also significantly involved the debate on education and teaching practices which we address in the following pages. To be precise, we analyze both the risks of a neoliberal recrudescence and the possibilities of a radical transformation starting from educational and social movement struggles.

Formal Education

With the explosion of the pandemic, formal education—and we particularly refer to school and university—had to adapt to an obligatory shift from classroom teaching to remote teaching. In times when deconstruction is seen as a method of knowledge of human complexity, where clear distinctions are certainly not suitable for describing the unpredictability of existence, where dichotomies are not allowed due to being too strict, in this very era of existential labyrinths, we are now in a dimension of clear and unavoidable separation between body and mind. With their minds, our students were able to experience unexplored, unprecedented, and surprising places. They could travel great distances and discover unthinkable places while their bodies were stuck between four walls for more than three months.

To be honest, the mind-body dichotomy is not a totally new entry onto the scholastic scene. Have we reflected on restrictions of the body in scholastic environments? The body has to deal with the impossibility of creating its own places; it is in an already given, instituted, purpose-built place that it must adapt to; it has to sit on its chair, behind a desk, in front of the teacher. Being restricted during the pandemic has led many specialists in the educational field to reflect on the theme of living. What relations exist between the body and the environment that is hosting it? Fragments that make up an ecology-based question: Does living mean adapting to the environment or imagining, devising, inventing, representing unprecedented places? Have we ever thought about why students, their bodies, are often attracted to virtual environments rather than so-called real places? Why do they seem to really need them? Why can they not do without them?

We understand that "remote teaching" cannot be self-sufficient but it does have potential when integrated with "classroom teaching." One cannot replace the other but they must integrate and be re-designed because remote learning leads to experiencing unthinkable, unknown, unexpected, and unimaginable places. Virtual is none other than that part of reality that is able to reinvent and make reality conditional, hypothetical, latent, and creatable. Education should not be confused with adapting to a prefabricated reality in a kit of pre-established skills to pursue and then certify. Going from classroom teaching to remote teaching has suddenly forced us to get to grips with a modality unfamiliar to many, often with inefficient network coverage that is not able to reach everyone. The difficult conditions were translated into a sensation of claustrophobia due to being confined to the home in front of a screen. Particular thought went to the many young people with disabilities who found themselves excluded and emarginated. Physical education activities, already inadequate before, were totally canceled and other problems of a purely didactic nature regarded modalities, methods, timing, relational, and communication potentialities and evaluations.

Let's start with a few questions: Is there any sense in changing a work method which already leads to conditions of estrangement or alienation into a digital modality? In short, is it right to put a knowledge transfer system onto digital platforms which imposes a pre-established program without any confrontation between different ideas that might alter or modify it or generate unprecedented or unexpected interpretations and further study? If this method has failed "in the classroom," why re-propose it through online learning where the distance is not only physical but also, and above all, relational, emotional, and communicative? If distancing implies spatial distance, alienation describes a condition of the soul. And this is what needs to be overcome.

It should be said that remote teaching did not originate with the health crisis. We did not invent it in 2020. Its history lies in the development of communication means. Thinking about it, written correspondence is a form of remote communication with educational potential. The radio and television have been transmitting extraordinary remote learning experiences since the 1950s, devising experimental and innovative forms of remote learning communication. For example, since its very onset, the RAI, Italian State Television, has paid particular attention to the field of education. From *Telescuola* to the literacy program presented by Alberto Manzi, a primary school teacher, who used the television in an extraordinarily empathetic and ingenious manner, managing to keep what he called "cognitive tension" high, or, in other words, the will to learn. His program *"Non è mai troppo tardi"* (It's never too late) integrated distance-learning methods and monitor-coordinated territorial groups to give televised lessons in cultural centers, parishes, squares, and schools.

This mixed modality could be studied as guidelines for work in small integrated groups with specific online lessons where technologies do not replace face-to-face lessons but integrate with them. Education needs a physical territorial place and the enormous potential lies in going beyond its limits, creating learning environments and forms of open and more easily divulged communication. When we use different teaching instruments, we should necessarily modify the modalities of communication, expression, and relations; invent unprecedented forms of learning and teaching and; be inclusive and encourage curiosity.

Nowadays, a large part of remote teaching has shifted onto the social media, creating unusual and extraordinary potential yet, at the same time, posing a question that is worth reflecting on: Can artificial intelligence be used as a control and ideological consent system? In many cases, the history of education itself has been subject to control by state devices or has bowed to private interests. An unsettling example is China, where, in schools—even prior to the pandemic and the shift to remote teaching—teachers are monitored, and software, through algorithms, examines student attention. Facial recognition is foreseen and even drones are used to film how much attention the children are paying.

There are several cases in which artificial intelligence is used as a means of surveillance. In this scenario, a dominating algorithm is able to gather data and return, as output, propaganda on the buying or, in some cases, the political tendencies suitable for our profile. A serious and critical reflection on remote teaching must also bear in mind aspects such as these if it wants to guarantee the freedom and intellectual autonomy of students and teachers. These values, in any experience and any modality, must be an undisputed condition. In our opinion, these are the topics that the debate should focus on so that transferring content and teaching modalities onto the web does not become an appetizing condition for financial giants and control organizations, for persuasion and manipulation through algorithms used as an instrument of power.

Non-formal Education

Non-formal education in Italy comprises multiple and heterogeneous experiences and is probably an educational sector that experiments the most innovative and vibrant practices. In its genealogy the jolt that Paulo Freire's pedagogy evoked in the field of adult education and the de-institutionalization movement led by Franco Basaglia, who both made a decisive contribution to affirming the approach to permanent education on an international scale back in the 1970s, played an important role. Even now, non-formal education features a capacity to intercept plural forms of social unease and to help particularly vulnerable people, such as the elderly, immigrants, convicts, minors, the homeless, the disabled, those with pathological addictions and mental illnesses, and so on. However, the current non-formal education system is considerably affected by the quality of relationships between public and private set-ups in the social state model that dominates in Italy. These relationships have very often flaunted the logic of delegation and outsourcing. In fact, private social players (cooperatives, associations, NGOs, foundations) are the main protagonists of this essential yet often precarious sector with its working conditions and social and institutional recognition of the numerous professions involved, above all, teachers and pedagogists.[1]

Unlike formal education, non-formal education has been practically absent in the infodemic that has unfolded in recent months. This aspect highlights the usual invisibility with which the public debate cloaks educational professions and the social groups to which they refer. Several spontaneous initiatives have risen up to counter this invisibility, including the "*#Noi ci siamo*" (We are here) social campaign through which, during the initial months of the health crisis, educators aimed to underline their commitment as well as the need to have personal protective equipment in order to protect their own health and that of the users. In fact, a myriad of services and essential-to-life activities continued to be offered mainly due to the ability of those involved to adapt to an unprecedented situation.

Services for disabled men and women are an emblematic example. During the lockdown, day-center activities—where disabled people spend part of their day—were often suspended and re-modeled either in the home or remotely.[2] Residential care centers—those where disabled persons live permanently— have, however, continued to function while respecting the regulations imposed nationwide (e.g., not allowing them to meet their family members). In both cases, socio-educational specialists really had to adapt their work. There were many and often contradictory experiences:

- difficulties in finding the right way to communicate and explain the disruption to daily habits which, for some people, are particularly important and reassuring;
- searching for new balance in conditions where either being close (in the case of residential facilities) or having to keep a distance (in the case of day-centers) is much more intense than usual);
- the drastic reduction in social relations which is generally both a means and a fundamental objective in education;
- giving up physical presence, contact, or facial expression, which are essential and often vital dimensions in educational relationships (e.g., lip-reading for the deaf);
- but also experimenting new possibilities of proximity, different activities, and unexpected and significant forms of collaboration with colleagues, the users' families and other organizations within the territory.

All this was happening in a framework that is often characterized by power disputes between the various levels of administration and considerable pressure to make further cuts to resources and staff.

From these reflections, it is obvious that the effects of the lockdown were not the same for everyone but, on the contrary, had a greater dramatic impact on the lives of the more fragile. In the following pages, we take a closer look at the reasoning, focusing on the situation of convicts and undocumented migrants. In particular, we try to bring to light both the effects of the pandemic and its management and the more farsighted responses that emerged and impose crucial questions on the society in which we live.

The Prisons

In March 2020, one of the priority requirements identified by the government was to ensure social distancing and contain infections. This led to an unprecedented closure of Italian prisons (Antigone 2020). First, all visits from family members were suspended as well as all educational, cultural, and sports activities.[3] Staff and volunteers involved in these activities were therefore forbidden access to the prison. This also led to a drastic reduction in communication from the outside,[4] spreading panic both among the convicts and their relatives. Initially, the overcrowded conditions prior to coronavirus[5] became considerably more serious due to the prisoners' no longer being able to enjoy special permits to work outside the prison walls. The shortage of personal protective equipment, lacking throughout the national territory, made the fear of infection worse and added to the already precarious hygienic conditions and compulsory close-living that occurs in prison. This explosive situation triggered a series of protests which, between March 7 and 9, consecutively involved the prisons in Foggia, Modena, Rome Rebibbia, Bologna, Melfi, Rieti, Bari, Palermo Ucciardone, and went on to affect fifty penal institutes throughout Italy. Even if there were some peaceful initiatives (hunger strikes, letters from the prisoners, etc.), in many cases, the protests turned into authentic clashes. The outcome was extremely severe: extensive damage to buildings and materials, tens of prison guards injured and fourteen prisoners killed in circumstances yet to be entirely understood.[6] Moreover, in the days to follow, the prisoners' families reported several episodes of violence that are currently under investigation.

In this atmosphere, actions taken to inform, sensitize, and support by associations such as Antigone and the national Authority for the rights of convicts or persons deprived of their freedom,[7] as well as the fears of political decision-makers about the devastating effects of coronavirus spreading in the prisons, led to the first positive results.[8] First of all, the number of convicts in prison was considerably reduced[9] (although it already grew again during the summer), not only due to fewer crimes being committed during the lockdown, but also to a greater resort to alternative detention measures.[10] This was mainly due to the decisions of magistrates who drew on preexisting juridical instruments, while the introduction of a new legislative provision, aimed at extending house arrest to other categories,[11] had a more modest impact because of a media campaign that suggested that the mafia was behind these prison releases. Among other things, this campaign inflated the number of mafia bosses condemned to a hard prison regime—there were actually four—who were granted house arrest for reasons linked to the health crisis.

It is, in fact, common for Italian public opinion to express judgments strongly influenced by the symbolic meaning that a hard prison regime denotes[12] every time that respect is called for in regard to prison sentences and living conditions. Reading about prison only from the prospective of 41 bis (from the Italian Prison Administration Act), however, gives distorted results: it puts the prisoners on an equal level which is, in truth, hard to generalize. The vast majority of the prison population is, in fact, made up of foreigners (33%), drug addicts (32% of prisoners are serving time for breaking drug laws), homeless people belonging to the poorest classes of society (the three most frequent regions of origin— Apulia, Sicily, and Campania—are those with the lowest pro capita GNP and the highest unemployment figures). This reality shows the correlation between prison and extreme marginality and suggests that—as numerous accounts in literature argue—adequate prevention interventions and hardship aid are the most effective and pertinent responses to the problem of overcrowding in prisons.

In recent years, repressive and security solutions have received new lifeblood from populist political forces which have shown to be skilled in manipulating and exploiting, for electoral consensus purposes, the punitive impulses connected to feelings of fear, frustration, and rage, particularly widespread in periods of economic crisis among the more underprivileged classes (Fiandaca 2020). Endorsing the inadequacy of a health system centered only on hospitals— institutions that, in many cases, have contributed to spreading the virus—the health crisis has shown that it is only possible to ensure safety, dignity, and care for everybody through widespread nationwide and synergically connected interventions (Antigone 2020). It is therefore necessary to focus again, and more radically, on a community that educates and is able to care. On the other hand, the experience that we have all had of being shut in our houses, away from our loved ones, not able to carry out activities that give our lives more sense, can perhaps encourage our ability to comprehend all those people who have had their freedom taken away and open new chinks of humanity. In this sense, proposals from associations and movements committed to protecting the rights of convicts move in two essential directions:

- To reaffirm the educational function attributed to punishments by the Italian Constitution[13] by relaunching the measures, treatments, and activities aimed at the convict's social re-integration and giving new impulse to alternative measures, which have proved to be more effective and also less costly than incarceration.
- To surpass the criminogenic system of some regulations, especially the one relating to drugs which, particularly in the last fifteen years, has been exploited by repressive instruments that are detrimental to socio-educational responses.

Undocumented Migrants

Italy, which has historically been a country of emigration, also began to be a country of immigration in the 1970s when neoliberalist policies led to the first signs of economic recession and impoverishment. Since then, the Italian response to immigrations has featured significant tragedies. Indeed, reflection on interculture— and especially on intercultural pedagogy—is extremely upscale and has been able to draw important lessons from the failures that were recorded in countries where immigration dates well into the past (Surian 2001). Moreover, several innovative hospitality experiences have been positively received, even managing, in some cases, to influence political decisions.[14] However, legal provisions promoted by governments that take a different view and which have succeeded each other since the 1990s to present day have had mutual ideas about cutting security and seeing immigrations as a public order problem more than a socio-educational question. It is impossible here to summarize the content of Italian immigration law but it is important to highlight one aspect: even if these provisions were justified by a public discourse against illegal immigration, increasingly reducing legalization channels[15] has produced further clandestinity or—in other words—has created a mass of men and women without rights that can easily be exploited by the black economy. It is unsettling to see the convergence of mafia interests, neoliberalist powers, and the political machine in this business (Palmisano 2017) which, depowered and subservient, fuels consent with rowdy and pointless public order response.

In this perspective, the interventions undertaken regarding immigration during the pandemic can be understood. It was indeed obvious that the lockdown measures would, on the one hand, have a dramatic impact on the Italian and migrant population involved in the black economy while, on the other hand, put crops and the agricultural industry at risk. The response to the health crisis was a draft legislation that aimed at bringing out and legalizing the clandestine immigrants working in agriculture and as carers. The measure was promoted by the Democrat Party minister of agriculture, Teresa Bellanova, who had herself been a farm laborer and trade unionist. Nevertheless, as expected, the initiative was the subject of a staunch trial of strength between the parliamentary forces, mainly using rhetoric and the media. The result was therefore a complete mess. First of all, the legalization process was extremely complicated bureaucratically speaking and only aimed at a few categories of workers. Moreover, it had a limited time, which proves that, more than giving "dignity to the invisible," the measure aimed at ensuring agriculture with a workforce, a sector that—in ordinary circumstances—survives precisely due to this malpractice. The ridiculously low prices imposed by large-scale retailers[16] are not compatible with contractual conditions and decent salaries.

However, the cultural atmosphere generated by the legalization measure contributed to creating the conditions for more radical actions. May 21 was a historical date because undocumented migrants working on farms started a national strike. The demonstration took place in Foggia—the epicenter of illegal hiring—and was followed by others just as the echo of anti-racist protests was sounding in Italy, urged on by shouts of "Black lives matter" on the streets in the United States. The climax of this rallying was the founding of the Farm Labourers' League on August 11, 2020, driven by trade unionist, Aboubakar Soumahoro. It is important to highlight that this was not a totally new initiative. In recent years, numerous experiences have sprung up which, aimed at reacting to the widespread hatred in society for immigrants, have created alliances between Italians and foreigners in regard to vital issues such as food production. An example is the *Fuori mercato* (off-market) network that promotes agro-ecological cultivation and trade channels totally different to the market logic that governs the agro-food industry and is founded on cooperation and respect of workers, consumers, and the environment.

During lockdown, we experienced a condition of vulnerability that even more greatly highlighted how much we really need each other and the planet. Will we be able to seize this precious opportunity to question our economic and political systems which create divisions and dispense death? Or will the fragility we experienced be fertile ground for strengthening hatred through which the oppressed, rather than freeing themselves, will crush those who are weaker? It is an open challenge for popular education.

Conclusion

This text has mainly focused on the first months of the health crisis, characterized by the lockdown and subsequent reopening measures. As we conclude, however, we are already into the so-called second wave of the epidemic which began in October, 2020, and is galloping at an alarming speed. The difficulties that the Italian government appears to be having to intervene in structural public system problems, from health care to education and transport, provoked by neoliberalist policies in the last few decades that have been insensitive to these problems seem to have undermined last spring's efforts (especially the national lockdown lasting three months) and highlighted the failure of this model. New restrictions are therefore being imposed on citizens' lives, on education, and on participation and basic organization.

Traces of this crisis, even when it has, hopefully, been overcome, will be indelible. The social characteristics that are indispensable to critical pedagogy and popular education have been heavily hit: socialization, encounter, contact, reunion, art, corporality, theater, music, assembly. Gatherings, or rather, convergences of groups of people in one place, have been banned. Nevertheless, other means of communication of a virtual nature have been found or strengthened that, if well integrated with physical presence, can be highly useful.

The fact remains that we are living in uncertain and distressing times, in the middle of a complex phenomenon that we are still trying to understand and it is therefore hard to draw definitive conclusions. Keeping faith with critical pedagogy, we have preferred to disseminate our written questions that outline the primary dynamics that cross Italian society, often in opposite directions. We believe that popular education is called upon to pause in this hiatus while carrying out its often silent yet indispensable daily activity of thought and action.

The time is ripe to strengthen historical sense through knowledge. Living in hard times without historical knowledge means totally losing the sense of direction. Instead, we need to look to the horizon to find the sense of social relations, which also means a social condition in which to take action. That is why, more than ever, the awareness of being part of history, not only of "barbarism" but also of resistance movements, fights for social justice, equity, and solidarity, also means searching for the keys to construct a democratic sense to our social living. We hope that this text will have made even the tiniest contribution to creating this awareness.

The Lost Generation? Educational Contingency in Viral Times

Malta and Beyond

Carmel Borg and Peter Mayo

Introduction

The general widespread rhetoric is that pandemics affect people of all backgrounds, a tune belted out over and over again to nauseating effect. An in-depth context analysis, that of the small Mediterranean island state of Malta, with an official population of 441,543, reveals that the effects vary according to social background. While people from middle-class families can be fatally hit by the pandemic, there are more significant per capita negative effects on people from the less well-to-do sectors of society, the working class. We view "working class" in a nuanced way. In our view, it includes people who have become déclassé marked by a deterioration in their living conditions; they might be more qualified than their parents but cannot enjoy their standard of living (English and Mayo 2012: 119).

Education, Middle-Class Jobs and the Class/Ethnic Divide

Education sites have endured sudden changes through the onset of Covid-19. As elsewhere, educational institutions have been, for a long period, "closed" sites with administration reduced to skeleton staff and educators urged to seek alternative ways of interacting with students. Questions arise: Are fully fledged, salaried educators engaged in "middle-class" work fostering a "middle-class" ethos even when working with predominantly working-class students? They are often said to be, in the words of the recently deceased Eric Olin Wright (Wright et al. 1989), in a contradictory class location. "The pandemic has complicated the class divide, by singling out a privileged class of those who can work from home in a secure labour condition"[1] (Della Porta 2020). Malta's streets remain full of people scampering around as their livelihood depends on this. Rife is the abuse and exploitation of those involved in the informal economy, key in Malta and other countries to partly sustain the formal economy (Borg 2020a).

Mental-health issues can affect people living in a restricted room or two. Contrast this with the palatial settings of others. Malta is hitherto spared the heart-wrenching sight of homeless people filing outside a Brussels megastore at closing time, waiting for their share of cardboard boxes which will serve as the only barrier between their bodies and a December cold night. This can be witnessed in many commercial streets the world over. "Socialism or Barbarism," Rosa Luxemburg once posed by way of contrast.

There is still a contrast, in Malta, as elsewhere, between those who can work safely and others who risk health to eke a living, often skirmishing on the periphery. Students, at all education levels, also face these contrasts. Certain educators and students can teach or learn in the comfort of their home. Others have limited space in their overcrowded homes which they constantly need to leave to carry out family livelihood chores, possibly even boosting family earnings in the "hidden economy." Social class and ethnicity are significant variables here. They increase one's chances of overcoming or succumbing to the pandemic. Quite vulnerable are those carrying out menial, often clandestine, work. This is the staple of immigrants' life, especially the life of undocumented immigrants (*sans papiers*—without papers). Age is a key variable here. Isolation compounds the issue.

The choice is often between exposure and starvation. Migrants are most likely to risk exposure to the virus. The coronavirus situation barred some of them coming by boat from entering Maltese ports, a few facing death by drowning or dehydration. This is aggravated by the Malta-EU standoff with regard to migrant responsibility. Despite widespread calls for cooperation and compassion, self-interest guides not only individuals, under neoliberalism, but also nation states. So much for the receding of the nation state under globalization!

All into Proper Perspective

This is the wider scenario in which we need to look at Maltese education in these times. We would assume Covid-19's negative effects on the disadvantaged to be a universal phenomenon but we will show this as being or potentially being the case with Malta. The effects we are considering include not only the incidence of death by Covid-19 but also opportunities available or not in other sectors of life. As elsewhere (Apple 2020), Covid-19 continues to have a deleterious effect on the Maltese educational experiences.

Malta witnessed a spike in Covid-19 cases, after a brief lull and subsequent relaxation of preventive measures. This spike disrupted teaching/learning processes. The shift in responsibility onto disadvantaged homes was devastating.

Covid-19 and Education Developments in Malta

The first case of Covid-19 in Malta was reported on March 7, 2020. In less than a week, and in response to the general concern expressed by the population at large, the then newly installed prime minister announced that schools, university and childcare centers were to close for seven days, eventually extended to the rest of the scholastic/academic year. The partial lockdown, coupled with effective enforcement and multiple solidarity initiatives, at different levels, yielded tangible results. With the number of active cases down to thirty-eight, following consecutive days of zero cases, the public health emergency was lifted by end of June.

On July 1, and with a sense of economic urgency, the Malta International Airport (MIA) was opened to mass tourism, a staple of Malta's economy, with minimum control at entry point. This was the beginning of a "Covid slide" that, at the time of writing, resulted in 85 deaths, a rate of 192 deaths per 1 million.[2] The mutual trust between local authorities and the public was gradually eroded, as many lowered their guard and unions disputed government's decrees and decisions. Economic considerations regained center stage.

Despite this, the education ministry announced that schools will open for face-to-face teaching and learning on September 28. Tension within the education communities, particularly in the pre-school and compulsory education sectors, took the form of a struggle between the two unions, representing the various grades of the teaching profession, and the Ministry of Education and Employment (MEDE). The struggle was over the timing of the opening of schools, the level of readiness in terms of health and safety protocols, the syllabi to be covered, and the procedures to be followed in case of an infection.

Unions adopted different strategies to force the Ministry into concrete and accountable action. The more established of the two unions, the Malta Union of Teachers (MUT), adopted a pragmatic and largely dialogical approach, while the recently established Malta Union of Professional Educators (UPE) was more militant and consistently advocated online learning. Tension between unions and the Ministry over school readiness in the area of health and safety resulted in the postponement of the opening of schools, eventually materializing in a staggered way. Parents were given the choice of compulsory children attendance either face-to-face or online. Twenty-five percent of state-school students stayed at home while benefitting from a range of non-physical provision (Cordina 2020). Live streaming of classroom-based teaching was opposed, by both unions, on security grounds.

Schooling Online

While the country's Information and Communication Technologies (ICT) infrastructure was up to scratch and allowed educators to move into a virtual relationship with their students within days, the same was not true of online teaching readiness. There was more emergency remote learning than genuine online learning. The former consisted of content-driven, coverage-obsessed, prescriptive, and transmission-mode relationships with students.

Neither was there much serious rethink of knowledge production within schools, nor robust attempts at puncturing what Dewey and Freire famously and respectively called "pouring in" and "banking education." The early virtual experience brought a general longing for return to face-to-face teaching. Emergency remote learning was seen as a momentary alternative to the "real thing," a stop-gap for which many educators were ill-prepared. Albeit with exceptions, the Covid-19 period constituted a missed opportunity to propel the Maltese education system into the future.

Teacher-Proof Systems and Cultural Imperialism

In quickly bridging the resources gap, Covid-19 brought about a local surge in the use of readily available internet tools and online educational packages. The situation calls for vigilance against educator-deskilling. The contingency can easily accommodate pre-packaged learning. This plays into the hands of commercial interests hovering over and around education. It has already been a recurring global feature of education that allows for cultural imperialism: an education that is contextually insensitive and can easily generate teacher-proof systems.

Social and Economic Gaps

Covid-19 continued to unveil and reinforce the social and economic gaps that characterize Maltese society. Several studies, including PISA 2019, have illustrated the strong correlation that exists between family socioeconomic status and educational achievement in Malta. The lack of pedagogical preparedness coupled with the weak response to the individual needs of the most disadvantaged students, presented a huge obstacle to social justice, which was already severely compromised before Covid-19; Malta scored low in the EU index of social justice in "equitable education" (Thorsten, Schmidt and Heller 2019). Research regarding online learning, in fact, shows that remote approaches to teaching and learning can only be effective and socially just if students have equitable access to fast internet and teachers are well prepared for digital teaching (Borg 2020b). Unfortunately, these basic requirements have been largely absent from many educational environments. Children with little or no support at home would emerge seriously damaged by Covid-19, resulting in high percentages of scholastic underachievement (Borg 2020c).

In addition, research on remote learning shows that this specific approach to teaching is maximized if personalized and sufficiently resourced to target diversity, learning differences and difficulties, as well as home circumstances. The emergency on a massive scale that the sudden closure of schools created, together with lack of experience in addressing remote learning for large groups, caused marginalization. The educational predicament of children became disproportionately dependent on the quality of remote provision, support services, emotional care, and assessment. It also exacerbates the class divide regarding not only access to state-of-the-art devices and physical-learning settings at home but also cultural, economic, and social capital (Bourdieu 1977) for "home schooling" (Apple 2004: 176); this can result in atomization (Giroux 2021).

Disengagement, frequently reported by teachers, ranging from poor return of homework to intermittent participation and complete disappearance from the education radar are symptomatic of an education system that has apparently failed to engage all students and their families through personalized and needs-oriented strategies (MFWS 2020). Contingency planning was found wanting in this regard.

The pandemic has exacerbated well-documented opportunity gaps that put low-income students at a disadvantage relative to their better-off peers (Borg 2020c). There are gaps regarding access to food and nutrition, housing, health care/insurance, financial relief measures (SILV-EU 2019), and especially devices and internet access. While not severe in the Maltese context, the digital divide made it virtually impossible for some students to learn during the pandemic. We often learn of students living in crowded spaces where the tranquility of online learning and home study in general is a luxury difficult to realize—all this while assuming that they can afford a computer and its accessories, some, at best, sharing one computer among several family members.[3] For many school children, the only source of formal education is their schooling, from which they can be easily disengaged, unless enticing and meaningful pedagogical approaches are adopted.

Several pre-Covid-19 studies have shown that reduced instructional time lowers academic achievement (Borg 2020b). The phenomenon of learning loss has been evidenced by studies measuring regression after the summer recess. They also illustrate how reduced instructional time mostly impacts children from disadvantaged backgrounds. These children have fewer school-relevant educational opportunities outside the formal education system. Willing and available parents, with a high level of education, were helping their children with learning. Some used their economic potential to support their children with private tuition, a thriving industry, and the hardware, software, and internet speed required to maximize virtual learning. Social networking and a computer for each household member ensure smooth learning procedures. Privileged home environments contrast sharply with home ecologies characterized by precarious living. Covid-19 hit hardest those families living close to the poverty line. Such families were impacted by job loss; severe reduction in working hours; the shrinking of the informal economy, an important lifeline for the precarious sector of the population. Health issues constitute some of the social realities, which could not be addressed because of limited income. The issues include: poor nutrition, crowded spaces, digital deprivation, social ghettoization, lack of contact with significant adults outside the home, and possible early leaving from school in an attempt to contribute economically to the family's lost income. Unless pro-active community action is adopted by governments and local governments in terms of providing safe public spaces for learning digitally outside the home, schools will widen rather than bridge social divides. Evidence also suggests that disadvantaged children were hit hardest by the uneven online provision. Students who were receiving low-quality remote learning, poor-home help, and reduced-support services would betray signs of academic stagnation when assessed.

A webinar organized by the Malta Foundation for the Wellbeing of Society (MFWS) in April 2020 revealed how students' routines were completely disrupted, and how the pandemic had distanced students from their social circles, their best friends, and their loved ones. At the same event, parents and educators shared stories of anxious students, uncertain about the immediate future. Many experienced lack of concentration and motivation, disorientation, frustration, anxiety, loneliness, and boredom (MFWS 2020).

In times of Covid-19, what we are left with is a schooling system which, more than ever, renders students largely dependent on the availability of parents and on family resources. Children of low economic status are generally overrepresented in the statistics reporting on educational underachievement in Malta. While affecting students across the board, the pandemic is exacerbating underachievement within the foregoing category of students for reasons outlined earlier. Children living in disenfranchised and marginalized contexts, such as homes experiencing poverty and mental-health issues, are disproportionately impacted by the pandemic. School shutdown is not only causing uneven losses for these students but is also leading to disengagement on a larger scale than normal. Some students have literally vanished from the school's radar.

While student engagement is correlated with home support, the magnitude of how much learning was lost through the closure of schools between March and June 2020 is also a function of access to quality online instruction. Maltese parents have reported uneven school engagement with their children. Parents of students with disabilities and of children with learning difficulties have been particularly vocal in this regard, with some feeling that their children have been gravely shortchanged by the system. While acknowledging that the shift from face-to-face to online engagement is logistically complex and pedagogically challenging, we argue that quality education should remain a commitment, irrespective of the learning environment and of the extraordinary historical moment prescribed by Covid-19.

Quality education is hereby defined by the school's willingness to employ inclusive practices in the most difficult of circumstances; reach out socially and emotionally to children; maintain strong home-school links; create communities of practice by engaging parents in their children's learning; adopt a policy of zero tolerance to truancy; engage in ongoing professional development; adopt assessment procedures that truly serve learning; meaningfully and respectfully engage and enable support staff to reach out productively to struggling students and parents; set up focus groups that inform policy, pedagogy, and curriculum in an educational context which is dynamic and fluid.

Regarding the probable results of scholastic achievement of the emergency remote learning on children, Dorn et al. (2020) note that while the best full-time, virtual schools perform at par with traditional schools, most studies have found that full-time online learning does not deliver the academic results of in-class instruction. This emerged from a detailed data analysis of the impact of Covid-19 on student achievement within the US education system. They further note that the emergency remote learning, from March to June 2020, in general, was less effective and reached fewer students. The data available suggests that students experiencing average-quality remote learning continued to progress, but at a slower pace than if they had remained in school. Students who were getting lower-quality remote learning and poor-home support were generally "stagnated" at their current grade levels. Those who ended off the radar, or were completely disengaged, "lost significant ground" from which it will be difficult to recover in future. There is thus, post-Covid-19, a stronger case for second-chance youth and adult education if the present generation, or large sectors of this generation, are not to be lost forever and become known, in a play on Gertrude Stein's words, the "lost generation."

While the estimates are not based on Maltese data and, therefore, results may not be generalizable for all student populations, they provide us with strong indications as to what Maltese and other children may experience in the near future. The data indicate that should schools continue to operate remotely, following the summer recess, which normally contributes to academic regression, students could lose three to four months of learning if they receive average remote instruction. They can lose many more months with lower-quality remote instruction. These losses are magnified further in the case of traditionally disenfranchised students.

Using a national sample of over 5 million students in grades three to eight who took MAP Growth assessments in 2017–2018, a study (Kuhfeld et al. 2020) compared growth for students who had completed a standard-length school year to projected growth in the context of the pandemic. The analysis predicts massive learning losses in the core subjects, mathematics in particular. Should the situation experienced as of March this year persist, the "Covid slide" can only be mitigated by high-quality online schooling and home schooling.

As indicated earlier, the academic dimension of education is not the only ongoing concern of educators and other significant adults. Recreational as well as significant curricular experiences were stopped or have been postponed. The pandemic has cut several children from their social circles and from meaningful, all-year social encounters. Unfortunately, many children and youth found themselves trapped within dysfunctional home environments. Confined largely to their homes, children were enduring, full-time, the harsh reality of alcoholic parents, physical, and sexual abuse; parental litigation; and domestic violence. For many of these children, time spent at school and outdoors is an escape from the carceral home. This might well be how school, often depicted as a prison, appears to certain students; a prison to some, a source of liberation to others. It is a complex and paradoxical world that educators are called upon to deal with in a spirit of human compassion.

Many were spending several hours on their own, in homes that are poorly equipped to educate children. Children are spending hours in front of different types of screens, often sleeping and eating irregularly. Some children are facing food insecurity and substantial loss in family income. The emotional toll on a good number of students is significant. Returning to schools in October meant facing students who are moderately to substantially behind in key areas of education, a situation vividly described by Paulo Freire regarding the effects of the Great Depression on Brazil and his upbringing (Freire 1994, 1996).

Covid-19 might have caught us by surprise in March 2020, but there should be no excuse for being ill-prepared this time round as it is likely to enter its second year. This situation calls for robust assessment of learning at school level. All children should be assessed formally and informally for prior learning before proceeding to addressing the curricular outcomes of the forthcoming scholastic year. The same applies to nutrition. There are cases, albeit not the norm, in Maltese primary schools when basic sandwiches, for the morning break, are prepared for certain students. This somehow recalls the activities of cooks in São Paulo's "Popular-Public" schools. Schools should expect greater variability in terms of scholastic-year-readiness, and should be prepared to employ differentiated pedagogical and nutritional strategies to address this variability. The need for personalized learning is expected to become more pronounced.

University Education

The University of Malta, the only public university on the island, was quick to move online, with many faculty members engaging in emergency remote teaching and learning which came in the form of synchronous learning, replicating the traditional teaching that still dominates the pedagogical scene at the only public university in Malta. In fact, during the emergency, transferring content was prioritized over online pedagogy. While the first few months of the Covid-19 experience exposed the lack of digital training within the academic community, the University of Malta fared well in the students' eyes, as evidenced by the response of the Maltese students participating in a global survey on the impact of the situation on higher education. Aristovnik (2020) revealed that, similar to students across all continents, Covid-19 has significantly increased the study workload. Despite this workload, University of Malta students reported that they managed well the new, exclusively virtual reality, with the University of Malta coming in second place when the 2,881 students from across the globe were asked to rate their level of satisfaction with their tutors.

The survey also looked at students' satisfaction with the shift from class-based learning to online provision. The University of Malta ranked first with regard to students' satisfaction with recorded videos and second with regard to the use of video conferences. University of Malta students were among the most satisfied surveyed students from over 150 universities in 100 countries and 6 continents.

A number of international studies have analyzed the impact of Covid-19 on higher education student productivity. Using a field experiment with 458 students from 3 different subject areas at the Universidad Autónoma de Madrid (Spain), González et al. (2020) divided students into two groups. The first group (control) covered academic years 2017/2018 and 2018/2019. The second group (experimental) covered students from 2019/2020, the group of students that had their face-to-face activities interrupted because of the pandemic. The study concluded that there is a significant positive effect of Covid-19 on students' performance. This effect is also significant in activities that did not change their format when transposed online. In addition, an analysis of students' learning strategies before moving online shows that students did not study on a continuous basis. Covid-19 changed students' learning strategies to a more continuous habit, improving their efficiency.

The careers of this year's university graduates can be severely affected by the Covid-19 pandemic. They have experienced major teaching interruptions in the final part of their studies. This includes their assessments. They are graduating at the beginning of a major global recession. Evidence suggests that poor market conditions at labor market entry cause workers to accept lower-paid jobs, and that this has permanent effects for the careers of some. Oreopoulos, von Wachter and Heisz (2012) show that graduates from programs with high predicted earnings can compensate for their poor starting point through both within- and-across-firm earnings, but graduates from other programs have experienced permanent earning losses from graduating in a recession. Restrictions of travel for work and further study might lead to lower economic returns on education owing to the graduate being confined to a specific labor market.

Undergraduates Disappearance

Many of the dysfunctional aspects of the contingency, outlined with regard to schools, apply to higher education institutions and need not be rehearsed again. They are important considerations that have to be taken on board when exploring higher education (HE) alternatives, from a social justice perspective, at the time of Covid-19 and after. Our guess and fear are that all this will continue to be given short shrift. Higher education institutions, and especially universities, by and large still accommodate a middle-class viewpoint.[4] Despite laudable and interesting experiments among peasants in Latin America[5] (de Sousa Santos 2017; Connell 2019; Mayo 2019; Mayo and Vittoria 2017) and also in Western Europe (Neary 2014; Earl 2016; Tarlau 2019), the institution, as we conventionally know it, and in which most academics work, remains, like most schools, a "bourgeois institution." Many institutions have gradually been transformed since the exclusionary past, often not in a democratic way as the business imperative holds sway.

The general ethos, however, remains bourgeois. Academics by and large work in privileged positions, some more than others. Yet there are issues to be raised with regard to these institutions' future if they are to be rendered more democratic (Connell 2019), less Eurocentric (de Sousa Santos 2017), and more community-engaged (Walcott 2020).

Standard Corona Response

During this period of Covid-19, educators have been urged, if not compelled, irrespective of their training for this purpose, to place their courses and carry out their teaching online. Lecturers can agree with students on what mode to adopt. This makes sense since professors generally go on teaching until seventy and also beyond and therefore fall within "vulnerable groups" as is the case with one of us. This has led many to herald online learning as the future. For many, the present period is the potential watershed in affirming this mode of delivery as par for the course in higher education. This is to be expected—in synch with the neoliberal tenets concerning mass-oriented education and individualistic learning. Unlike schools, online learning might well persist in HE. It might be here for the long haul.

The history of education is full of episodes when necessity, as in the case of the clandestine Polish Flying University, led to creative alternatives (Puiu 2020). The present crisis makes those who are resistant to modern digitally mediated technology take the plunge, whether adequately trained for this purpose or not. Many educators from Greece, Italy, Cyprus, and the UK told Mayo (2020a) that online learning is a new experience taken up by the uninitiated.[6] There are universities that have been well versed in this as a number of their students are distant online participants. Most likely, the educators concerned are constantly given adequate training in this mode of delivery. Open university tutors in the UK spent a year's preparatory period before taking on online teaching commitments. This is a far cry from the situation concerning the majority of academics in the country or worldwide who had to make the sudden switch.

This approach can extend beyond a crisis contingency. It can turn out to be a lucrative venture in the long run. Again, this is in keeping with neoliberal tenets: a course's "validity" is often said to be gauged by its ability to be "sold" internationally (Mayo 2019). It would allow for the creation of a global market. It is argued that online learning can reach students anywhere and at different times. Yet this requires great planning, preparation, and thinking. The generation of good learning settings, digital or otherwise, requires important skills and solid teamwork. It involves educators, communities, and learning designers. There is also the danger of surveillance when talks are recorded which can render participants less inclined to talk for fear that the streamed conversation ends up in the "wrong hands." Some foreign students fear intelligence services back home.

Consumer Product or Public Good?

How can we achieve an online and "face-to-face" teaching balance at universities? There is also the issue of online learning taking HE further down the much-marketed business pathway (Mayo 2019). Does the idea of HE as a public good still hold or is it seen in economistic terms and therefore according to the business model? The issue of resources for online learning, mentioned earlier, resurfaces here. Maltese students receive a stipend at undergraduate level. It should at least be of an amount that suffices in this regard.

Covid-19 and Neoliberalism

Covid-19 allows hope for imaginative and social justice educators to teach against the grain (Simon 1992). This means going against the flow. But the flow attracts educators who appear to be "with it." This is where we are worried. There is an unequal scenario that education can confront if it is driven by a vision of a just world which can come into being. Covid-19 has "outed" neoliberalism even further. Shredding a social contract meant to transcend capitalism (Giroux 2020) has led to a few public resources available to counter the pandemic. Hopefully, the much spoken about sense of solidarity can lead to a rethink of education at all levels. The genuine human and ecological factor in research and education remains key. Once the crisis is hopefully overcome, will education be transformed as a result of a general rethink, both nationally and globally? Beyond the Covid-19 Pandora box there lies hope which springs eternal.

Lessons from Teacher Organizing

Disputing the Meaning of Teaching and Teachers' Work During the Coronavirus Pandemic in Chile

M. Beatriz Fernández, Iván Salinas Barrios, and Andrea Lira

This chapter presents a critical analysis of Chile's institutional responses as well as teachers' responses to the Covid-19 sanitary crisis in the context of the sociopolitical crisis that preceded it since October 2019. We begin describing Chile's educational policies, examining neoliberal and New Public Management policies set in place before the social-political crisis of October 2019 and the pandemic outbreak in March 2020. Using rhizomatic theory (Deleuze and Guattari 1987), we then discuss the dispute for the meaning of teaching and the reconfiguration of teachers' work through the examination of the different stages of the Ministry of Education's responses, as well as new teacher organizations and unions' responses to the pandemic. Finally, we discuss what we have learned from the work of teacher organizing and the potential for the post-pandemic future.

Chile as an Early Adopter of Neoliberal and New Public Management Policies

Chile adopted neoliberalism as a renovated phase of capitalism during the 1980s under Pinochet's dictatorship (Harvey 2005). New public management (NPM) developed as a privatization approach derived from neoliberal policies that fragments public services in small units, makes them responsible for their budget, distinguishes users and providers, and promotes a culture of managerialism aiming at achieving measurable results (Verger, Fontdevila, and Zancajo 2016). The Chilean education system has been organized under this approach. During the 1980s, Pinochet's dictatorship implemented neoliberal reforms to change the landscape of education. The reform decentralized public education provision from the state to municipalities, changing the public education funding scheme by defunding it in order to promote privatization through state subsidies (school vouchers). Subsidized private schools were allowed to charge small amounts of tuition and have tax exemptions. The government also divided national state universities in regional branches, withdrawing their main source of funding and creating a tuition-based funding scheme, while promoting entrepreneurial new universities. Teacher and student movements that opposed the reforms were heavily repressed by the government. A national standardized test for all schools (SIMCE) was created and applied since 1988. A day before the dictatorship ended, in 1990, Pinochet signed the Constitutional Education Organic Law.

In the 1990s, elected governments promoted policies for addressing pressing consequences of the dictatorship's reforms. In 1991, the government passed the Teaching Statute, which regulates teachers' hiring and firing, labor rights, work schedules, and wages (Ley 19.070). This was modified in 1995 to include financial and symbolic competitive incentives for teachers working in schools that obtained measurable results in standardized tests (Ley 19.410). Ever since 1995, the government published SIMCE scores, making it the measure of quality education. Also, focalized programs for curriculum change (MECE) and for assisting the poorest schools (P900) were implemented. In 1997, the government started a curricular reform, setting an agenda for a full-day working schedule (Ley 19.532).

By the year 2000, public enrollment in schools had decreased to 55 percent from 78 percent in 1981 (Fundación Sol 2011). The government passed reforms that address the quality of education, implementing focalized programs for students dropping out of high schools (*Liceo para Todos* and *Liceos Prioritarios* programs). It also updated SIMCE tests to make it possible to follow up cohorts of students and compare year to year information. Chile's inclusion into OECD in 2003 made it a participant in the PISA tests, forewarning politicians about the comparatively low performance of Chilean school students. Concerns about quality led the government to implement the creation of performance standards for teacher education, economic incentives for "pedagogical excellence," a network of highest-rated teachers (*maestros de maestros*), and standards for good teaching (*Marco para la buena enseñanza*), which marked the start of teacher evaluation in the public school system in 2004, as well as making mandatory to have a high-school diploma for all. With a liberalized higher education entrepreneurial system, private universities had opened by dozens and increased their rates of enrollment (Orellana 2018). To address the demand for higher education, the government proposed a state-guaranteed student loan system, reinforcing tuition-based higher education and opening a new market for private for-profit institutions to rely on.

Quality being the official discourse of the 2000s, large secondary students revolts surprised politicians in 2001 and 2006. In 2001, students protested by the thousands in downtown Santiago demanding free fares for public transportation and more involvement from the state in administering public transportation for students. The movement was named *mochilazo* (which refers to mochila, or backpack, a common accessory in school-aged youth in Chile), and forced the Ministry of Education to create a national card for student fares in public transportation and be in charge of its administration. In 2006, secondary students initiated larger protests in a powerful national movement known as *Revolución Pingüina* (which makes reference to the resemblance that school uniforms in Chile have had with the colors of penguins). The movement was fueled by the precarious conditions of schools in many places of the country. It visibilized a strong social agenda against markets in education, quickly garnering national social support and political advocacy from university student federations, teacher organizations, and workers' unions. The movement gained political content requesting to "stop for-profit education" and the end to Pinochet's constitutional laws that organized education. The government announced a presidential committee in order to discuss the issues raised by the protests, which resorted to a political agreement among parties for reform in education (Domedel and Peña y Lillo 2008). In 2008, the government created a focalized funding system for the most vulnerable schools (Ley 20.248), and in 2009 passed a new organic law for education, creating two new state institutions for external control and assessment: the Agency for the Quality of Education and the School Superintendency.

In 2010, public (municipal) schools shared about 42 percent of the total student enrollment (Fundación Sol 2011). Following the agreements of 2007, congress passed in 2011 a law to create the Education Quality Assurance System (Ley 20.529), which increased accountability by extending the power of standardized testing for sanctioning lower performing schools. In the same year, a university student movement shook the political environment and quickly garnered social support, demanding to stop the market-based education system, which was generating large student debt (Simonsen 2012; Figueroa 2013). The movement was summarized with the demand for "free quality education," which became the basis for a reform agenda of a new elected government in 2014.

The agenda included a reform to teacher professional career, including merit-pay, classification of teachers in a scale of performance based on standardized norm-referenced disciplinary-content tests, and an accountability reform to teacher education, which increased vigilance through tests and accreditation processes and imposed consequences for teacher education programs based on accreditation results (González et al. 2020). This reform was heavily opposed by teachers at the base, and provoked a disengagement with the National Teacher Association leadership, which was politically linked to the government, and the spread of locally based organizations and teacher collectives that protested the reform (González 2015; Navarrete 2020). Other three reforms were a focalized free-tuition law for the poorest 40 percent of higher education students within a higher education reform (Ley 21.091), an inclusion law (Ley 20.845) that ended school tuition in state-funded schools, and a centralized school admission system was created. In 2008, another student-started movement, the "Feminist May," garnered social support for an agenda of cultural change, against patriarchy and patriarchal violence, and for institutional changes that acknowledge historical and cultural oppression against women (Brito 2020; Zerán 2018).

This brief account shows the most relevant policies implemented under NPM principles in Chile's education. In most cases, policies had been contested by demonstrations from agents such as organized students and teachers (e.g., Thielemann 2016). Those who are teaching in Chilean classrooms today embody these reforms either as a generation who saw them imposed, or a generation who has lived them as school students and prospective teachers. Young teachers today have experienced standardized testing, student debt, and the constraints of NPM to their professional work. These are the educational experiences that are the backbone of those teachers who received the news and political response to the Covid-19 pandemic.

The People's Rebellion of 10/18 before the Pandemic

This social and economic model went into crisis right before the pandemic outbreak in Chile. On October 18, 2019, several protests emerged around different metro subway stations in the Chilean capital. A week before, high-school students had protested the rise of public transportation fares by 30 Chilean pesos (equivalent to 40 US cents), announced on October 6. Students organized fare evasions, massive jumping over metro station turnstiles, and encouraged passersby to do it as well including disseminating their message on social media. The government-sanctioned police violence used to deter the growing fare evasion movement was broadcast across mass and social media receiving widespread criticism. On October 18, the metro company decided to close some crucial stations and interrupt the transportation service near the end of the workday on a Friday. Protests erupted as a response to the lack of transportation, and people complained and organized through social media, spontaneously gathering to protest in downtown Santiago and other points of the metropolitan region. That night, while social media broadcast protesters being violently repressed by riot-geared police, several metro stations were arsoned. The government announced a state of emergency and curfew for the following days in the capital.

The shock of this moment is hard to express. From one day to the next the military were in charge of the streets after curfew and the less monied neighborhoods faced increased repression, home invasions, and use of riot and war gear, like tear gas and water cannons. There was no spokesperson of this public resistance movement, nor any affiliation to a specific political group. Riots erupted in several other cities, as the media named the events "*estallido social*" or "social burst," or "social revolt." People marched across the country to protest against an unjust system that did not provide decent social security pensions, education, health, and housing. In a few days, the government declared a state of emergency in fifteen out of seventeen regional capitals. The sentence "it's not 30 Chilean pesos, it's 30 years" became a slogan of the revolt, making it clear that the rise in fares was only a spark that set the fire. After almost a month of protests around the country and multiple human rights violations, members of all political parties signed the "agreement for social peace and a new constitution" on November 15, 2020 (Biblioteca del Cogreso Nacional 2020). The agreement set the agenda for a national plebiscite in 2020 to ask if people wanted to change the constitution, approved under the dictatorship in the 1980s. The plebiscite would also ask what kind of political organism should write a new constitution. The elections held in the midst of the pandemic resulted in the first ever constitution that will be written by 50 percent elected women.

While some educators tried to generate curriculum materials to address the social unrest in schools, the Ministry of Education announced a law proposal to punish political indoctrination in schools at the end of November 2019 (Diario Uchile 2019). The Ministry declared that indoctrination was a form of violence against students and announced high-stakes consequences for schools, such as the loss of official authorization to work. The proposal received criticism from teacher organizations and academics (El Periodista 2019; Cabaluz 2019).

Despite not being approved by congress, it caused great concern and fear among teachers. At the national level, while the massiveness of protests declined over the summer, people continued protesting in the main cities until the beginning of March 2020, when the first Covid-19 cases were detected.

Teacher Organizations' Rhizomatic Responses to the Covid-19 Pandemic Educational Crisis

We propose the concept of rhizome (Deleuze and Guattari 1987) to understand the teacher's responses to both the pandemic and the currently ongoing social movement in Chile. "Rhizome" is a term for a form of plant that spreads like dandelions or ginger. These plants do not have individual roots or a beginning point. They develop a network of roots and nodes underground that bloom or push through the surface at any point and each node can develop and create its own network (Geerlings and Lundberg 2018). Even if the network is severed at any point it can continue to develop and multiply at any point. The tree is the figure that is commonly used as a metaphor for knowledge and social phenomena. In the tree the trunk is the nucleus and every branch and growth comes from one set of roots that grows into the trunk that then bifurcates. Different from the understanding of knowledge as a tree, Deleuze and Guattari explain that

> A rhizome has no beginning or end; it is always in the middle, between things, interbeing, *intermezzo*. The tree is filiation, but the rhizome is alliance, uniquely alliance. The tree imposes the verb "to be" but the fabric of the rhizome is the conjunction, "and . . . and . . . and . . ." This conjunction carries enough force to shake and uproot the verb "to be." (1987: 25)

We propose that the varied reactions and organizations that stem from both the pandemic and the social revolt can be understood as rhizomes, with the different groups and forms of organizing framed as lines of flight and moments of territorialization and deterritorialization. This contrasts to the arborescent view of social movements, organized by leaders with groups of followers that branch and act from this leadership. The response to the Covid-19 pandemic in education has the complexity of a rhizome, where it is difficult to track the origin and end (Deleuze and Guattari 1987). We use the rhizome to analyze the growth of teachers' responses around different themes or controversies that arose on this pandemic time.

Broadening Teachers' Voices

Shortly after classes moved from face-to-face interactions to remote emergency education, different groups of teachers organized webinars to discuss education, teachers and students struggles, and to share resources during the pandemic. Webinars gave the opportunity to several teacher groups to express their reflections and experiences without investing the onerous resources needed to organize presence-based seminars. Also, webinars allowed the broadening of the public voice of teachers from the National Teachers' Association (*Colegio de Profesores*) discourse to several small groups of teacher organizations that interconnect and diverge in their concerns and members. Some of these groups were the Movement for Teacher Unity (MUD), the Special Education Movement (MED), the Feminist Teachers Network (REDOFEM), the Network of Philosophy Teachers of Chile (REPROFICH), and the Autonomous Network of teachers of Magallanes (RAPROMAG) among others.

These groups existed before the pandemic, but their voices reached a larger audience during this time. Their origins could be traced back to different periods and political contexts. For example, the National Teachers' Association (*Colegio de Profesores*) was founded after an executive order of Pinochet's dictatorship that replaced the Single Education Workers Union (SUTE), and acquired its democratic character only in the middle of the 1980s (Colegio de profesoras y profesores de Chile 2020a). Meanwhile the Feminist Teachers Network began in Santiago during the 2018 movement called Feminist May (Zerán 2018), and the Autonomous Network of teachers of Magallanes (RAPROMAG) emerged after the Social Revolt of October 2019 in Patagonia, in the south of Chile.

Social media and online resources allowed more diversity of speakers as well as topics. For example, the Feminist Teachers Network pioneered demands for socio-emotional support, and the need for a "pedagogical break," denouncing the work overload of women teachers, who represent the 74 percent of teachers in the country, working from home during the pandemic (El Mostrador 2020). Social media resources created by this network explained reproductive work, why women teachers were doing teaching and care work during the pandemic, the percentages of women in teaching, early child education, and special education, and the feeling of workload in women and men working from home. This network also introduced debates about anti-sexist education and anti-racist education during this time (Red Docente Feminista 2020)[1].

The Movement for Teacher Unity (MUD) emphasized teachers' work conditions for online teaching, protection for teachers fired from their schools, defense of the Social Revolt's detainees, exposure of police violence, the role and characteristics of education in the constitutional debate, and the defense of special education during the Covid-19 sanitary emergency (Movimiento por la Unidad Docente 2020). Materials generated by the Movement for Teacher Unity showed their explicit commitment to condemn oppression on the streets. This movement has also maintained close relationships with international educational workers' organizations in Latin America, participating in webinars related to the future of public education, and has collaborated with the National Workers' of Education Federation (FENATED), posing demands related to educational assistants' concerns. They participated in the world education congress to defend public education against neoliberal policies, which is another form of rhizomatic appearance among teacher organizations beyond the limits of national action. That is, teacher and educational workers´ organizations used the interactive conditions of the pandemic for connecting and acting in alliances that broadened their voices[2].

The Network of Philosophy Teachers of Chile (REPROFICH) created a virtual "laboratory" to collectively discuss questions related to the possibilities of emancipatory education, transformative curriculum and educational quality, teacher organization, and political activism during the pandemic among other topics.

The virtual aesthetics of each group also speaks to the diverse messages, approaches, and imagined audiences. With the feminists of REDOFEM, for example, we see informative messaging, centering the experience of women in education and explaining the complexities of gender-based violence in education. With MUD, the other organization featured earlier, the messages focus on denouncing the violation of human rights and on calls for protesting the deplorable state of the education system in Chile and its systemic inequalities as a result of neoliberal policies. The virtual dissemination of ideas through arts and graphic content during the October revolt that increased during the pandemic has been central to the reach of ideas across physical distance and to this diversity of approaches to organizing in movements against the current education system. Despite this new diversity, a sharp distinction among members at the ground level is difficult to make. Some members of these groups participate in other teacher organizations, their organizations worked in several initiatives together, and/or they are political allies. Some of these groups became closer to each other after the Social Revolt of 2019 in searching for more influence facing oppression on streets. Also, most of these groups publicly agreed to oppose the implementation of the national standardized test for students and the national teacher evaluation for teachers during the pandemic, in their criticism toward the minister of education and his pressure to return to schools buildings without sanitary conditions for teachers and students, and the demand for better online connectivity, and the nuclearization of curricular goals.

The Dispute for Defining What Matters in Education

One of the most important public discussions during this time was the definition of what teachers should teach during the pandemic and what the focus of their work should be. The tight accountability system over schools, expression of the NPM policies, coupled with the Ministry of Education calls for maintaining the focus on the yearly national curriculum goals and evaluations for "saving the school year" restrained teachers' possibilities of action during the pandemic (González et al. 2020). However, several groups of teachers and scholars pointed out the importance of connecting teaching with students' well-being and their contexts. Despite differences among teacher organizations, most of them demanded better work conditions and the need to work around learning goals connected with local contexts.

The National Teacher Association (*Colegio de Profesores*) released a document with proposals to face the Covid-19 emergency in the middle of May. The Ministry of Education pressured for continuing business as usual and returning to school buildings during the pandemic outbreak, the proposal focused on returning to face-to-face classes, financials, and a pedagogical proposal of curricular flexibility to work around core learning objectives, nuclearization, diversity, and socio-emotional aspects (Colegio de profesores 2020b). Members of a regional branch also denounced difficulties in accessing remote classes with half of students and, therefore urged the need to consider the trajectory of each student and provide emotional support to reduce the negative aspects of the pandemic (Valenzuela 2020).

Despite their differences, several teacher organizations agreed on the need to weigh the socioeconomic and emotional outcomes of the pandemic and used social media and opinion letters to demand less bureaucratic work and less external evaluation over teachers and students. While the Ministry of Education strongly promoted the evaluation of students and teachers using learning and equity as a source of legitimation for this proposal, teacher organizations emphasized the inadequacy of these evaluations because of the unequal contexts for learning, the need to invest on support for students and teachers, and the negative consequences of pressuring students and teachers to perform well on these tests (González et al. 2020). Underneath arguments from the Ministry of Education and teacher organizations were the disputes for what the priorities of the educational systems should be under a sanitary emergency and its main goals on a regular basis. Protecting the NPM logic and its gear assembly was confronted by the logic of the protection of well-being, social justice in education, and relevant learning. In connection with the educational system goals, teachers' role and mission was exposed, debated, and recreated by teacher organizations. For example, one flyer for a webinar organized by MUD stated that the role of school during the pandemic was to provide emotional support and organization.[3]

The Dispute for Embracing Normalcy or the New Normal

The push for normalcy was another important aspect strongly defended by the Ministry of Education. Students' return to school buildings had a central role in this debate as a material expression of a normal state of operation in the educational and economic system. The Minister of Finance made the rationale for the government's insistence on reopening school buildings explicit: schools need to be open to reactivate the employment market. He stated: "It is key that we start talking about re-opening. Not only about pre-schools, but also schools. It is fundamental. Normalcy, daily life, return to work, cannot be resumed if you have your kids at home and have no one to leave them with. And this is valid for an infant, but also for a primary school child" (Castro 2020, free translation). This rationale was quickly captured and responded by teacher organizations using social media resources. For example, the Feminist Teacher Network portrayed a picture of the Minister of Labor and the Minister of Finance labeled "schools are not daycare for your business."[4]

While the president and his minister pushed for a return to face-to-face activities even when detected Covid-19 cases were high, teacher organizations exposed health concerns and poor schools' conditions, which made a plan for return unrealistic. Also, these organizations claimed the importance of situating students' and teachers' safety at the center of this decision and listening to school communities. This concern is expressed in an editorial opinion piece written by a member of the Feminist Teachers Network, a member of the Movement for Teacher Unity, and a scholar:

> The government imagines an "ideal" school, absolutely removed from the concrete reality lived by the majority of our schools [...]. The danger of a gradual return to classes in the current conditions implies a very large risk for the life of those who

make up school communities. [. . .] Education must provide certainties, starting with the one that signals a contribution to defend life and integrity as a central task. [. . .] Our return to schools must include a radical return to democracy, which allows us to listen among ourselves as a national community in order to take care of each other. (González, Olivares, and Salinas 2020)

This idea is disseminated also by social media resources generated by the Movement for Teacher Unity, clearly stating that "we [the teachers] will not return to face-to-face classes until the danger is over."[5]

Behind this teachers' resistance to returning to school buildings, there lies a dispute for recognizing the effects of the pandemic in the educational system and teachers' work. While the government pushed to overshadow the lack of schools' conditions to return to face-to-face classes and tried to impose a sense of normalcy, teacher organizations expressed their proposal for embracing the new normal of the pandemic situation and used it as an aspect to contextualize their teaching.

Lessons from Teacher Organization around Teachers' Work and Teaching

The responses from teachers to the pandemic in Chile have been mediated by the structure of the Chilean educational system and the history of social movements in the country. Different from previous ways of teacher organization around struggles when teachers' voices were either coming from the National Teacher Association (*Colegio de Profesores*) or in opposition to it, the pandemic scenario shows a broad spectrum of teacher organizations' perspectives, messages, aesthetics, and forms of organizing. This response to the pandemic cannot be understood as separate from the social revolt of October 18, 2019, but rather in conjunction with the organizing that these groups had already begun to create with this movement.

Social media was a powerful tool for organizing teachers across the country despite the geographic distances and allowed them to share a message with minimal resources. Online resources facilitated teacher's creation of their own aesthetic, quickly responding to the changing environment, and creating spaces for discussing ideas and reflecting about teaching at an uncertain time.

Despite the diversity of approaches and points of view about the education system these groups provide a complex and visible network that disputes the discourse of the new public Management about teachers and teaching in Chile. We have used Deleuze and Guattari's (1987) concept of rhizome to show the way in which these organizations relate to each other and develop, shift, and change through multiple lines of flight.

The efforts of these groups during Covid-19 show the beauty and power that comes from diverse voices and bodies of teachers organizing to dispute the meaning of teaching and teacher's work. While the government continues to respond to teachers without including their voices, we hope that, in this analysis, we have shown the ways in which the organizing of teachers in Chile demonstrates how they take back their place as experts in what their work is and what the potential is to be. We hope the new normal includes more of this work, more disruption of the normalcy of an education system with experts who are not teachers and where the work of schools is designed with little input and autonomy of the professionals who actually do the work.

This new scenario of diverse teacher organizations is promising for its implications in the process of construction of a new constitution in Chile. Secondary and university students have been the main propellers of much of the social movement placing the education system as one of the main points of debate and change. The discussions and the elections of the people who will be writing it will certainly center the issue of public education, and we hope that given this expansion of teacher organizations teachers will now be able to participate in the debate and play a fundamental role in the construction of a new public education.

Environmental Education

For a Critical Renovation alongside the Traditional Peoples

Carlos Frederico B. Loureiro

Introduction

The intensification of the process of capital accumulation based on material dispossession and destruction of natural reserves increases conflicts against those who have a mostly communal form of sociability and non-capitalist ways to connect with the land and reproduce their livelihood. The same process prevents these groups from accessing basic social rights—which imposes upon them a higher degree of fragility in the context of the Covid-19 pandemic, or even in potential futures marked by the disease.

In Brazil, artisanal fisherpeople, indigenous, and maroon populations are among several groups identified as traditional peoples, all of which have their territories currently threatened by the federal government's policies and face Covid-19 death rates above national averages.[1] To make matters worse, environmental and educational policies suffer intense dismantling and ideological persecution—which also applies to environmental education. All federal institutions responsible for its implementation have been extinguished. Such context leads us to reinstate the importance of developing environmental education processes with these peoples so as to find ways to overcome social relations ruled by capital and reconstruct policies which grant the right to education and to the environment as a common good.

Generally speaking, traditional peoples are groups that have a high degree of connection and dependence on their territories. Their productive activities involve little market interaction and enable practices of organic bonds with their land. It is paramount to recognize this specific point. Losing their vital ties to a territory which their culture produces and attributes meaning to is losing what they hold most sacred. Life for them has no price, and their territories cannot be exchanged in the form of commodities.

Traditional peoples' access to basic social rights and specific rights is either made difficult, denied, or often questioned. Their historically constructed social invisibility leads to difficulties with participating as equals in political decision making—something only recently achieved, after intense social organization and struggle. Otherwise, losses are glaring.

This chapter thus starts by outlining some considerations about the circumstances of dispossession which characterize policies of extermination of traditional peoples in Brazil, as well as the role of critical education as a prerequisite for anti-systemic struggles. Second, it presents the importance of critical knowledge about reality as a condition for a problematizing stance toward society. A consideration follows concerning the importance of dialogue as a way for education to take the other into consideration, as well as the necessary reflection about the material conditions under which linguistic and communicational exchange takes place in an unequal society. Finally, it distinguishes ancestry as a category which demands immense sensitivity from educators willing to understand its subtleties and its position as a precondition for trust and exchange between people, as well as for education to take place.

Colonialism, Capitalism, and Environmental Collapse

Enrique Dussel's (1993) classic *1942: El encubrimiento del Otro* (*1942: The Covering of the Other*) finds the stepping stones of the Eurocentric model of civilization in the economic and political practices of the late fifteenth century which were paramount to the consolidation of capitalism as the prevailing social form in Europe. This process involved two main movements. The first was the expansion of trade and mercantile exchange, along with the violent private appropriation of lands and the elimination by military and state forces of any form of sociability involving communal, non-patriarchal and religiously plural relations incompatible with the social project of the bourgeoisie in Europe (Federici 2017). The second occurred outside the continent and involved the covering, subalternization or even the elimination of other civilizations, peoples, and customs in the Americas and later in Africa through colonization. This included brutally plundering knowledge and natural wealth, as well as crushing sociabilities other than the ones imposed from Europe.

These originary forms of land and knowledge dispossession led to the destruction of ecosystems, to the violent occupation of rural areas, to the eviction of populations for land privatization and to the intensive extraction of land and underground resources. Such practices ensured the accumulation of capital in Europe and its expanded reproduction, as well as the subsequent spread of capitalist social forms around the world (Marx 2013).

During the first decade of the twenty-first century, rising prices of mineral commodities made mineral extractivism in Latin American territories expand (Petras 2014). This contemporary phenomenon, called neo-extractivism, is a development model based on economic growth with low industrialization and technological capacities, on the appropriation of natural resources, on supply chains of little diversity and on a subordinate form of geopolitical and geo-economic involvement.

The state, controlled by ruling-class fractions which benefit from such pattern of accumulation, has an active role in that system, which attempts to legitimize in many ways. First comes the bold assertion, radicalized by the federal government which took office in 2019, of the growth of the market economy as a path to prosperity and high living standards, as well as about the market's ability to regulate environmental impacts on its own. Moreover, such hegemonic discourse is based on disregard for the importance of social relations for the education of individuals, who in turn become exclusively responsible for whatever happens to them, making their success or failure a mere matter of personal merit. The government's defense of the mining sector, the oil industry, and the agribusiness finally takes tones of cynicism when it proposes that Brazil has too many protected areas, and indigenous and maroon lands stand in the way of economic activity.

The scale of neo-extractivist production in Brazil, anchored in rural violence and in the intensification of natural resource use, is little diversified, very centralized, and controlled by a small number of families, which leads not only to environmental injustice and inequity, but also to a policy of extermination of traditional peoples. This is expressed by the exponential increase in deaths in the midst of conflicts involving the occupation of traditional territories—even legally protected ones—and by the absence of public policies to fight the pandemic, which denies these people the right to health care and safety.

This model of economic development is legitimized by ideologies which vulgarize socio-environmental barbarism in the name of "economic health," as if it were not possible to have different economies, cyclic and compatible with both human and ecological needs. In a similar fashion it vulgarizes deaths, justified in the name of economic interest.

Unifying the array of existing anti-systemic stances is both an urgent need and a set of challenges in the current context of capitalist crisis (Fontes and Miranda 2014). One of these challenges refers to the role of environmental education as an enabler of solidary practices and of dialogue between knowledges and science. This dialogue must be characterized by the construction of a knowledge independent from hegemonic discourse and by the recognition of the value of traditional knowledge and of the practices of workers who are pushed by job scarcity and by the precarization of working conditions.

Pedagogically speaking, having concrete subjects and situations as a starting point brings to the fore the conflictive dimension at the root of prevailing social relations. This in turn facilitates the understanding of the non-neutrality of environmental themes, as well as the impossibility of solving them with technical intervention or individual moral desire. Historicity is thus a constituent of pedagogical practices, since simply acknowledging problems or relying on individual will as a solution is no longer enough. Problematization is vital for an understanding of causal dynamics and of social agents involved in each problem, as well as for organized collective action toward recognition and enforcement of rights through universalistic policies.

This intentionality is responsible for politicizing environmental education and requiring subjects to adopt a stance toward different projects for society and sustainability. The need to take a stance leads to a reflexive attitude toward reality, to a complex understanding of the rights and responsibilities of individuals-groups-classes, and to practices which operate both in daily life and in political organization for social struggles.

These circumstances reinforce the urgency of discussing and understanding categories which are strategic for struggles and for the construction of socially just policies. Our experience suggests that discussing three of these categories is fundamental: the act of knowing, dialogicity, and ancestry.

The Act of Knowing Critically

For critical thinking, simple analogies between realizations and products of distinct historical times risk on anachronism and cause misunderstandings by ignoring specific social mediations. They miss the most important part, namely, the ability to explain something based on its own determinations and modes of existence in/of a society and its social relations. Concepts are not mental creations isolated from material social conditions and cannot therefore be understood as if they were independent ideas, detached from the historical moment and social totality in which they occur. Concepts are efforts to understand, define and linguistically express some existing being. The same concept may take different forms in different societies or even in different historical moments of the same society.

In the field of environmental education, conceptual confusions persist such as the idea that nature has always been destroyed. This idea lies in equating natural destruction with natural transformation for the creation of ways of living, claiming any form of use to be inherently harmful. Also, this gives universal and atemporal content to destruction by treating it the same way in different historical moments and favoring fatalistic and immobilistic discourses. This way a basic ability is lost, namely the ability to answer: in which society and, consequently, what kind of person presides over what is and what is not environmental destruction?

In *The German Ideology*, Marx and Engels (2007) remarked that what lacks an explanation is not the fact that we are nature, but rather what led to the nature-society metabolic rift, to the ideologies which consider humans to be detached from nature. Why do they emphasize that? Precisely because they want to highlight the need to put into question what is unique and singular and therefore distinguishes one historical moment from another, one social formation from another, so as to be able to envisage the creation of practical alternatives.

More than that, critical thinking does now define the act of knowing as describing and systematizing phenomena, organizing reality in a certain way. Neither does it mean formally deploying a method which gathers research techniques which lead us to knowledge. It is much more than that. It is the confrontation between previous knowledge, which one carries in one's worldview, and reality. This process moves one toward new knowledge, which in turn mobilizes one to certain goals. It is the methodological movement of understanding reality by shedding light on the relations which compose a totality. It is turning a relational complex into something understandable.

Environmental degradation and destruction are the immediate given with which we are confronted and also points of departure as issues which mobilize us and which we want to overcome. What is the concrete aspect of these phenomena? What is currently specific to them and thus differentiates them from previous forms of metabolic interaction between nature and society?

Capitalism makes a qualitative inversion which is decisive in relation to any other social formation we know. The production of surplus, that is, of an amount of products larger than the one necessary to meet immediate survival needs, was a condition for the development of social life beyond staying alive and fighting threats from nature and other peoples. Industrialization led to productivity gains and, therefore, to the materialization of surplus in the form of capital (Marques 2016).

The private appropriation of both the means of production and the wealth produced is a core feature of these relations of production, under which surplus concentrates in the hands of very few people. As a consequence, surplus becomes the goal toward which production is directed, reproducing a form of sociability which is hierarchical, domineering, and divisive. Also, it leads the state, the economy, and politics into the hands of capital holders. Thus surplus, which previously ensured safety and survival, now takes the form of capital and threatens our survival as it gradually destroys nature and subordinates human creative activity to economic imperatives.

This kind of social structuring prevents the universalization of basic sanitation, electricity, water, and so on, since these are not immediately profitable. It also multiplies older forms of environmental impact in productive processes, because populations led into misery eventually push deforestation, water pollution, disorderly land occupation, and so on.

More than ever, hence, it is necessary to consider education as a historically determined social practice. Criticism is an epistemological and ontological requirement of our historical time in the pursuit of the determinations of being and of explanations based on the manifestations of complex relations. This process leads one to detach from the world of market exchange, its superficiality and its binaries.

It follows that all critical pedagogies state that education is an intentional activity—that is, aimed at achieving certain goals—determined by the contradictions of a class society, dialogic—because it always involves the other and the exchanges with them, even when in positions of inequality—with the purpose of acquiring and constructing knowledge which support processes of emancipation (Loureiro 2007).

For these pedagogies, knowing is the foundation both for consciousness of the world in which one lives and for intervention thereupon. For critical traditions, human beings must be understood as creative beings who, through their activity in the world, change reality and produce culture. This tradition does not consider concepts and symbols regardless of objective conditions of living. Understanding and being conscious of the worlds, interpreting it, being the world are all events which only happen in society. Wondering, knowing, understanding, interpreting, and acting are processes in which human beings unlock their potential and mobilize their ability to opt, to decide, to choose, even when under systemic coercion. By exercising their choice during their actions, not only do humans change the world, but they also change their stance toward the world.

Dialogue

In education, dialogue is a requirement for the promotion of encounters of diverse knowledges, organizing practices, and fostering the free creation of knowledge. Its relevance is rather consensual among educators who see it as a prerequisite, regardless of their concern for environmental issues.

Dialogue is the interaction between people who speak, exchange ideas, communicate in several ways while they listen to each other. Speaking and listening are active and inseparable moments, because the process of understanding the meaning of something happens in the speaker-listener relation, and not from one to another. Radically thinking, it is relations themselves that give rise to potential meanings. One understands something based on their existence as much as on what is revealed in the interaction (Grondin 2012). As a consequence, people participate in what is said, understood, and objectivized. Non-participatory dialogues are, by definition, monologues, acts of imposition. And imposition in any of its forms is the negation of education.

However, recognizing listening as an active ability does not abolish the need to acknowledge the importance of previous knowledge, which is defined by the culture to which one belongs, as well as their ideologies. It is no barrier to but rather a part of dialogue. As for dialogue based on disguised stances and lies, it is a non-dialogue. Participants must expose their values and intentions, bringing previous experience into consciousness and reflecting about it, so that the situation may bring about something new, leading to an interpretation which is open to the other.

This movement ensures not only objectivity in education, but also collective agreement about what is at stake and acceptance of proposed intentionalities—which is not the same as neutrality. The idea of neutrality assumes that it is possible to disregard previous ideas and worldviews when looking at an object. It presupposes that a method can guarantee the distanced production of unbiased knowledge. As for the idea of objectivity we propose, it assumes the impossibility of neutrality. It highlights the role of critical consciousness about the place from which each speaker engages in interaction, while keeping methodological and argumentative rigor.

This process creates a kind of understanding which translates the meaning of something, expresses it linguistically and objectivizes it in praxis, transcending particularities and reaching universality. Such universality does not qualify as abstract and based on atemporal law, but starts in particular and historical relations and moves on to create what is common in public life.

Dialogue establishes an understanding which does not deny explanation, systematic knowledge of facts, phenomena, their relations, and complex causalities. In any educational process, understanding and explaining are vital for knowing the world, being in the world, acting in the world and developing consciousness of one's place in the world. Thus, it is not enough to be open to dialogue. It is necessary to exercise rigor in listening, as well as to practice study and research. That is the reason why Freire (2001) was emphatic in his non-adherence to the pedagogical defense of spontaneity and voluntarism. Education demands systematic study and fondness for knowledge.

Dialogue always occurs between people who belong to groups and classes. This implies legitimate or denied identities, identity flows, diverse and often opposing needs and interests, which are constituted by economic and power relations materialized in state and civil society organizations (Loureiro 2005). Therefore, emancipatory education processes are not built with any subject, but with those who bear the material deprivation characteristic of the alienated relations which rule contemporary social forms. It is no matter of individual good will, but rather of consciousness of the contradictions instituted by a social totality. Dialogue by itself does not emancipate, but rather social processes which adopt dialogue as a prerequisite and a practical requirement, built by social agents in the midst of their movements of social transformation, materializing desired changes.

Dialogue is no mere methodological device. It is used as a form of communication in which issues concerning different places of enunciation are overcome in favor of difference as a quality, as a value of qualification, as a way to promote knowledge interchange in a learning environment. Thus, it organizes practices and supports their connection to the social totality, in which the social appropriation of knowledge is at stake.

Advocacy for difference is undeniably a contemporary prerequisite for the construction of different social standards. Issues of gender, ethnicity, race, religion, generation, personal choice, and are directly related to human differentiation in the social production of existence and to each person's singularity. However, for critical thinking this movement belongs in the same sphere as the struggle for equality, since they are not opposing movements. Quite the contrary: they are complementary in emancipation. Difference is defined by political, economic, and institutional social relations. Hence in capitalism these relations are shaped by the very same context as the one shaping processes of discrimination and inequality which cannot be mistaken by respect for difference. Unequal is not the same as plural. The opposite of unequal is equal. The opposite of difference is indifference or economic and cultural homogenization. Each one's free expression is connected to overcoming historically constructed material conditions of dispossession and domination (Loureiro and Layrargues 2013).

In face of that, dialogic educational practices should adopt an attitude of permanent suspicion, challenging and reflecting about everything. In contemporary society, the ideologies and interests of the ruling classes are diffused by school, state, and mass communication mechanisms, among others, which universalize their truths and forms of sociability. Besides, the recent fake news phenomenon, consisting of lies deliberately told to an astonishing number of readers at lightning speed, prevents counter-argumentation, denies facts, confuses opinions, and creates false truths. Thus, it produces intolerant, individualistic, and anti-scientific subjectivities.

Therefore, worldviews and ideologies, either in a broad sense—as a view of the world or a set of truths and particular ideas stated as universal, ensuring social cohesion and muffling conflicts and contradictions—or in a narrow one—as a false presentation of reality—cannot be simply accepted as a part of communicative action. They must also be challenged. Every criticism to ideology is a kind of self-criticism, both of which comprise environmental education by keeping an "alert state" which is not the same as moral distrust in people's conduct. This attention is directed at transparency in educational processes, activities, and routines; at the way duties and responsibilities are shared; at consensus about pedagogical principles and guidelines; at the consciousness of the transformative intentionality of critical environmental education; at the joint definition of contents and activities; at the clear presentation of goals; at the problematization of contents and the purposes thereof; and finally at the permanent participatory evaluation of every step of the process.

Ancestry

The struggle of traditional peoples for territorial sovereignty, cultural diversity, and their recognition by the state is not only a matter of historical debt to be overcome, and it is not a demand for praise of practices which please curiosity, affection, and taste. It is rather the struggle for the enforcement of social rights and rights of existence of livelihoods which differ both from the interests of capital and from its civilizational standards. These same livelihoods nourish and educate us to face political struggle.

The transmission of customs, moral codes, memories, and rites ensures tradition is preserved and occurs mostly in the repetition of essential behaviors, either through oral communication or intergenerational experience. This is why elders are deeply respected and valued as the living memory of communities, as the guardians of millenary wisdom who have much to teach us about how to live respectfully toward others and nature. Oral tradition—or orality—plays two important roles in this process. First it favors intergenerational respect— something rather neglected by a society which treats older people as a burden at the moment they are no longer available as either labor power or as proper consumers. Second it engenders knowledge based on concrete experience and on a pace of learning distinct from the speed prescribed for workers under capitalism. Learning through other languages and rhythms is also a significant challenge for environmental educators, and also a source of difficulty and tension when educational processes disregard such specificities.

As Postone (2014) reminds us, capitalist relations of production and industrialization universalized the organization of labor time and daily tasks based on the hours of the clock—and the adoption of this instrument to measure time. In this social form, labor time is the fundamental measure which defines the economic value of commodities. Thus, humankind naturalizes the organization of life around the clock and unlearns other healthy kinds of time: the time of natural cycles, the time to develop an argument, the time to contemplate nature and beauty, the time of bodies, the time of relationships with others.

The generalization of industrial production destroyed previous forms of life for which work itself as an activity or dimension external to social life was a strange notion, whereas time was observed in natural processes—such as the duration of days, tides, rains, and crops—in analogies with tasks—such as cooking rice, frying something, or boiling eggs—and in religious rituals—the time to pray the rosary for Catholics, for example. This reorganization of material life imposed abstract and linear experiences of time measured by the clock as the norm, to the detriment of remaining ways of living and experiencing temporality. This particular form of time enables its own conversion—at least in the way society sees it—into a unit of measurement which acts *externally to phenomena*, being thus able to index them. This point promotes the historical encounter between two homogenizing forces: the intensifying association of time with money, which in turn assumes the role of defining the concrete life of people, who since then have these two abstractions as the foundations of social life.

Studies and research about traditional peoples suggest that in the past their ancestral practices have led to the management of biomes and favored biodiversity. Hence existing biological diversity is not driven solely by natural factors, but also by the interaction with social forms of coexistence which do not degrade the conditions which enable life. Currently it is possible to affirm without doubt that biological diversity is intimately connected with cultural diversity. Therefore, traditional knowledge mobilizes subjects and has much to teach humanity, helping materialize alternative practices and problematize the Eurocentric urban-industrial capitalist way of life (Moutinho da Costa 2011).

These aspects reinforce the importance of reconsidering a narrow view of tradition in environmental education processes. According to this view, the tradition of traditional peoples is something static, destined to disappear along the process of scientific and material progress. This stagist perspective was promoted by colonization and hegemonic bourgeois thought. It helps justify the domination and destruction of others by spreading that capitalism is the only social form loyal to human nature—selfish, competitive, individualistic, utilitarian, and so on—and to the full accomplishment of human potential. The elimination of other civilizations and cultures thus seems to be acceptable and even natural, as if in a selection process.

Paying heed and learning from traditions does not mean sticking to a hypothetically more sustainable past, nor does it prescribe general conversion into indigenous, maroon or *caiçara* individuals. It is not a matter of traveling in time to search for something lost. It is a matter of politically opting for the construction of another possible world, in dialogue with those who, along with overexploited wage workers, bear the objective negation of what destroys and subordinates life to the accumulation of material wealth produced through violence and suffering.

Their traditional character is marked by a way to read the present while considering the past, which enables envisioning a future without significant losses in terms of customs, values, cultures, and forms of coexistence which have historically been viable and decisive for the reproduction of certain social groups. It is then far from static: it is a movement of permanently interpreting what is realized, identifying what binds past, present, and future. Tradition is respect. The cultural practices and rituals of the traditional peoples, therefore, aim directly at preserving the groups' existence through constant change without losing cultural traces fundamental for their identity and sense of belonging.

This aspect impacts the social, political, and educational relevance of tradition. As indicated by Hobsbawn (1984), society often resorts to tradition in moments when its form of organization is hit by severe crisis. According to him, the dynamics of tradition enable the objective consideration of alternatives to the current state of affairs to depart from deeply rooted foundations.

As for those of us who mostly reproduce ruling standards, the usual reaction to the discovery of the crisis is immobility or dissatisfaction, both of which lead to individual action ranging from charity to indifference toward human suffering. Traditional peoples and their ancestral practices may teach and exemplify ways collective action can encounter the new without losing respect for a people's history and ancestry.

No social practice is possible for traditional people without remembering, reverencing or bringing ancestry into presence. It is a delicate element, which manifests in several languages and facilitates unique learning opportunities—a fact the understanding of which is vital. Some aspects of ancestry are explicit, while others are subtle and require attention, and some others are only revealed through practice and coexistence. Actually, most things about ancestry are not written, but experienced and understood. It follows that dialogue and respect to ancestry are a prerequisite, otherwise the educational process will not take place.

The most visible dimension of ancestry is the acknowledgment and appreciation of the legacy passed on by ancestors. Cultural practices, meetings, workshops, and other group activities are based on the gratitude to those who created and transmitted the wisdom required for the realization of something in the present. Legacy is the point of departure, from which we create and adapt according to our own circumstances. There is hence an aspect of respect and reverence in remembering the names and families who contributed to the construction of what exists today, as well as an aspect of historical recovery in shedding light on the roots from which trunks, branches, leaves, and fruits developed. Ancestry helps understand historical consciousness and values the lives of all who take part in what we are as humankind.

This first aspect helps prevent one specific process from being obliterated. Although the meaning of linguistic expressions often refers to historical relations, stories of life and needs met through work, their interpretation frequently ignores this background. An African dance, for example, is not a mere set of sexy and aesthetically beautiful harmonious movements to be repeated by any person interested in learning them. Each movement has a reason and generally expresses types of work and spiritual beliefs representative of certain worldviews. Dance thus does not consist of body movements which enable pleasure, but rather of movements which convey historical wisdom and the taste for sharing life with others through body language. This same language associates with other languages, which also have a lot to say. The colors and kinds of clothing and turbans speak and communicate the worldviews and values which rule these cultures.

Educational activities with these traditions involve fundamentally storytelling, narratives, bodily experiences and the development of contents brought about by these practices, which lead to transcending experience. Our example enables potentially interesting subjects, such as labor relations, slavery, racism, social rights, interactions with nature through work and culture, religiosity, spirituality, tolerance, and cultural diversity.

The second dimension of ancestry to be approached here is not as immediately noticeable. It refers to a joint understanding of past and future, sacred and profane, society and nature as being together at all times. This is expressed in gestures such as greeting the earth with one's hand or head, bowing before an elder—or expressing humility and gratitude somehow—walking barefoot in certain spaces, dancing with hips and steps strongly directed at the earth. They indicate the acknowledgment of the fact that one can only exist because one's ancestors and elders made on earth a path to guide their walk, and the earth is the floor on which one acts, works, and feeds. Without the earth, there would be no human life or learning. One exists today with one's ancestry.

For education, this dimension leads to the development of collectivist values, such as humility, respect, solidarity, and gratitude, while enabling refined and integrated collective understandings about nature, humankind, and time.

Finally, the notion of cycles contained in ancestry is the third dimension to be developed here. For traditions, life is a permanent cycle of birth, growth, and death. The latter is not an absolute end, since ancestors return through ancestry. Regardless of belief in rebirth, it is paramount to understand that, despite human finitude, possibilities in praxis and legacy are endless. This creates a sense of responsibility for present and future generations which is extremely value for environmental debates.

Conclusion

Fields like the environment and education are under intense pressure in current political, economic, and ideological circumstances, when ruling forces adhere to absolute economic liberalization and state deregulation while supporting and normalizing conservative ideologies. Hence the extermination of traditional peoples and their knowledge consists of a crime and a serious threat to their integrity and the reproduction of their livelihoods.

Under those circumstances, taking the dialogical and transformative path cannot rely on the options created by the ruling-class fractions which control the state. It depends fundamentally on dialogue between grassroots movements of education workers, unions, and environmentalists, as well as on the struggle for exposing the contradictions of a class society. Also, it is necessary to make the state more democratic and occupy it so as to enforce rights—a process both contradictory and incipient in recent history. Common agendas are still modest, often fragmenting coalitions and only slightly challenging ruling standards.

This chapter has aimed at proposing some theoretical considerations about the foundations for practices of critical environmental education with traditional peoples. It has emphasized a stance which understands education as a permanent process of human development, to be thought and implemented with all its contradictions and possibilities in the capitalist social totality in which we live and which we attempt to transform.

Note

The chapter was translated from Portuguese to English by Jun Shimada.

Resisting and Re-Existing on Earth

Politics for Hope and "*Buen Vivir*"

Luiz Katu, Celso Sánchez, and Daniel Renaud Camargo[1]

Daniel Renaud Camargo: This chapter presents the dialogue between Celso Sánchez—university professor with an extensive trajectory as an activist alongside traditional and indigenous populations in Brazil—and Chief Luiz Katu—who is a leader from the Potiguara ethnicity, an indigenous people from Northeast Brazil also known as the *comedores de camarão* (shrimp eaters), hence having a strong connection with waters. The dialogue was on distance and online streamed on May 4, 2020, being subsequently translated from Portuguese to English. The authors discussed the current context of resistance of indigenous peoples facing the historical occurrence of cultural erasure and persecution, as well as new threats such as the Covid-19 pandemic and the current state of politics in Brazil.

   Chief Luiz Katu: First of all, I would like to express my gratitude for being here at this moment. Greetings to everyone on the other side, reading this text, and also to Professor Celso. Even though we have just met, it seems like we have been friends for decades. This is important that we feel this connection, even if we are apart, this is nonetheless *buen vivir*.[2] I want to let you know that, as a Potiguara indigenous person, as the resisting people of this country and of the Americas, we will bring up the resistance experience from the time being—how we, indigenous peoples, have been withstanding, what our political and *buen vivir* practices are, so as to keep resisting to all of this situation and others: what has happened, the current scenario, and our post-pandemic perspectives. For the indigenous peoples, it has been frequent to occupy these spaces of resistance, so it would not be different this time around, especially with everything that is going on nowadays. Clearly the current state of things is worrisome, so we need to strengthen our cause with the indigenous groups and allies to the cause.

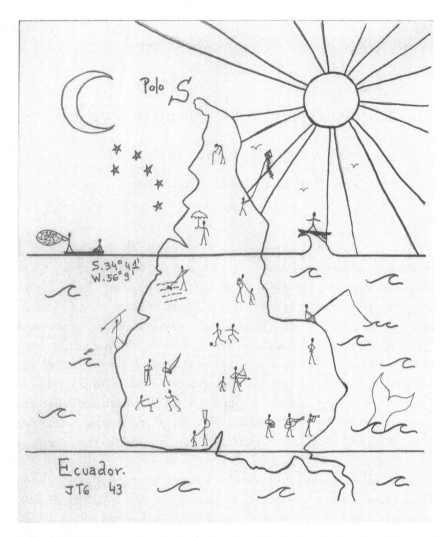

Figure 11.1 América Latina Povoada (Populated Latin America) by Daniel Renaud Camargo, 2020.

This is the kind of politics we bring to conversations, so that we can talk a bit about how the indigenous peoples have united and what we have been doing, united not only in Rio Grande do Norte and in Northeast Brazil, but in all states of Brazil, toward resisting and acting to effectively overcome the current situation. Because we know that it has not been easy for indigenous peoples, that they are at the frontline, fighting on behalf of other brothers and sisters who are isolated, and we know what the arrival of outsiders—who are not inserted in their context—what this arrival may cause these people.

Celso Sánchez: What an honor to be part of this conversation with you, comrade Luiz, with all of your wisdom, strength. . . . What a pleasure, what an honor to meet you. It is such a shame we are not physically together so I could give you a hug. Because of times like this we learn to appreciate the value of a hug, the importance of physical presence, of staring at one's eyes. . . . Affection is such an important thing! When this is over, I hope our society learns to appreciate hugging, eye contact, a handshake, and empathy, but these will not come easily! It will happen if we build this together, and to build a society that appreciates affection it is absolutely necessary to listen to words like Luiz's, plus the other voices from the indigenous peoples' resistance that demand "Demarcation now."[3] If we understand the historical process that has been in place for the past 520 years, which represents a covering of the other, a silencing and an erasure of the other sides of history and the dehumanization of people. A project of a single story is already in place, like that Nigerian writer Chimamanda Ngozi Adichie (2009) says. We need to start taking these encounters with originary, traditional, and popular knowledges as departing points for our thought, constantly valuing the indigenous people and the social movements. Nowadays, we join the fight of many of these people and the fight for the right to be alive. You see, we are talking about something so basic, which is the right to be as one can fully be in life, in every possible way. And now, in this context, we are appropriating these new technologies and we will surely have them as a legacy from this moment. Undoubtedly, we will need to start meeting more, and listening to one another, because we are part of a society that erases and silences people, and it is beneficial to those in power that we do not debate and get to know each other, that we do not take into consideration that the struggle in Rio Grande do Norte, in Northeast Brazil, is similar to the struggle of other indigenous peoples in Brazil and in the Americas. But now I want to hear a bit about the story of your people.

Chief Luiz Katu: We are Potiguaras from Catu Valley.[4] The Katu village is located on the southern coast of Rio Grande do Norte, and it belongs to the continuous line of villages which starts in Paraíba state and goes all the way to the southern coast of Rio Grande do Norte. It comprehends thirty-five Potiguara villages spread around this territory. One thing I always say is that, although the territory is divided in states, our people have never been divided, and we continually keep our migratory movement. It's a common practice; although they try to break us every day, we are still united. Here on the south coast, where the Katu village is located, we are connected to the Jacu and Sagitrabanda villages, in the city of Baía Formosa, in Rio Grande do Norte. Our people have been facing one of the worst genocides of indigenous peoples ever. The reason behind this is the fact that we are close to the location where the known Massacre of Cunhaú[5] took place.[6] Because of everything that happened in Cunhaú, the indigenous peoples in this region, who have been persecuted, are also suffering with a high level of prejudice and false accusations. Still, the Potiguara-Katu manage to resist and stay at Catu Valley. The Catu River meets the sea at two of this state's beaches: Sibaúma and Barra de Punhaú, both in Canguaretama city. And let me tell you, this is a strong name. Canguaretama means "to be close to the skeleton region" in Tupi, quite a strong name. Nowadays, there are 203 families in the area, which totals 800 indigenous peoples in this place of resistance. Since the 2000s, the Potiguara-Katu have been joining forces, participating in several actions to reshape the original historiography which is constantly told in Rio Grande do Norte. The historiography here in Rio Grande do Norte was extremely cruel to the indigenous peoples, not only to the Potiguaras, but also to other ethnic groups, such as the Tapuias, Paiacús, Taraieriús. Nowadays these ethnic groups resist together and fight bravely to change this single story, insisting on the need to reexamine the true history of the indigenous peoples of Rio Grande do Norte, to rewrite what was documented about our people, especially with concerns about referring to this location as an ancient burial ground. For example, when it is said that there are no indigenous peoples left here in Rio Grande do Norte and in Piauí state, the intention is really to erase us from history—and we have been fighting all those stereotypes, all those attempts to silence our history. It has been a strenuous battle against the largest institutional racism inflicted upon indigenous peoples of Rio Grande do Norte. Institutional racism in Rio Grande do Norte is undeniable, and we are at the frontline, fighting to break with the stigma about indigenous peoples. So, Katu is one of the villages which have been challenging this, with the understanding that it is imperative for us to become the protagonists of our own existence, of our own resistance, and if someone were to rewrite and retell how the indigenous peoples have persevered until now, this someone should be the indigenous peoples themselves. In 2005, the Potiguaras-Katu, the Potiguaras-Mendonças[7] from the city of João Câmara and the Caboclos de Assu[8] joined forces and held a public hearing at the legislative assembly of Rio Grande do Norte. It was only in 2005 that we were able to raise some awareness and be heard, so that the indigenous peoples of Rio Grande do Norte were seen, at national level, as an organized people, reassuring our resistance, announcing we are still alive, we have been persecuted, attacked, and often cast aside, but we are still in our settlements. The speeches at this public hearing were very harsh, we had to sit and listen to government representatives who are unaware of our existence, because they were reluctant to let go of

Câmara Cascudo.[9] We acknowledge the importance of Câmara Cascudo to Brazilian literature and historiography, he was indeed a renowned folklorist and this cannot be taken away from him. However, when it comes to the indigenous peoples, to the ethnic population of our country, especially of Rio Grande do Norte, he played a major part in the construction of the image of disappearance, of empty villages, of the occupation of indigenous territories by colonial projects and the resulting exodus of these people. For this reason, the assumption that indigenous peoples of Rio Grande do Norte were not organized escalated as a result of some of Câmara Cascudo's writings, and it is our mission, that the Potiguaras-Katu stand up to this and collaborate to the rewriting of our erased history. To resist, as we are resisting right now through these pandemic times. We now live in a situation of indispensable isolation which is crucial to avoid the risk of the virus reaching our settlements, and this is just another example of how we will remain resistant throughout time. Today I put forward a cry from the indigenous peoples of Rio Grande do Norte. Presently, I can assure you we have more than 5,000 self-identified indigenous people, considering only those settled in villages. If we add to this number those not settled—taking into account the 2010 census—then this number rises to nearly 8,000 indigenous.

Since we are settled in a valley which is our main place for coexisting and living in harmony with mother earth, with nature, we end up standing in the way of the interests of the sugarcane agribusiness.

We are a group of Potiguaras indigenous peoples, the "shrimp eaters," and currently the Canguaretama Valley was seized by multinationals which control the exploitation of shrimp aquaculture, shrimp farms. As a result, the Potiguara indigenous peoples are no longer able to harvest the very shrimp which denominates our ethnic origin, thus forcing our people into picking wild fruits as a means of subsistence. We resorted to picking these fruits, featuring the Potiguaras-Katu among the largest *mangaba* gatherers[10] in Rio Grande do Norte. We are the largest organized group, numerous families spend around six months a year, every day, picking *mangaba*. It is something we show deep respect to, these families being able to maintain this ancient practice of picking *mangaba* and *batí*.[11] During this period, with the invasion of sugarcane agribusiness, which is awful to our people, the biggest harm to the Potiguara-Katu is the occupation of this territory used for sugarcane cropping, as this monoculture seized all our territory, including the *capoeiras*[12] and woodlands where the *mangaba* trees grow, thus making it scarce and forcing natives to walk close to 30 kilometers every day through sugarcane fields before reaching a woodland area to find only a few *mangaba* trees to be picked, and then return home at the end of the day with their baskets filled with *mangabas*. They start their day at around three or four in the morning, to return home at the end of the day, when the sun is setting. They risk their lives crossing these sugarcane fields and are often threatened by the farmers for doing it. We are talking about circumstances in which indigenous territories have been fenced in, and they are on the other side of this fence witnessing *mangabas* falling off the trees and rotting on the floor, unable to do anything about it, unable to cross over and pick these fruits, because they run the risk of getting shot for trespassing. We have been struggling to put into effect a project called "Free Mangaba," and we have been asking for support from institutions, politicians, and allies for funds and endorsement to help us carry out this project so that we, the indigenous peoples, are granted access to these *capoeiras* and woodlands and pick these fruits—allowing us to keep this ancient practice of traditional peoples alive. Nevertheless, despite all the struggle, we still pick some twenty, thirty crates of *mangaba* every week, which sums up to about one ton of *mangaba* per week—during the *mangaba* harvest period.

When the pandemic hit, we started adapting to quarantine and isolation, after all, there are a considerate number of elders living in the village, and we need to prevent them from getting infected, for some of them are still involved with the process of going to the farmers' markets to sell the *mangaba*, and the Covid-19 outbreak had an impact on the bulk sale of the *mangaba* at these markets, plus the aggravation of *mangaba* being a really perishable product. You pick the *mangaba*, and then—as we call it—you smother it with layers of *covaçu*[13] leaves, and in two days it is ready for consumption. However, you cannot transfer it from the crate they have been ripening on into a different crate, because the fruit is so delicate that it would break open. That is how perishable the *mangaba* is. This situation was very harmful to the indigenous peoples, the increase of *mangaba* loss pushed us to keep resisting, it gave me the opportunity to speak about it on the internet. The support we received was important, it allowed us to start a partnership campaign on the internet and on social media, and it attracted a lot of attention and help. And I say so because no help is too small for us. All the help we can get, with partnerships, is extremely important. And then we made a question that was very gratifying for me: the indigenous themselves started to have their *mangabas* and they earned a fair value for their fruits, a value negotiated with him based on research about the value they could earn in street markets. Then they delivered their *mangabas*, got paid, and still had the right to take some *mangaba* home. The remaining fruits were distributed in the village among all the indigenous. Many times, because the indigenous needed other things which were unavailable in their village—which is also due to the destruction of our Atlantic Forest, game and fish became very scarce—and this makes our people buy products in nearby cities and they still had to market their *mangaba*, so they often sold all this *mangaba* and ended up unable to try the *mangaba* they collected themselves.

Besides, I also need to say that family farming today, which is very strong in the village, is harmed in this moment because its production is also directly traded in street markets by these indigenous. We are the biggest producers of organic potatoes in this region of the state of Rio Grande do Norte, and we also have the potato festival[14] in the Katu village. We pray to our father Tupã[15] for this pandemic to end. Our *pajés,*[16] our relatives, always pray to our Encantados[17] so that we can overcome it fast, because we want to celebrate the potato festival on November 1, the day of all saints, the day when all peoples are able to celebrate. Paracatu, as we call it, is an important day, because we knew how much the Gramació[18] mission, that this is the place where our people was secluded and isolated, where their language was usurped and removed, where Christianism came in such a perverse fashion in that moment that today we can see how much of the strength of our cultural practice was removed. Gramació is a Tupi word that means "to corner into the bush." Check this: to corner into the bush. It is a place where the Potiguaras came from, came up the margins of the Katu River and stayed in its fountainhead. We are the water people, the protecting guardians of the fountains of Piriqui-Una Environmental Protection Area.[19] So this family farming practice, growing potatoes, has helped our people a lot. The potato festival is an example of resistance, an example of a moment when our people joins the Black people, the Quilombola[20] communities, and so many other peoples to celebrate, to gather, and to share. In Vale do Catu, which means the Katu River Valley, resistance is offered by traditional peoples: the Potiguares in the riverhead, near the fountain, and the maroon community called Quilombo do Sibaúma[21] in the river delta. It is important to say this resistance today is important. We have been fighting alongside our people so they will not leave the village and the potato festival was one of the parties created to keep our people in the settlement, because the exodus was too intense. We have many Potiguar-Katu indigenous people in Rio de Janeiro, in São Paulo, in Minas Gerais, who live in cities under subhuman working conditions and often cannot return to the village. This is a huge concern for us, and that was why we started to value and strengthen our agriculture, our millenary practice of collecting native fruits and growing sweet potatoes, and today it changed a lot. Now we do not see such an intense emigration of the village's indigenous, but it remains a matter of worry, because, you see, I mentioned organic products. We are the biggest growers of organic food on this coast, but we are never awarded organic certification, and do you know why? Because around us tens and tens of pesticides are spilled every year by sugarcane farms. And then indigenous farmers, who are working directly, respecting the cycles of mother earth, are prevented from earning a certification that adds value to their product. That is why I say that for us demarcating our lands is important and necessary.

Celso Sánchez: I would like to take advantage of the opportunity to salute my Guarani brothers and sisters, who I have had the privilege and joy to follow and walk with for the last twenty-five years. And I also have the privilege of having been baptized and having a Guarani name, which is an honor for me, something I am deeply grateful and proud of, and I proudly call myself Karaí Pyaguassú. The Guarani people say things that resemble what you are saying. The history of the Guarani villages and territories is very similar to what Luiz told us, unfortunately. A history of struggle, resistance, and defense of their territories. Here we also fight for demarcation and we see constant attacks against the villages, known as *tekoás*. It is not a random coincidence, because it comes from a project of inventing a certain Brazil based on genocide. A genocide followed by ecocide and ethnocide. I really like a Colombian author who is also a friend of us, a struggle comrade, professor Santiago Arboleda, who had to leave Colombia due to all the persecution suffered by Afro-Colombian communities in the South Pacific region. He went to Ecuador, where he became a professor of the Símon Bolivar Andean University, home to many indigenous people. And professor Santiago Arboleda tells us about an ecogenethnocide (Quiñonez 2019) in progress, and that is what we have witnessed for the past 520 years, a programmed project of erasure and monoculturalization of life. It is not only a sugarcane, banana, or coffee monoculture, but also a monoculture of ideas, of thoughts, as termed by Vandana Shiva (Geremias 2012). One of these days I was talking to my Guarani comrades and they told me that the *xeramoï*[22] already knew we would live a terrible moment like this, and they told me that the *xeramoi* had a dream. The Guarani dream a lot and dreams have a central role in their culture. In this dream, they said: "a moment will come when you, the white, the *juruás*"[23]—which is how they call us—"will contaminate even the air that we breathe, and a disease will spread through the air, and we will be saved by our way of being, our traditional way of being"—which the Guarani call *nhanderekó*.[24] And this disease that comes through the air and infects the air itself is what they call *tatatiná* and it is very similar to what we see in the case of this virus, something that spreads through the air as we sputter. And Mr. Messias

Bolsonaro[25] is the biggest sputterer, who not only spreads the poison of the virus, but also the poison of the monoculture of ideas, the poison of a certain worldview directed at a single path, a single truth, which he wants to impose. It is a truth that both benefits him and his privileges and supports his allegedly superior caste. So he is a white supremacist, educated, as all white supremacists, by an entire tradition of people who thought and laid the foundations for racist thought in Brazil. Câmara Cascudo is only one example, but I could mention thousands of cases and names, such as Monteiro Lobato himself. No one can deny his importance for literature, but, while he was a committed racist and eugenicist, he defended a certain notion of white supremacy as the basis for those ideas, and there is no doubt about that. Therefore, it is paramount to build other historiographies. And other geographies too, because the present one is a geography that divides us not only between states and cities, but also between countries! Latin America is seen by the eyes of the indigenous, for example, is recognized as *Abya Yalla*, and *Abya Yalla* is a single territory, a single mother. We have a mother and we behave as ungrateful and impolite children who cannot even acknowledge her, our nourishing mother, our original womb. I really like to remember Eduardo Galeano when he said that, up in the Andes, where the earth is called *Pachamama*, they bury lovers' hair curls and newborns' navels, so that the earth shall always feed them and be witness to their love (Galeano 1999: 38). We have to remember, think, and connect these things . . . Galeano also has a passage that says that 1492 was the moment when Columbus supposedly discovered America, in line with this I really like an author called Enrique Dussel, an Argentinian philosopher rooted in Mexico, who says 1492 was not at all about discovering America, but rather about covering the other, because people were already here, then there was no discovery. There was a covering! They had their diversity covered, along with their plural forms of existence, of being and being with the world, with others, and with nature. Our Western society, thus, is a society against nature and against diversities, whereas originary societies, from indigenous and traditional communities, are societies with nature—and inside them are existing and resisting libraries of survival, libraries of wisdom about the earth, libraries of knowledge, libraries of respect for nature. We have to learn that respect, because it is not something we are born with the ability to practice. How to respect is something to be learned. And in this moment we have a chance to realize that either we learn how to respect or we die. Respecting earth as survival is fundamental. Then in 1500 they arrived in this place that is called Brazil today, but used to be called Pindorama[26] and to be inhabited by the Pindoramic people, as termed by Nego Bispo, a wise master from Maroon communities from the state of Piauí. Nego Bispo also points out that we have to embrace these moments for counter-colonizations, to go in the opposite direction of colonizations and learn from communities of resistance their knowledge about resistance, which are the knowledges of the earth. That is why it is so important to re-discover and dis-cover. But back to Galeano, he says that, until 1492—which by the way is the supposed moment when Columbus and the European arrived in the Americas—this territory was called *Abya Yalla* and then started being called America as a tribute to Américo Vespúcio, a genocidal colonizer who came here and robbed our originary peoples, a land robber! And until today we name our territory after this usurper, this robber. Then, this invention of America needs to be deconstructed immediately! The biggest representative of these bloody caravels, which keep arriving at our beaches, is Jair Messias Bolsonaro. He needs to be immediately removed from the post of colonizer, and he colonizes not only territories, but also minds. When he sputters his droplets, as a virus, infecting people with his ideas and single stories, he keeps bringing damn caravels of blood in every droplet. The pandemic has obviously already arrived in the slums and made its victims. By the way it is important to mention that this virus may be democratic in the way it kills both the rich and the poor, but despite affecting and killing rich and poor alike, the pandemic is visibly racist and unequal. There is something that we are calling pandemic injustice. Because those who are not rich die more easily from Covid-19, since they are note even tested, they have no access to the public health system, and the public health system is already collapsing. In the case of Rio de Janeiro, the system had already been collapsing for some time, and the poor know that, because they experienced such collapse on a daily basis, and that is called pandemic injustice (Sato 2020). This injustice reveals that the virus may be democratic, but the pandemic is unequal. Inequality is right there, and then we have people and populations who are more vulnerable than others. Peoples such as the Kaingang, Bororô, Xavante, Krahô, and many others, with their great wisdom, and people such as Daniel Munduruku, who has been writing for so many years, not to mention the great Ailton Krenak, who has been producing a legacy as an intellectual. They are all people who are reading, studying, writing, producing, and even joining Western universities. And I repeat: we urgently need to listen to these people, who need to be part of the basic curricula of those who daily struggle. People such as Luiz Katu himself, who Brazil does not get to know. That is why it is very important to have spaces like this, which allow us to hear what these people and these traditional peoples have to tell us. Indigenous and traditional peoples, which include Maroon communities, Caiçaras,

Sertanejos, Ribeirinhos, and many others which are made of many wise people. It is precisely this diversity, this people, this wisdom that Bolsonaro wants to destroy, because he knows he is no match to this diversity. Brazilian biosocial diversity is what can help us face the ecogenethnocide. So, the challenge is: building a plural, diverse society, with a politics focused on listening, and that is why we must say and repeat: "Demarcation Now" and "Down with Bolsonaro and His Scum"!

Daniel Renaud Camargo: While this text was typed, on September 2020, Covid-19 cases spiked in Brazil, which became a hotspot for the pandemic, which also reached several indigenous ethnic groups and caused them immense trouble. There have also been numerous attacks on indigenous villages, including Chief Raoni's village, as well as the process of dismantling policies for the protection of indigenous and traditional peoples by the Bolsonaro government.

Note

The chapter was translated from Portuguese to English by Jun Shimada.

Afterword

Inny Accioly and Donaldo Macedo

Each chapter in this book, *Education, Equality, and Justice in the New Normal: Global Responses to the Pandemic*, represents a robust denunciation of neoliberal casino capitalism and its anti-ethical ideology which endanger the permanence of life on this planet as we know it. Written by leading scholars and activists from Brazil, Canada, Chile, Greece, Italy, Malta, the United Kingdom, and the United States, this book situates the analyses of the responses to the pandemic within the complex social and political consequences suffered by societies in which the elimination of the social contract has proceeded unchecked for decades under the guise of "the market knows best."

The coronavirus pandemic, like the devastation wrought by Hurricane Katrina in New Orleans in 2005, made abundantly clear that the human misery caused by dreadful poverty is a socially constructed virus that has claimed the lives of millions who, due to no fault of their own, become undeserved victims of geography and of political systems whose raison d'être is to exact human misery through violence, wars, and exploitation. Hence, it should not be surprising that the year 2020 left cruel blemishes on the history of humankind to the extent that the confluence of poverty and the pandemic, and manifold other tragedies, brought to light the continuity of a long and brutal history of inequality and injustice. It should not at all surprise us that millions of coronavirus-related fatalities worldwide were linked to a lack of material resources needed to comply with preventive sanitary measures, social distance, and shelter in, or to ensure access to ventilators for the ill. Market solutions did not protect people in abject poverty from being caught in the usual dilemma between starving or taking risks of being infected. Neither should we be surprised that, while the coronavirus spread its poison without regard to ethnicity, race, class, and gender, the populations that were most adversely impacted by its lethal contagion were those who had been enslaved, colonized, contained, and exploited. Thus, when we analyze the pandemic from a historical perspective, it is not difficult to understand why Indigenous groups, Afro-Americans, and Latinxs were disproportionally more vulnerable and more likely to succumb to the pandemic. For the impoverished living dead and oppressed people corralled in the world's ghettos and shanty towns, it follows that their day-to-day survival is almost always locked to an "emergency situation." For the oppressed, the pandemic emergency alert is not an exception, but the rule under which their lives are governed and controlled. Their daily existence consists of a check list of attempts to overcome emergency after emergency in a quest to establish a semblance of stability, safety, and humanity which regretfully is almost always postponed.

Rather than losing hope in the face of the current savage form of capitalism, which is substantially worse than the Gilded Age, or viewing the reality of the oppressed as "not inexorable or unchangeable," we need to understand that history is not a heap of disconnected facts and actions. History is a complex set of forces and conditions that shift and change, but continue to exert power over subjugated peoples who are exploited and oppressed, continuously suffering the inhumanity and indignities of pillage and plunder. Against the prevalent manner of viewing history as a neat and tidy continuum of facts and events, there is an urgent need to dismantle the linearity of history which is usually presented and taught in schools. However, such a break requires the development of critical and independent thinking skills so to be able to make the necessary linkage among historical events and social conditions in order to comprehend reality in its totality and globality. Consequently, the analysis of history from the perspective of the oppressed will enable us to more easily comprehend that the oppressed, by and large, were and continue to be victims of the Western-white colonizers' history—a history that summarily denied and continues to deny millions and millions of peoples, and their respective communities, the right to be agents of their own history. This denial made it nearly impossible for the oppressed to maintain and build their languages, their traditions, and their cultures. Yet, in asserting agency over their history, it is necessary that the oppressed connect the conditions of their struggle to the plight of others, including the victims of the coronavirus plague, so they can reject the deterministic view of their victimhood propagated by dominant narratives of history, and instead understand both their oppression and the millions of unnecessary deaths entailed by the pandemic to be by-products of unrestrained and pervasive capitalist greed. The rejection of a deterministic view of history has become part of a tradition among the Latin American grassroots movements, which require their members to call out aloud three times the names of their dead comrades. The calling of names aloud is then followed by subsequently repeating the word "present." By remembering the dead, it reaffirms that their memory remains alive within every person who is committed to the liberation struggle—a struggle that commits each individual to fighting for the right to a dignified life in the process of reclaiming his or her humanity.

The coronavirus plague demands from all of us a critical response that likewise refuses to forget in the face of an overwhelming temptation to return to "normal." We must reject a resigned acceptance of both the unspeakable losses entailed by the pandemic and the persistence of worsening life conditions for the remaining hundreds of millions around the globe who continue to struggle for their daily survival. More than ever, critical educators have the ethical duty to fight for all lives that have been lethally suffocated throughout history and for the lives of those who are still victims of the savageness of capitalism, particularly in view of the looming socio-environmental and economic catastrophe. A language of critique is the starting point that animates the struggle for life; however, it is not possible to criticize the current system without the recognition of the "other" (whose life is denied to the limit) as an autonomous subject, free and equal in their humanity. Therefore, we contend that, for those of us who dare to imagine a world that is less evil and more humane, we need to struggle toward the eradication of privileges of class, race, gender, and ethnicity. In our view, any form of privilege points to ossified structural inequities that undergird a market economy which perpetuates its power through shameless calls for "adaptability to situations that constitute a denial of humanization [and which] are acceptable only as a consequence of the experience of being dominated or enslaved" (Freire 1998: 72).

In other words, the conception of a "new normal" in the aftermath of the coronavirus pandemic can only be truly new if "normality" is collectively reconstructed so that no single person is made to accept or even consider adaptability to a political and economic (dis)order in which policymakers and corporations put profits first and relegate whole groups of people to human misery. It should be unacceptable in the approaching future, for instance, to speak of democracy in the United States, which is the richest society in the world and a country in which millions of homeless people, including entire families and around 16 million children, go to bed hungry every night. Moreover, it should be a point of shame rather than pride that the United States, a nation that praises itself for its abundant food production, pays farmers not to plant the land so that food scarcity and high prices can always guarantee obscene profits for agribusiness. This example, along with many others, makes a mockery of any claim of the United States to support its citizens equally. It should also be unacceptable that in a country like Brazil, where there is a robust public health system and a long tradition of vaccination campaigns, the current government hinders the delivery of coronavirus vaccination programs while coronavirus patients and premature babies die because the state ran out of oxygen supply, particularly in the state of Amazonas, where there are already more deaths due to inadequate resources. We could not agree more with Chomsky when he affirms that "what we are seeing in countries such as Brazil is a crime against humanity" (Chomsky 2021). As poignantly captured by Fernanda Almeida, the neoliberal normality went so far as to literally asphyxiate the future:

> The images and reports from Manaus [in state of Amazonas] present a real scenario of war, unimaginable, unbearable, unforgivable: death due to shortness of breath—suffocation, and despair. [. . .] I insist on the symbolic appeal: there is a lack of air for people who live in the forest presented as the lungs of the world. In this merciless episode there is no lack of symbolic elements. Nothing seems more absurd than 60 premature babies without air! Yes, 60 premature babies could have died from lack of oxygen in neonatal intensive care units. (Almeida 2021, our translations)

Such societies point to democracy's decay within a regime of private wealth and profiteering decadence whose ruling-class minions have put civil societies everywhere under siege. With the meager social contract on life support and societies worldwide on a downward spiral toward collapse, we must refuse the moral degeneration and obscene greed that preceded the fall of past empires. A critical approach to education is now imperative at the current historical juncture. It is not enough to teach only the subject matter disarticulated from other historical events. We must exhort, for example, elitist Classics departments to teach students not only how to translate Latin into English but also the needed critical tools so students can deconstruct the underbelly of cruelty and decadence that destroyed the Roman Empire and understand its ramifications for the twenty-first century. The same critical tools that will allow students to grasp the collapse of the Roman Empire will also serve them well in comprehending why other empires ceased to exist and why US imperialist aspirations have brought American society to the precipice of decadence and decline.

We contend that the new normality must be urgently reconstructed around commitments that the US government ceases to promote or finance wars abroad, stop behaving like guardians of democracy as a ruse to impose "the market knows best" ideology on the rest of the world, and confront the reality that American culture, the American way of life, and a myopic conception of America as the embodiment of democracy displayed their utter fragility during the coup d'état attempt in January 2021. While most US citizens experienced shock and outrage when far-right elected officials and the followers of the ex-president Donald Trump engaged in the Trumpist coup attempt, they usually remain unmoved when the US government routinely sponsors coups abroad against any government whose citizens choose their own political paths, and especially when those paths do not conform with the dictates of US imperialistic aspirations. This includes the resounding silence in response to the 1953 CIA coup to topple Iran's prime minister, Mohammad Mossadeqh, a democratically elected government, and impose the Shah of Iran, resulting in Mohammad Reza Pahlavi's decades-long brutal and murderous dictatorship; the United States' direct support of homicidal despot Augusto Pinochet's coup in Chile to oust the democratically elected Salvador Allende; the many coup attempts against Fidel Castro in Cuba; and the sponsorship of the Contras war against the Sandinista government in Nicaragua, just to mention a few examples in a long murderous record of the United States' direct and indirect involvement in coups abroad. A genuinely "new" normality would also make it unacceptable for the United States to impose sanctions on Cuba, Venezuela, Iran, or any other country that follows its own path of development. New normality would mean that the United States, the United Kingdom, and the European Union governments cease disrespecting the dignity, the humanity, and the rights of people from Africa, Latin America, and the Middle East. Simply put, "there is no theory of socio-political transformation that moves [people] if not grounded in an understanding of the human person as a maker of history and as one made by history. If it does not respect men and women as beings of decision, rupture, and option . . . [then the theoretical formulation transgresses] the ethical code indispensable for human living" (Freire 1998: 115).

The purpose of *Education, Equality, and Justice in the New Normal: Global Responses to the Pandemic* is, therefore, to serve as a critical resource for analyzing the current historical moment and to urge all those who consider themselves agents of change to embrace what Freire called "appropriate ire" (Freire 1998). For future generations of readers, we anticipate that this book will be a useful tool in the critical analysis of the multiple contradictions of these dark times, and serve as a historical record which, while in the midst of the racist, reactionary, and far-right ultra-neoliberal wave, demonstrates resistance and struggles animated always by hope—a radical hope anchored in the knowledge that, as agents of history, it is always possible to create humane structures that enable submerged voices to emerge. This hope, grounded in an understanding of human potential, is poetically captured by Amanda Gorman, a 22-year-old African American youth poet laureate (Gorman 2021):

When the day comes we ask ourselves,

where can we find light in this never-ending shade?
The loss we carry,
a sea we must wade
We've braved the belly of the beast
We've learned that quiet isn't always peace
And norms and notions
of what just is
Isn't always justice
And yet the dawn is ours
before we knew it
Somehow we do it . . .
The new dawn blooms as we free it
For there is always light,
if only we're brave enough to see it
If only brave enough to be it.

Notes

Preface

1 Žižek, S. (2020). *PANDEMIC! Covid-19shakes the World*. New York: Or Books.

2 Arendt, H. (1978). *The Life of the Mind*. New York: Harcourt.

3 See: https://www.theguardian.com/commentisfree/2020/feb/28/coronavirus-outb
reak-migrants-blamed-italy-matteo-salvini-marine-le-pen

4 Arendt 1978 (p. 4).

5 Cook, J (2020). "Why Is the World Going to Hell? Netflix's the Social Dilemma Tells
only Half the Story" in *Jonathon Cook Blog* (September 25).

6 Baldwin, J. (2007). *Giovanni's Room*. New York: Penguin Classics (p. 56)

7 Pegg, D. (2020). "What was Exercise Cygnus and What did it Find?" in *The
Guardian* (May 7).

8 See: https://www.hsph.harvard.edu/c-change/subtopics/coronavirus-and-climate
-change/

9 See: https://www.ecdc.europa.eu/en/geographical-distribution-2019-ncov-cases

10 See: https://time.com/5815367/coronavirus-deaths-comparison/

11 Trilling, D. (2020). "Migrants Aren't Spreading Coronavirus—but Nationalists are
Blaming them Anyway" in *The Guardian* (February 20).

12 Wallace, R. A. Liebman, L. F. Chaves, and R. Wallace (2020). "COVID-19 and
Circuits of Capital" in *Monthly Review* (May). https://monthlyreview.org/2020/05/0
1/Covid-19-and-circuits-of-capital/#en38backlink

13 See; https://www.pbs.org/newshour/nation/todays-racial-wealth-gap-is-wider-
than-in-the-1960s

14 See: https://ourworldindata.org/global-economic-inequality

15 See; https://www.oxfam.org/en/5-shocking-facts-about-extreme-global-inequality-a
nd-how-even-it

16 See: https://www.oxfam.org/en/press-releases/just-8-men-own-same-wealth-half
-world

17 Booth, R. and C. Barr (2020). "Black People Four Times more likely to Die from
Covid-19" ONS finds in *The Guardian* (May 7).

18 See: https://www.bbc.co.uk/news/health-54924121

19 See: https://www.aspeninstitute.org/blog-posts/the-Covid-19-eviction-crisis-an-e
    stimated-30-40-million-people-in-america-are-at-risk/#comments

20 See: https://www.cnbc.com/2020/07/10/looming-evictions-may-soon-make-28-mil
    lion-homeless-expert-says.html

21 Walicek, T. (2021). "Cities are Razing Homeless Encampments despite Record Cold
    Weather and COVID" in *Truthout* (February 20).

22 See: https://www.aa.com.tr/en/analysis/analysis-the-consequences-of-global-Covid
    -vaccine-inequality/2131116

23 See: https://www.wsws.org/en/articles/2021/01/13/food-j13.html

24 See: https://www.aamc.org/news-insights/54-million-people-america-face-food
    -insecurity-during-pandemic-it-could-have-dire-consequences-their

25 See: https://www.democracynow.org/2020/11/24/food_insecurity_raj_patel

26 See: https://teachertaskforce.org/news/Covid-19-highlights-digital-divide-distance
    -learning

27 See: https://observatory.tec.mx/edu-news/teacher-training-challenge

28 See: https://www.weforum.org/agenda/2020/09/Covid-19-has-intensified-the-di
    gital-divide/

29 See: https://www.forbes.com/billionaires/

30 See: https://www.statista.com/statistics/266288/annual-et-income-of-amazonc
    om/

31 See: http://qpol.qub.ac.uk/performing-artists-in-the-age-of-Covid-19/

32 See: https://voxeu.org/article/Covid-19-will-raise-inequality-if-past-pandemics-are
    -guide

33 Nivens, J. (2019). "Tories say There's no Magic Tree Until They Need It for
    Themselves" *The Daily Record* (August 4).

34 Žižek, S. (2020).

35 Robinson, W. I. (2019). *Into the Tempest. Essays on the New Global Capitalism.*
    Chicago: Haymarket Books (1).

36 Bell, K. and Green, J. (2016). "On the Perils of Invoking Neoliberalism in Public
    Health Critique," *Crit Public Health* 26: 239–43.

37 See: https://www.bbc.co.uk/news/business-55170756

38 See: https://www.aa.com.tr/en/analysis/analysis-the-consequences-of-global-Covid
    -vaccine-inequality/2131116

39 Sullivan, H. (2021) "South Africa Paying more than Double EU Prices for Oxford
    Vaccine" in *The Guardian* (January 22).

40 Goodman, P. (2020) "One Vaccine Side Effect: Global Economic Inequality" in *The
    New York Times* (December 25).

41 hooks, b. (2008). Interview in *Talking about Revolution*. Cambridge, MA: Southend
    Press.

42 Translation: The people united, will not be defeated!

Chapter 1

1 *The Nation*, December 14, 2020. Available at https://www.thenation.com/article/w orld/one-health-pandemic/

2 *The Boston Globe*, January 2, 2021, p. D2.

3 *Democracy Now*, January 7, 2021.

4 *The Nation*, December 14, 2020. Available at https://www.thenation.com/article/w orld/one-health-pandemic/

5 #MinersOutCovidOut campaign, The Yanomami and Ye'kwana Leadership Forum, November 17, 2020. Available at https://www.socioambiental.org/pt-br/ node/7054

6 Marx21, "Coronavirus: The agricultural industry would risk millions of deaths," interview with Rob Wallace, March 11, 2020. Available at https://www.marx21.de/ coronavirus-agribusiness-would-risk-millions-of-deaths/

7 "Jair Bolsonaro claims Brazilians 'never catch anything' as Covid-19 cases rise," *The Guardian*, March 27, 2020. Available at https://www.theguardian.com/global-devel opment/2020/mar/27/jair-bolsonaro-claims-brazilians-never-catch-anything-as -covid-19-cases-rise

8 Kim Chipman, "Water joins gold and oil for first time as traded commodity on Wall Street amid fears of scarcity," *Financial Post*, December 8, 2020. Available at https:// financialpost.com/investing/water-joins-gold-and-oil-for-first-time-as-traded -commodity-on-wall-street-amid-fears-of-scarcity

9 Ronald Reagan, Inaugural Address, January 20, 1981. Available at https://www.rea ganfoundation.org/ronald-reagan/reagan-quotes-speeches/inaugural-address-2/

10 IMF Blog, November 2, 2020. Available at https://blogs.imf.org/2020/11/02/the-cri sis-is-not-over-keep-spending-wisely/

11 Rebecca Henderson, "How COVID-19 Has Transformed the Gig Economy," *Forbes*, December 10, 2020. Available at https://www.forbes.com/sites/rebeccahend erson/2020/12/10/how-covid-19-has-transformed-the-gig-economy/?sh=22c4 dfef6c99

12 Paula Froelich, "Brazilian President Bolsonaro claims COVID vaccine could turn people into alligators," *New York Post*, December 19, 2020. Available at https://ny post.com/2020/12/19/brazilian-prez-bolsonaro-claims-covid-vaccine-could-turn -people-into-alligators/

Chapter 2

1 The dialogue between Amy Goodman and Noam Chomsky is revised version of Democracy Now! Daily Show Broadcast aired on April 10, 2020.

Chapter 3

1 Arundhati Roy, *Financial Times*, Aril 3, 2020. Available at https://www.ft.com/c
   ontent/10d8f5e8-74eb-11ea-95fe-fcd274e920ca

2 Amartya Sen, *The Indian Express*, April 8, 2020. Available at https://indianexpress.
   com/article/opinion/columns/coronavirus-india-lockdown-amartya-sen-economy
   -migrants-6352132/

3 Steven Methven, London Review of Books, April 16, 2020. Available at https://www.
   lrb.co.uk/blog/2020/april/staying-angry

4 VICE co-founder Shane Smith interviews famed whistleblower Edward Snowden in
   "Shelter in Place," a new series on VICE TV. April 9, 2020. Available at https://www.
   vice.com/en/article/bvge5q/snowden-warns-governments-are-using-coronavirus-
   to-build-the-architecture-of-oppression

5 Slavoj Žižek, coronavirus is "Kill Bill"-esque blow to capitalism and could lead to
   reinvention of communism, February 27, 2020. Available at https://www.rt.com/op-
   ed/481831-coronavirus-kill-bill-capitalism-communism/

6 Jonathan Cook, Counterpunch, April 3, 2020. Available at https://www.counterp
   unch.org/2020/04/03/the-bigger-picture-is-hiding-behind-a-virus/

7 Ejeris Dixon, *Truthout*, April 11, 2020. Available at https://truthout.org/articles/fasci
   sts-are-using-covid-19-to-advance-their-agenda-its-up-to-us-to-stop-them/

8 Ishaan Tharoor, *The Washington Post*, March 31, 2020, Available at https://www.was
   hingtonpost.com/world/2020/03/31/coronavirus-kills-its-first-democracy/

9 Selam Gebrekidan, *The New York Times*, March 30, 2020. Available at https://www.
   nytimes.com/2020/03/30/world/europe/coronavirus-governments-power.html

10 Betsy Woodruff Swan, *Politico*, March 21, 2020. Available at https://www.politico.
   com/news/2020/03/21/doj-coronavirus-emergency-powers-140023

11 *The Guardian*, March 30, 2020. Available at https://www.theguardian.com/us-news/
   2020/mar/30/trump-republican-party-voting-reform-coronavirus

12 Anthony Dimaggio, *Counterpunch*, March 27, 2020. Available at https://www.cou
   nterpunch.org/2020/03/27/misinformation-and-the-coronavirus-on-the-dangers-of
   -depoliticization-and-social-media/

13 Susan Sontag, *Fascinating Fascism*, February 6, 1975. Available at https://www.nyb
   ooks.com/articles/1975/02/06/fascinating-fascism/

14 Joel Bleifuss, December 20, 2019, *In These Times*. Available at https://inthesetimes.com/
   article/fox-news-trump-ukraine-fake-news-independent-journalism-in-these-times

15 Binoy Kampmark, *Counterpunch*, January 13, 2017. Available at https://www.cou
   nterpunch.org/2017/01/13/liquid-modernity-zygmunt-bauman-and-the-rootless-c
   ondition/

16 Jonathan Freedland, *The Guardian*, June 22, 2018, Available at https://www.the
   guardian.com/commentisfree/2018/jun/22/trump-world-1930s-children-parents-e
   urope-migrants

17 Peter Thompson, *The Guardian*, April 22, 2013. Available at https://www.theguard
ian.com/commentisfree/belief/2013/apr/22/frankfurt-school-walter-benjamin-f
ascism-future

Chapter 4

1 Except where otherwise specified, all indicators were extracted from Brazil's
2018 Higher Education Census (Brasil 2019).
2 The New School movement rose in the 1930s in Brazil as a part of the movement
for Progressive Education, influenced by Pestalozzi, Dewey, Montessori, and
Kilpatrick. Its main references in Brazil are Anísio Teixeira and Fernando
Azevedo.

Chapter 5

1 Some parts of this conversation were published in Solomon MAG (September 14,
2020). English translations by Gigi Papoulias and Stavros Tsiakalos.
2 Georg Lukacs (1981): *The Destruction of Reason*. Atlantic Highlands, N.J.:
Humanities Press.
3 See Giorgio Agamben: Una domanda. Published in Quodlibet—Rubrica di
Giorgio Agamben, April 13, 2020. Available at: https://www.quodlibet.it/giorgio
-agamben-una-domanda. Translated into English by Adam Kotsko. Available at:
https://itself.blog/2020/04/15/giorgio-agamben-a-question. Accessed on January 3,
2021.
4 Slavoj Žižek (2020): *PANDEMIC!—COVID 19 Shakes the World*. New York •
London, OR Books, p. 56.
5 See Luděk Stavinoha and Apostolis Fotiadis: Asylum Outsourced: McKinsey's
Secret Role in Europe's Refugee Crisis. Article published by BalkanInsight on June
22, 2020. Available at: https://balkaninsight.com/2020/06/22/asylum-outsourced-
mckinseys-secret-role-in-europes-refugee-crisis. Accessed on January 3, 2021.
6 Chiara Loschi and Alessandra Russo (January 13, 2020): Whose Enemy at the
Gates? Border Management in the Context of EU Crisis Response in Libya and
Ukraine, Geopolitics, DOI: 10.1080/14650045.2020.1716739. Available at:
https://www.tandfonline.com/doi/full/10.1080/14650045.2020.1716739. Accessed
on January 3, 2021.
7 Announcement available at: https://www.ecchr.eu/pressemitteilung/new-investig
ation-challenges-european-court-of-human-rights-ruling-on-pushbacks. Accessed
on January 3, 2021.

8 Post-Synodal Apostolic Exhortation Ecclesia in Africa of the Holy Father John Paul II to the Bishops Priests and Deacons Men and Women Religious and All the Lay Faithful on the Church in Africa and Its Evangelizing Mission toward the Year 2000. Available At: Http://Www.Vatican.Va/Content/John-Paul-Ii/En/Apost_Exhortations/Documents/Hf_Jp-Ii_Exh_14091995_Ecclesia-In-Africa.Html. Accessed on January 3, 2021.

9 Article published on May 22, 2018, in *The New Humanitarian*. Available at: https://deeply.thenewhumanitarian.org/refugees/articles/2018/05/22/niger-europes-migration-laboratory. Accessed on January 3, 2021.

10 See article published by *El País* on March 25, 2020. Available at: https://elpais.com/elpais/2020/03/25/opinion/1585138497_451554.html. Accessed on January 3, 2021.

Chapter 6

1 https://www.washingtonpost.com/outlook/2019/11/26/trumps-xenophobia-is-an-american-tradition-it-doesnt-have-be/
2 https://www.washingtonpost.com/news/fact-checker/
3 https://www.unhcr.org/5ee200e37.pdf
4 https://reporting.unhcr.org/node/40
5 https://www.e-ir.info/2017/09/18/securitization-of-refugees-in-europe/
6 https://www.nbcnews.com/think/opinion/trump-s-wall-mexico-follows-footsteps-authoritarian-leaders-throughout-history-ncna956411
7 https://www.unhcr.org/en-us/news/stories/2019/6/5d0a078d4/message-worlds-refugees-unhcr-chief-filippo-grandi.html
8 https://www.unhcr.org/globaltrends2019/
9 https://www.rescue.org/article/fragile-countries-could-see-1-billion-coronavirus-cases-heres-why
10 https://www.govinfo.gov/content/pkg/CHRG-116hhrg37284/html/CHRG-116hhrg37284.htm
11 https://www.ohchr.org/en/professionalinterest/pages/cat.aspx
12 https://www.oxfam.org/en/research/hunger-virus-how-COVID-19-fuelling-hunger-hungry-world
13 https://www.washingtonpost.com/immigration/kids-in-cages-debate-trump-obama/2020/10/23/8ff96f3c-1532-11eb-82af-864652063d61_story.html
14 https://www.oxfam.org/en/research/hunger-virus-how-COVID-19-fuelling-hunger-hungry-world
15 https://www.unicef.org/press-releases/150-million-additional-children-plunged-poverty-due-COVID-19-unicef-save-children
16 https://www.unwomen.org/en/news/stories/2020/5/press-release-the-shadow-pandemic-of-violence-against-women-during-COVID-19

17 https://www.un.org/development/desa/indigenouspeoples/COVID-19.html

18 https://www.refugeesinternational.org/ https://www.refugeesinternational.org/

19 https://refintl.squarespace.com/reports?category=Report&offset=148958630746

20 https://www.govinfo.gov/content/pkg/CHRG-116hhrg37284/html/CHRG-116hhr g37284.htm

Chapter 7

Following the provisions of the Italian National Agency for the Evaluation of Universities and Research Institutes (ANVUR), the authors declare that this chapter is the result of the collaboration and discussion between two authors: Paolo Vittoria wrote the part relating to formal education while Mariateresa Muraca wrote the introduction and the part on non-formal education. The conclusions were jointly written.

1 An important step forward was taken with law 2443 of 2017, which, for the first time, outlined the professions of professional socio-pedagogic and pedagogist educators.

2 "Cura Italia" Decree, approved on March 16, 2020.

3 In some cases, lessons were attended remotely in the following months but rather inconsistently and with notable limitations, mainly due to the difficulty in setting up a stable connection inside the prison (Antigone 2020).

4 A penitentiary administration memo dated April 26, 2010, authorized prisoners to use state smartphones to video call their families.

5 According to the Antigone association's 2020 report: "at the end of February, there were 61,230 prisoners in facilities designed for 50.931. The women totalled 2,702, 4.4 percent of the total, while there were 19,899 foreigners, 32.5 percent of the total. The official overcrowding rate was, therefore, 120.2 percent, even if we know that, then as now, the real number of places available was about 4,000 less which meant that the overcrowding rate was about 130 percent. But even if we take the official rate, in places like Taranto or Como, it was higher than 195 percent. [. . .] Italian prisons are among the most crowded in Europe, second only to those in Belgium" (p. 11). The report also points out that some of the regions more seriously struck by the epidemic were also those with the highest levels of overcrowding (Lombardy 140%, Liguria 137%, Veneto 135%, Emilia Romagna 130%).

6 Official sources speculate that the cause of death was by overdose after ingesting methadone and drug poisoning.

7 This is a non-juridical, collegial, and independent authority that oversees all forms of deprivation of freedom. In Italy, it was set up by Law Decree No. 146 del 2013.

8 In general, these measures were effective in limiting infection and death among the prisoners (211 infections and 4 deaths on May 15) and penitentiary workers (320 infections and 4 deaths on May 15) (Fiandaca 2020).

9 On May 15, there were 52,679 people in prison compared to 61,230 on February 29.

10 These include house arrest, that is, the chance to serve time, or part of it, in your own home; probation at social services as part of a programme which includes the obligation to work, voluntary activities, specific rules, treatment in the case of addictions, and periodical meetings with social workers; partial freedom, on the basis of which the prisoner leaves prison during the day to go to work; and suspension of proceedings with probation in exchange for observing a programme that includes a series of activities.

11 As an exception to paragraphs 1, 2 and 4 of art. 1 Law 199/2010, article 123 of Decree Law no. 18 of March 17, 2020, allowed condemned convicts with no more than eighteen months still to serve to request, by June 30, 2020, to finish the time in their own homes or another public or private place of care. This measure was denied to prisoners convicted of some categories of crime or who had participated in riots; moreover, it foresaw applying electronic control devices for prisoners with more than six months still to serve.

12 Hard prison regime is a detention regime featuring solitary confinement and special surveillance. Governed by article 41 bis of Law no. 663 of 1986, it was introduced in 1992 during a period of organized crime massacres which caused the death of leading anti-mafia figures such as the two judges, Giovanni Falcone and Paolo Borsellino. The main aim of 41 bis is to prevent mafia bosses from continuing to give orders from prison and its significance is therefore hard to dispute.

13 According to paragraph 3 of article 27 of the Constitution: "Punishments cannot consist of treatments contrary to the sense of humanity and must tend towards re-educating the convict."

14 The most emblematic example is at Riace, a town in Calabria that reacted to the risk of depopulation by transforming itself into a hospitality town for men, women, and children from all over the world. The experience in Riace and other Italian municipalities encouraged the creation of the Protection System for Asylum Seekers and Refugees (SPRAR), a nationwide system founded in collaboration between the state and local authorities. SPRAR was significantly depowered by the Northern League and 5 Star Movement government between 2018 and 2019.

15 Currently, the only way to access legal immigrant status in Italy is to obtain an international protection permit or marry an Italian citizen.

16 Furthermore, during the pandemic, large-scale distribution recorded a 10 percent increase in sales with peaks of 30 percent (Mediobanca 2020).

Chapter 8

1 https://www.facebook.com/donatella.dellaporta. Not all "smart work" is "middle class" and not all "middle class" work can be done at home.
2 November 11, 2020. Available at: https://www.worldometers.info/coronavirus/
3 We thank students in the University of Malta MA Adult Education class ACA5001 for this point.
4 This section on higher education draws on material from Mayo (2020b).
5 These include higher education institutions connected with social movements such as the Escola Nacional Florestan Fernandes, connected with the Landless peasant movement (MST) in Brazil, and the UNITIERRA in Chiapas, Mexico.
6 Electronic exchanges with one of the present authors during the Covid-19 lockdown.

Chapter 9

1 The text in the social network resources translate: "What is reproductive work? The activities that sustain life. That is, taking care of home and family. This work has been historically the responsibility of women, and contrary to productive work (goods and services), it is not paid, even as it is fundamental for the whole society. #TeacherMay1st"; "We women teachers also have children who do not attend school due to Covid-19 like everyone else. This implies that besides teaching work we must do care and reproductive work. #TeacherMay1st"; "Women are 73% of the teaching force. Women are 99% of early childhood educators. Women are 94.5% of special education teachers. #TeacherMay1st"; "Telework. 56% of women, 36% of men feel they work more at home. #TeacherMay1st." Images available at the following links: https://www.facebook.com/redofem/photos/3922052261168333; https://www.facebook.com/redofem/photos/3922052231168336
  https://www.facebook.com/redofem/photos/3922052187835007
  https://www.facebook.com/redofem/photos/3922052167835009
2 Examples of MUD's social media resources translate: "The police started shooting and Pedro got two shots of rubber buckshot in his leg. While he was trying to stand up, he was captured by five or seven unidentified police agents that hit him and kicked him in his head and different parts of his body." Image available at https://www.facebook.com/MUDNacional/photos/3389237457800546
3 The flyer is available at https://www.facebook.com/MUDNacional/photos/3088779671179661
  The text in the flyer translates: "Role of the school during the pandemic: containment and organization. Voices and experiences from the urban and rural. Participants [names of participants]. Movement for teacher unity."

4   The text in the social media resources translates: "Schools are not daycare for their businesses." Image available at https://www.facebook.com/redofem/photos/461441 3848598834

5   The text in the social media resources translates: "We will not return to classes until the danger is over." Image available at: https://www.facebook.com/MUDNacional/ photos/a.247857871938536/3052331311491164

Chapter 10

1   Whereas international literature and legislation has consecrated the term "indigenous and tribal peoples," also present in Convention 169 of the International Labor Association, we have opted to be coherent with Brazilian terminology and maintain "traditional peoples." This option echoes presidential Decree No. 6,040/2007, which defines traditional peoples as "culturally different groups which recognize themselves as such and have their own forms of social organization, occupying and using territories and natural resources as a condition for their cultural, social, religious, ancestral and economic reproduction with the aid of knowledge, innovations and practices created and transmitted by tradition."

Chapter 11

1   Text editor.

2   The term, usually translated as "the good living" or "living well," draws from indigenous terms such as "*sumak kawsay*" (Ecuador), "*suma qamaña*" (Bolivia), "*nhandereko*" (Guarani), "*shiir waras*" (Ashuar), and "*küme mongen*" (Mapuche). It represents the proposal of a substantial alternative to development, based on traditional indigenous values concerning nature and community, as well as on Western critical thought about the environment, gender, and care. (Gudynas 2015).

3   "*Demarcação já*" has been an increasingly popular slogan, repeated by indigenous activists and allies throughout Brazil in the last few years. It intends to raise public attention to the need to grant the rights of indigenous peoples to their lands, which is recognized by the Brazilian constitution.

4   Catu Valley—or *Vale do Catu*—is officially written with a "c" because of earlier transliterations of the Tupi word for "good," which today is spelled *katu*.

5   Cunhaú means Women's River in Tupi.

6   According to the official historiography of Rio Grande do Norte, the Massacre of Cunhaú was the assassination of Portuguese settlers allegedly attributed to an

alliance between the indigenous peoples and the Dutch. However, the indigenous peoples of Rio Grande do Norte stand by an alternative version of this story, according to which not only did they not participate in the massacre, but also they were the actual victims, because they were persecuted and banned from the Cunhaú region.

7 Indigenous family group living in the João Câmara (RN) municipality.

8 Multiethnic peoples composed of indigenous from different groups of the Macro Jê language family, who define themselves as the Caboclos from Assu Valley (Vale do Assu).

9 Important Brazilian historian, anthropologist, lawyer, journalist, and folklorist.

10 Native fruit of the *mangabeira* or the *mangaba* tree (*Hancornia speciosa*).

11 Also known as *batiputá ou jabutapitá*, it is a native fruit of Brazil (*Ourotea parviflora*).

12 Woodland areas that underwent a slash-and-burn process.

13 Also popularly known as *coaçu* or *pajeú*, it is a plant of the *Polygonaceae* family, native to Atlantic Forest.

14 This ecumenical event is celebrated every on November 1 by the indigenous peoples of Rio Grande do Norte. For a long time it ceased to happen, but was recreated by Chief Luiz Katu in 2002 as a tribute to the resistance of traditional peoples, family farming, and indigenous culture.

15 "Tupã" is the Tupi term for God.

16 The word "*pajé*," from the Tupi language, is used as a general term to identify the guardians of religious, natural, and medical knowledge in ethnicities from Brazil, similarly to the use of shaman in North America.

17 Encantados—the Portuguese word for "enchanted" or "charmed"—represents spiritual beings in several indigenous and African-Brazilian religious traditions. They are usually connected to ancestry and to nature.

18 This was the main Catholic mission in the state of Rio Grande do Norte.

19 The area, located in the state of Rio Grande do Norte, encompasses the cities of Canguaretama, Spirit Santo, Goianinha, and Pedro Velho.

20 Quilombolas—or maroon communities—are traditional Brazilian populations who descend from African people who settled in communities to escape slavery.

21 A community located in the city of Tibaú do Sul (Rio Grande do Norte).

22 The elders, the grandparents, the guardians of wisdom in Guarani villages.

23 The white, the non-indigenous.

24 The Guarani way of life.

25 Brazilian President Jair Messias Bolsonaro, elected in October 2018.

26 The indigenous term means "land of the palm trees."

References

Adichie, C. N. (2009). "The Danger of a Single Story," *TEDGlobal*, July. Available online: https://www.ted.com/talks/chimamanda_ngozi_adichie_the_danger_of_a_single_story (accessed October 31, 2020).

Agamben, G. (2020). "Lo stato di eccezione provocato da un'emergenza immotivata," *Il Manifesto*, 26 February: 15.

Almeida, F. (2021). "Os 60 bebês do Amazonas: retrato de um futuro asfixiado" [The 60 babies from Amazonas: portrait of a asphyxiated future], *Outras Palavras*, January 23, 2021. Available at https://outraspalavras.net/crise-brasileira/os-60-bebes-do-amazonas-retrato-de-um-futuro-asfixiado/?fbclid=IwAR2F_60luTP1CCO0I4FtusCjAWDiRAhTnPdWCCArKhmkjwOFg8kpEeyrj8o

Antigone (2020). *Il carcere al tempo del Coronavirus. XVI Rapporto di Antigone sulle condizioni di detenzione*. Roma: associazione Antigone. Available online: https://www.antigone.it/upload/ANTIGONE_2020_XVIRAPPORTO%202.pdf (accessed November 6, 2020).

Apple, M. W. (2004). *Ideology and the Curriculum*, 3rd ed. New York and London: Routledge-Falmer.

Apple, M. W. (2020). "Critical Analysis and Discussion of the Covid-19 Crisis," *Global Thursday Webinar*, University of Ankara, July 9. Available online: https://www.youtube.com/watch?v=Xv0HhB_3gNQ (accessed November 14, 2020).

Arendt, H. (1978). *The Life of the Mind*. New York: Harcourt.

Arenilla, S. L. (2015). "Violations to the Principle of Non-Refoulement Under the Asylum Policy of the United States," *Anuario Mexicano de Derecho Internacional*, 15(1): 283–322. https://doi.org/https://doi.org/10.1016/j.amdi.2014.09.005

Aristovnik, A., Kerzic, D., Ravselj, D., Tomazevic, N., and Umek, L. (2020). "Impacts of the COVID-19 Pandemic on Life of Higher Education Students: A Global Perspective," *Sustainability 2020*, 12: 8438.

Ataiants, J., Cohen, C., Riley, A. H., Tellez Lieberman, J., Reidy, M. C., and Chilton, M. (2018). "Unaccompanied Children at the United States Border, a Human Rights Crisis That Can be Addressed with Policy Change," *Journal of Immigrant and Minority Health*, 20(4): 1000–10. https://doi.org/10.1007/s10903-017-0577-5

Baldwin, J. (2007). *Giovanni's Room*. New York: Penguin Classics.

Bell, K. and Green, J. (2016). "On the Perils of Invoking Neoliberalism in Public Health Critique," *Crit Public Health*, 26: 239–43.

Benjamin, W. (1987). "Teses sobre o conceito de história," in *Obras escolhidas. Vol. 1. Magia e técnica, arte e política. Ensaios sobre literatura e história da cultura*, 222–32. São Paulo: Brasiliense.

Biblioteca del Congreso Nacional (2020). "Acuerdo Por la Paz Social y la Nueva Constitución," *Biblioteca del congreso Nacional*. Available online: https://www.bcn.cl/procesoconstituyente/detalle_cronograma?id=f_cronograma-1

Booth, R. and Barr, C. (2020). "Black People Four Times more likely to Die from Covid-19, ONS Finds," *The Guardian*, May 7.

Boothman, D. (2017). "Transformismo," in G. Liguori and P. Voza (eds.), *Dicionário gramsciano*. São Paulo: Boitempo.

Borg, C. (2020a). "Analiżi | Il-pandemija żiedet l-abbuż u l-isfruttament fuq il-ħaddiema fl-ekonomija 'informali' daqs qatt qabel" (Analysis| the pandemic has increased abuse and exploitation of workers in the informal economy as never before), *illum*, April 29, 2020 (in Maltese).

Borg, C. (2020b). "Sena Delikata ghas-Sistema Edukattiva" (A Delicate Year for the Education System) *Dossier*, Edition 1, September (in Maltese).

Borg, C. (2020c). "200 Days of Covid. An Educational Perspective," *Malta Today*, September 20, 2020.

Borg, C. and Mayo, P. (2021). "The Lost Generation? Educational Contingency in Viral Times: Malta and Beyond," in *Education, Equality and Justice in the New Normal: Global Responses to the Pandemic*. London: Bloomsbury.

Borg, C., Mayo, P., and Raykov, M. (2016). *Adult Learning in Malta. Insights into Current Participation, Content and Forms of Adult Learning*. Malta: University of Malta.

Bosoer, F. (2020). "Fukuyama do 'fim da história' atualiza diagnóstico em 'modelo 2020,'" *Folha de São Paulo*, July 15. Available online: https://www1.folha.uol.com.br/mundo/2020/07/fukuyama-do-fim-da-historia-atualiza-diagnostico-em-modelo-2020.shtml (accessed August 13, 2020).

Bourdieu, P. (1977). *Outline of a Theory of Practice*. Cambridge: Cambridge University Press.

Brasil de Fato (2017). "Maior greve geral da história do país contou com 40 milhões de brasileiros," *Brasil de Fato*, April 28. Available online: https://www.brasildefato.com.br/2017/04/29/40-milhoes-param-no-pais-ato-em-sp-reune-70-mil-e-termina-com-repressao-da-pm/ (accessed October 31, 2020).

Brasil. Instituto Nacional de Estudos e Pesquisas Educacionais Anísio Teixeira – Inep. (2013). *Censo da Educação Superior 2012: notas estatísticas*. Brasília.

Brasil. Instituto Nacional de Estudos e Pesquisas Educacionais Anísio Teixeira – Inep. (2017). *Censo da Educação Superior 2016: notas estatísticas*. Brasília.

Brasil. Instituto Nacional de Estudos e Pesquisas Educacionais Anísio Teixeira – Inep. (2019). *Censo da Educação Superior 2018: notas estatísticas*. Brasília.

Brito, S., ed. (2020). *Por una constitución feminista*. Santiago: Pez espiral.

Butsch, R. (2019). *Screen Culture: A Global History*. London: Polity.

Cabaluz, F. (2019). "Violencia Escolar: Del aula segura al adoctrinamiento ideológico," *Punto de Vista*. Available online: http://www.academia.cl/comunicaciones/columnas/violencia-escolar-de-aula-segura-al-adoctrinamiento-ideologico

Castro, M. (2020). "El ministro Figueroa no está solo: La Moneda se cuadra por el retorno seguro a clases," *El Líbero*, September. Available online: https://ellibero.cl/actualidad/el-ministro-figueroa-no-esta-solo-la-moneda-se-cuadra-por-el-retorno-seguro-a-clases/

CDC (2020). *Order Suspending Introduction of Certain Persons from Countries Where a Communicable Disease Exists*, March 20, 2020. https://www.cdc.gov/quarantine/order-suspending-introduction-certain-persons.html

Center for Disease Control-CDC (March 20, 2020). *Order Suspending Introduction of Certain Persons from Countries Where a Communicable Disease Exists*. https://www.cdc.gov/quarantine/order-suspending-introduction-certain-persons.html

Chomsky, N. (2021). "Why Neoliberal Leaders Who Failed to Protect Their Countries From COVID-19 Must Be Investigated," *Counterpunch*, January 22, 2021. Available at https://www.counterpunch.org/2021/01/22/why-neoliberal-leaders-who-failed-to-protect-their-countries-from-covid-19-must-be-investigated/

Chouhy, C. and Madero-Hernandez, A. (2019). "'Murderers, Rapists, and Bad Hombres': Deconstructing the Immigration-Crime Myths," *Victims & Offenders*, 14(8): 1010–39. https://doi.org/10.1080/15564886.2019.1671283

Colegio de profesoras y profesores de Chile (2020a). "Historia," *Colegio de profesoras y profesores de Chile*. Available online: http://www.colegiodeprofesores.cl/historia/

Colegio de profesoras y profesores de Chile (2020b). "Propuestas para enfrentar la crisis en el sistema de educación en el momento actual de la pandemia," *Colegio de profesoras y profesores de Chile*, May. Available online: https://www.colegiodeprofesores.cl/wp-content/uploads/2020/05/Analisis-y-propuesta-CP-para-la-crisis-covid-19.pdf

Comissão Pastoral da Terra (2020). *Conflitos no campo: Brasil 2019*. Goiânia: Centro de Documentação Dom Tomás Balduíno. Available online: https://www.cptnacional.org.br/component/jdownloads/send/41-conflitos-no-campo-brasil-publicacao/14195-conflitos-no-campo-brasil-2019-web?Itemid=0 (accessed September 5, 2020).

Connell, R. (2019). *The Good University: What Universities Actually Do and Why It's Time for Radical Change*. London and New York: Zed Books.

Cook, J. (2020). "Why Is the World Going to Hell? Netflix's the Social Dilemma Tells only Half the Story," *Jonathon Cook Blog*, September 25. Retrieved from: https://www.jonathan-cook.net/blog/2020-09-25/netflix-social-dilemma/

Cordina, J. P. (2020). "During Pandemic, 1 in 4 Stay Out of School," *Newsbook Portal*. Available online: https://newsbook.com.mt/en/during-pandemic-1-in-4-stay-out-of-school/ (accessed November 11, 2020).

Darder, A. (2017). *Reinventing Paulo Freire: A Pedagogy of Love*. New York: Routledge.

De Sousa Santos, B. (2017). *Decolonising the University: The Challenge of Deep Cognitive Justice*. Newcastle-upon-Tyne: Cambridge Scholars Publishing.

deCook, J. (2020). "Coronavirus and the Radical Right: Conspiracy, Disinformation, and Xenophobia. How Is the Radical Right Using the COVID-19 Pandemic to Advance Their Political Agenda?" *OpenDemocracy*, March 13, 2020. https://www

.opendemocracy.net/en/countering-radical-right/coronavirus-and-radical-right-co nspiracy-disinformation-and-xenophobia/

Deleuze, G. and Guattari, F. (1987). *A Thousand Plateaus: Capitalism and Schizophrenia*, trans. B. Massumi. Minneapolis: University of Minnesota.

Della Porta, D. (2020). "The Pandemic Has Complicated the Class Divide…" (post on Facebook). *Facebook*, March 5, 2020.

Departamento Intersindical de Estatística e Estudos Socioeconômicos (2020). *Estudos e Pesquisas, Balanço das Greves de 2019*. Report number: 93. Available online: https://www.dieese.org.br/balancodasgreves/2019/estPesq93balancoGreves2019. html (accessed September 4, 2020).

Diario Uchile (2019). "Mineduc presenta proyecto de ley para frenar 'adoctrinamiento' en colegios," *Radio Universidad de Chile*, November. Available online: https://radio .uchile.cl/2019/11/25/mineduc-presenta-proyecto-de-ley-para-frenar-adoctrinam iento-en-colegios/

Dillon, M. and Neal, A. (2008). *Foucault on Politics, Security, and War*, 168. Hampshire: Palgrave Macmillan.

Domedel, A. and Peña y Lillo, M. (2008). *El Mayo de los Pingüinos*. Santiago: Ediciones Radio Universidad de Chile.

Domenici, T. (2020a). "Após uso de robôs, Laureate agora demite professores de EAD," *Agência Pública*, May 13. Available online: https://apublica.org/2020/05/apos-u so-de-robos-laureate-agora-demite-professores-de-ead/ (accessed September 28, 2020).

Domenici, T. (2020b). "'É cruel': professores relatam de aulas on-line com 300 alunos a demissões por pop-up," *Agência Pública*, September 22. Available online: https://ap ublica.org/2020/09/e-cruel-professores-relatam-de-aulas-on-line-com-300-alunos-a -demissoes-por-pop-up/ (accessed September 28, 2020).

Dominijanni, I. (2020). "L'io alterato," *Libreria delle donne di Milano*, May 25. Available online: https://www.libreriadelledonne.it/puntodivista/lio-alterato/ (accessed November 6, 2020).

Dorn, E., Hancock, B., Sarakatsannis, J., and Viruleg, E. (2020). "COVID-19 and Student Learning in the United States: The Hurt Could Last a Lifetime." Available online: https://www.mckinsey.com/industries/public-and-social-sector/our-insights /covid-19-and-student-learning-in-the-united-states-the-hurt-could-last-a-lifetime (accessed November 14, 2020).

Duarte, N. (2001). "As pedagogias do aprender a aprender e algumas ilusões da assim chamada sociedade do conhecimento," *Revista Brasileira de Educação*, (18): 35–40. Available online: https://www.scielo.br/pdf/rbedu/n18/n18a04 (accessed August 25, 2020).

Dussel, E. (1993). *1492 O encobrimento do outro: A origem do "mito da modernidade"*. Petrópolis: Vozes.

Earl, C. (2016). "Doing Pedagogy Publicly: Asserting the Right to the City to Rethink the University," *Open Library of the Humanities*, 2(2): 1–32.

Edling, S. and Macrine, S. L. (2021). *Transnational Feminist Politics, Education and Social Justice: Post Democracy and Post Truth.* London: Bloomsbury Press.

El mostrador (2020). "Organizaciones docentes proponen 'receso pedagógico' en pro de la salud mental en pandemia," *El mostrador*, July. Available online: https://www.elm ostrador.cl/noticias/pais/2020/07/10/organizaciones-docentes-proponen-receso-ped agogico-en-pro-de-la-salud-mental-en-pandemia/?fbclid=IwAR1448zGy1TC_w 9upMUlP0VSpwM86mJ5ado4vyMPfpoMuZcYvhU2G8zQH6I

El Periodista (2019). "Cubillos propone medidas contra 'adoctrinamiento político' en colegios y jardines infantiles," *El Periodista*, November. Available online: https://ww w.elperiodista.cl/cubillos-propone-medidas-contra-adoctrinamiento-politico-en-co legios-y-jardines-infantiles/

Empoli, G. (2019). *Les Ingénieurs du chaos.* Paris: J-C. Lattès,

English, L. and Mayo, P. (2012). *Learning with Adults: A Critical Pedagogical Introduction.* Boston and Leyden: Brill/Sense.

Federici, S. (2017). *Calibã e a bruxa. Mulheres, corpo e acumulação primitiva.* São Paulo: Elefante.

Fernández, M. B., Barrios, I. S., and Lira, A. (2021). "Lessons from Teacher Organizing: Disputing the Meaning of Teaching and Teachers' Work during the Coronavirus Pandemic in Chile," Em: *Education, Equality and Justice in the New Normal: Global Responses to the Pandemic.* London: Bloomsbury.

Ferraz, A. S. (2018). "Quando os trabalhadores param? Reinterpretando a ocorrência de greves no Brasil," *Lua Nova: Revista de Cultura e Política*, (104): 167–200. Available online: http://www.scielo.br/scielo.php?script=sci_arttext&pid=S0102-644520180 00200167&lng=en&nrm=iso (accessed September 15, 2020).

Fiandaca, G. (2020), "Scarcerazioni per motivi di salute, lotta alla mafia e opinione pubblica," *Sistema penale*, May 19. Available online: https://www.sistemapenale.it/it/ opinioni/fiandaca-scarcerazioni-per-motivi-di-salute-lotta-alla-mafia-e-opinione-pu bblica (accessed November 6, 2020).

Figueroa, F. (2013). *Llegamos para quedarnos: Crónicas de la revuelta estudiantil.* Santiago: LOM.

Fontes, V. (2020). "Tempos atrozes: fios históricos da dominação de classes no Brasil e contradições," *Esquerda Online*, May 23. Available online: https://esquerdaonline.co m.br/2020/05/23/tempos-atrozes-fios-historicos-da-dominacao-de-classes-no-brasil -e-contradicoes/ (accessed September 20, 2020).

Fontes, V. and Miranda, A. (2014), "Pensamento crítico e as populações do campo, da floresta, das águas e... das cidades," *Tempus, Actas de Saúde Coletiva*, 8(2): 305–16.

Foucault, M. (1926–1984 (1978)). *The History of Sexuality.* New York: Pantheon Books.

Foucault, M. (2003). *Abnormal: Lectures at the Collège de France, 1974–1975*, trans. Graham Burchell, English series editor Arnold I. Davidson, 213. New York: Picador.

Foucault, M. (2007). "Global Society Must Be Defended: Biopolitics Without Boundaries," *Social Text 91*, 25(2): 57.

Freire, P. (1970). *Pedagogy of the Oppressed.* New York: Seabury.

Freire, P. (1973). *Education for Critical Consciousness.* New York: Seabury.

Freire, P. (1994). *Pedagogy of Hope: Reliving Pedagogy of the Oppressed.* New York and London: Continuum.

Freire, P. (1996). *Letters to Cristina. Reflection on my Life and Work.* New York and London: Routledge.

Freire, P. (1998). *Pedagogy of Freedom: Ethics, Democracy, and Civic Courage.* Lanham: Rowman & Littlefield.

Freire, P. (2001). "Carta de Paulo Freire aos professores," *Estudos Avançados,* 15(42): 259–68.

Freire, A. and Macedo, D. (1998). *The Paulo Freire Reader.* New York: Continuum.

Friedman, M. (1970). "The Social Responsibility of Business Is to Increase Its Profits," *The New York Times Magazine,* September 13.

Fundación Sol (2011). "El desalojo de la educación pública," *Serie: Ideas para el buen vivir,* Fundación Sol. Available online: https://fundacionsol.cl/cl_luzit_herramientas/static/wp-content/uploads/2011/12/Ideas-1-Institucionalidad-y-Desarrollo.pdf

Galeano, E. (1999). *Memórias de fogo: as caras e as máscaras.* Porto Alegre: L&PM.

Geerlings, L. and Lundberg, A. (2018). "Global Discourses and Power/knowledge: Theoretical Reflections on Futures of Higher Education during the Rise of Asia," *Asia Pacific Journal of Education,* 38(2): 229–40.

Geremias, O. F. B. C. (2012). "*SHIVA, Vandana. Monoculturas da Mente: perspectivas da biodiversidade e da biotecnologia.* São Paulo: Gaia, 2003," *Agrária,* 0(17): 132–7.

Geyer, M. (1989). "The Militarization of Europe, 1914–1945," in J. R. Gillis (ed.), *Militarization of the Western World.* New Brunswick: Rutgers University Press.

Giroux, H. A. (2019). *The Terror of the Unforeseen.* Los Angeles: Los Angeles Review of Books.

Giroux, H. A. (2020a). "An Interview with Henry. A. Giroux on Critical Issues in Education," *Global Thursday Webinars,* Ankara. Available online https://www.youtube.com/watch?v=tRA3ZMbPaDc&fbclid=IwAR3EVVTEoVqQ8jUWsEM-gqwpvCNLrXB9juxTt3JWeRctas5UOBRb-fm0jCs (accessed August 11, 2020).

Giroux, H. A. (2020b). *On Critical Pedagogy.* London: Bloomsbury Publishing.

Giroux, H. A. (2021). *Race, Politics, and Pandemic Pedagogy: Education in a Time of Crisis.* New York and London: Bloomsbury Academic.

Giroux, H. A. and Filippakou, O. (2021). "Militarization in a Time of Pandemic Crisis," in *Education, Equality and Justice in the New Normal: Global Responses to the Pandemic.* London: Bloomsbury.

Goldstein, R. A., Macrine, S., and Chesky, Z. N. (2011). "Welcome to the 'new normal': The News Media and Neoliberal Reforming Education," *Journal of Inquiry & Action in Education,* 4(1): 6.

González, Á., Fernández, M. B., Pino-Yancovic, M., and Madrid, R. (2020). "Teaching in the Pandemic: Reconceptualizing Chilean Educators' Professionalism Now and for the Future," *Journal of Professional Capital and Community,* 5(3/4): 265–72. https://doi.org/10.1108/JPCC-06-2020-0043

González, E., Olivares, R., and Salinas, I. (2020). "¿Retorno gradual a clases? Cuando no se conoce la escuela que se tiene," *El mostrador*, April. Available online: https://www .elmostrador.cl/noticias/opinion/2020/04/29/retorno-gradual-a-clases-cuando-no-se -conoce-la-escuela-que-se-tiene/

González, L. E. (2015). *Arriba Profes de Chile: De la precarización neoliberal a la organización docente*. Santiago: América en Movimiento.

Gonzalez, T., de la Ruba, M. A., Hincz, K. P., Comas-Lopez, M., Subirats, L., Fort, S., and Sacha, G. M. (2020). "Influence of COVID-19 Confinement on Students" Performance in Higher Education," *Plos One*, 15(10): e0239490.

Goodman, A. and Chomsky, N. (2021). "Chomsky on Trump's Disastrous Coronavirus Response, Bernie Sanders & What Gives Him Hope," in *Education, Equality and Justice in the New Normal: Global Responses to the Pandemic*. London: Bloomsbury.

Goodman, P. (2020). One Vaccine Side Effect: Global Economic Inequality in *The New York Times* (December 25). Retrieved from: https://www.nytimes.com/2020/12/25/ business/coronavirus-vaccines-global-economy.html

Gorman, A. (2021). *The Hill We Climb: An Inaugural Poem for The Country*. Available at https://www.theamandagorman.com/

Gramsci, A. (2007). *1891–1937 Cadernos do cárcere*, volume 3, trans. C. N. Coutinho. Rio de Janeiro: Civilização Brasileira.

Grondin, J. (2012). *Hermenêutica*. São Paulo: Parábola Editorial.

Gudynas, E. (2015). "Buen vivir," in G. D'Alisa, F. Demaria and G. Kallis (eds.), *Degrowth: Vocabulary for a New Era*, 201–4. New York and London: Routledge.

Guerrero, J. (2020). *Hatemonger: Stephen Miller, Donald Trump, and the White Nationalist Agenda*. New York: HarperCollins US.

Guterres, A. (2005). "UNHCR-United Nations High Commissioner for Refugees [speech]." The UN Refugee Agency. http://www.unhcr.org/cgi-bin/texis/vtx/events/ opendoc.htm?tbl=EVENTS&id=42afe751

Harvey, D. (2005). *A Brief History of Neoliberalism*. New York: Oxford University Press.

Hathaway, J. A. (2005). *The Rights of Refugees Under International Law*, 261. Cambridge University Press. ISBN: 978-0-521-83494-0. https://assets.cambridge.org/97805218 /34940/frontmatter/9780521834940_frontmatter.pdf

Haywood, M. (2007). "Applying Post-critical Approaches to Refugee-Centred Education," MA (Applied Language Studies), AUT University (unpublished). http:// aut.researchgateway.ac.nz/bitstream/handle/10292/221/HaywardM.pdf?sequence=2

Hobsbawn, E. (1984). *A invenção das tradições*. Petrópolis: Paz e Terra.

hooks, b. (2008). Interview in *Talking about Revolution*. Cambridge, MA: Southend Press.

International Rescue Committee (2020). "What does a Joe Biden Presidency Mean for Refugees and Asylum Seekers?" *IRC*, November, 2020. https://www.rescue.org/ar ticle/what-does-joe-biden-presidency-mean-refugees-and-asylum-seekers

Kanno-Youngs, Z., and Shear, M. D. (2020). "Trump Virtually Cuts Off Refugees as He Unleashes a Tirade on Immigrants," *New York Times*, October 1, 2020: 16–21. https:/ /www.nytimes.com/2020/10%20/01/us/politics/trump-refugees.html

Katu, L., Sánchez, C., and D. R. Camargo (2021). "Resisting and Re-existing on Earth: Politics for Hope and 'buen vivir,'" in *Education, Equality and Justice in the New Normal: Global Responses to the Pandemic*. London: Bloomsbury.

Klein, N. (2020a). "Coronavírus pode construir uma distopia tecnológica," *The Intercept*, May 13. Available online: https://theintercept.com/2020/05/13/coronavirus-governa dor-nova-york-bilionarios-vigilancia/ (accessed October 14, 2020).

Klein, N. (2020b). "Não temos que aceitar voltar ao status quo pré-Covid piorado" [interview by K. Viner], *Carta Maior*, July 15. Available online: https://www .cartamaior.com.br/?/Editoria/Saude/Naomi-Klein-Nao-temos-que-aceitar-voltar -ao-status-quo-pre-Covid-piorado-/43/48154 (accessed October 14, 2020).

Kuhfeld, M., Soland, J., Tarasawa, B., Johnson, A., Ruzek, E., and Liu, J. (2020). "Projecting the Potential Impacts COVID-19 School Closures on Academic Achievement," *Educational Researcher*, October 28. https://doi.org/10.3102 /0013189X20965918

Lakhani, N. (2020). "US using Coronavirus Pandemic to Unlawfully Expel Asylum Seekers, Says UN," *The Guardian*, Friday, April 17, 2020. https://www.theguardian.c om/world/2020/apr/17/us-asylum-seekers-coronavirus-law-un

Lauterpacht, E. and Bethlehem, D. (2003). "The Scope and Content of the Principle of *Non-refoulement: Opinion*," in E. Feller, V. Türk, and F. Nicholson (eds.), *Refugee Protection in International Law: UNHCR's Global Consultations on International Protection*, 193–219. Cambridge: Cambridge University Press.

Leher, R. (2020a), "Guerra cultural e universidade pública: O Future-se é parte da estratégia de silenciamento," in J. Giolo, R. Leher, and V. Sguissardi (eds.), *Future-se: Ataque à autonomia das instituições federais de educação superior e sua sujeição ao mercado*. São Carlos: Diagrama. Available online: https://www.diagramaeditorial. com.br/project/future-se/ (accessed August 30, 2020).

Leher, R. (2020b), "Nas garras da autocracia: interferência governamental na escolha de reitores e liberdade de cátedra," *Carta Maior*, September 21. Available online: https://www.cartamaior.com.br/?%2FEditoria%2FEducacao%2FNas- garras-da-autocracia-interferencia-governamental-na-escolha-de-reitores-e-l iberdade-de-catedra%2F54%2F48786&fbclid=IwAR1V1-ui9Uopya_yPq0pdJ0A yClVnoojXzFO_gwAkvyDtJcbnSa26Aaiexk#.X2ntFwoIhJQ (accessed September 27, 2020).

Leher, R. (2021). "The 'new normal' in Education Is Ultra-neoliberal: In Defense of the Strategy that Breaks with the Time Continuum," in *Education, Equality and Justice in the New Normal: Global Responses to the Pandemic*. London: Bloomsbury.

Loureiro, C. F. B. (2005). "Teoria Crítica," in L. A. Ferraro Junior (ed.), *Encontros e caminhos: Formação de educadoras(es) ambientais e coletivos educadores*, Vol. 1. Brasília: Ministério do Meio Ambiente, Diretoria de Educação Ambiental.

Loureiro, C. F. B. (2007). "Pensamento crítico, tradição marxista e a questão ambiental: Ampliando os debates," in C. F. B. Loureiro (ed.), *A questão ambiental no pensamento crítico: Natureza, trabalho e educação*. Rio de Janeiro: Quartet.

Loureiro, C. F. B. (2021). "Environmental Education: For a Critical Renovation Alongside the Traditional Peoples," in *Education, Equality, and Justice in the New Normal: Global Responses to the Pandemic*. London: Bloomsbury.

Loureiro, C. F. B. and Layrargues, P. P. (2013). "Ecologia política, justiça e educação ambiental crítica: Perspectivas de aliança contra-hegemônica," *Trabalho, Educação e Saúde*, 11(1): 53–71.

Macedo, D. (2006). "Literacy for Stupidification: The Pedagogy of Big Lies," in *Literacies of Power*. New York: Routledge.

Macedo, D. P. and Bartolomé, L. I. (1999). *Dancing with Bigotry: Beyond the Politics of Tolerance*. New York: St. Martin's Press.

Macrine, S. L. (2016). "Pedagogies of Neoliberalism," in S. Springer K. Birch, and J. MacLeavy (eds.), *Handbook of Neoliberalism*, 294–305. New York: New York: Routledge.

Macrine, S. L. (2020). *Critical Pedagogy in Uncertain Times: Hope and Possibilities*, 2nd ed. New York: Palgrave Macmillan. https://link.springer.com/book/10.1007/978-3-030-39808-8

Macrine, S. L. (2021). "Coronavirus Pandemic and the 'Refoulment' of Refugee/Asylum Seekers," in *Education, Equality, and Justice in the New Normal: Global Responses to the Pandemic*. London: Bloomsbury.

Macrine, S. L. and Edling, S. (2021). "The Refugee Crisis is a Feminist Issue," in S. Edling and S. L. Macrine (eds.), *Transnational Feminist Politics, Education and Social Justice: Post-Democracy and Post-Truth*. London: Bloomsbury Publishers.

Marques, L. (2016). *Capitalismo e colapso ambiental*. Campinas: Edunicamp.

Marx, K. (2013). *O capital*, Vol. 1. São Paulo: Boitempo.

Marx, K. and Engels, F. (2007). *A ideologia alemã*. São Paulo: Boitempo.

Mason, S. (2009). "How Does Racism Provide a Metric for Biopolitics of Security?" E-International Relations (www.e-ir.info), July 7, 2009. https://www.e-ir.info/2009/07/07/how-does-racism-provide-a-metric-for-biopolitics-of-security/

Mattos, M. B. (2020). *Governo Bolsonaro: Neofascismo e autocracia burguesa no Brasil*. São Paulo: Usina.

Mavelli, L. (2017). "Governing Populations Through the Humanitarian Government of Refugees: Biopolitical Care and Racism in the European Refugee Crisis," *Review of International Studies*, 43(5): 809–32. https://doi.org/10.1017/S0260210517000110

Mayo, P. (2019). *Higher Education in a Globalising World: Community Engagement and Lifelong Learning*. Manchester: Manchester University Press.

Mayo, P. (2020a). "Higher Education in the Time of Corona," *RSA*, 23 March 2020. Available online: https://www.thersa.org/comment/2020/03/higher-education-in-the-time-of-corona (accessed November 14, 2020).

Mayo, P. (2020b). "The Corona Challenge to Higher Education," *Culture e Studi del Sociale*, 5(1) Special issue: 371–6. Available at: http://www.cussoc.it/index.php/journal/issue/archive (accessed November 14, 2020).

Mayo, P. and Vittoria, P. (2017). *Saggi di pedagogia critica oltre il neoliberismo. Analizzando educatori, lotte e movimenti sociali.* Florence: Società Editrice Fiorentina (In Italian).

McCoy, J. and Somer, M. (2019). "Toward a Theory of Pernicious Polarization and How It Harms Democracies: Comparative Evidence and Possible Remedies," *The ANNALS of the American Academy of Political and Social Science*, 681(1): 234–71. doi:10.1177/0002716218818782

McCoy, T. (2014). How ISIS and other jihadists persuaded thousands of Westerners to fight their war of extremism. *The Washington Post*, pp. 1–6. Retrieved from http://www.washingtonpost.com/news/morning-mix/wp/2014/06/17/how-isis-persuaded-thousands-of-westerners-to-fight-its-war-of-extremism/.

McLaren, P. (2015). *Life in Schools. Critical Pedagogy in the Foundations of Education,* 6th ed. Boulder: Paradigm Publishers.

Mediobanca. (2020). *Osservatorio sulla Gdo italiana e i maggiori operatori stranieri.* Milano: Ricerche e studi Mediobanca. Available online: https://www.mbres.it/sites/default/files/resources/rs_Focus-GDO-2019.pdf (accessed November 6, 2020).

MFWS (Malta Foundation for the Wellbeing of Society). (2020). Unpublished report on a webinar encounter with teachers, parents, administrators, academics and children, May.

Miguel, L. F. (2019). *O colapso da democracia no Brasil: Da Constituição ao golpe de 2016.* São Paulo: Expressão Popular.

Moutinho da Costa, L. (2011). "Territorialidade e racismo ambiental: Elementos para se pensar a educação ambiental crítica em unidades de conservação," *Pesquisa em Educação Ambiental*, 6(1): 101–22.

Movimiento por la Unidad Docente (2020). "Untitled." *Facebook Movimiento por la Unidad Docente*, n.d. Available online: https://www.facebook.com/MUDNacional/

Muschert G. W. (2019). "Book Review: Deep Inequality: Understanding the New Normal and How to Challenge It," *Frontiers in Sociology*, 4(4). https://www.frontiersin.org/articles/10.3389/fsoc.2019.00004/full

Navarrete, A. (2020). *La Primavera Docente: Profesoras y Profesores, un actor en movimiento. Chile 2014–2016.* Concepción: Escaparate.

Neary, M. (2014). "The University and the City: Social Science Centre, Lincoln – Forming the Urban Revolution," in P. Temple (ed.), *The Physical University: Contours of Space and Place in Higher Education*, 203–16. London and New York: Routledge.

Nelson, T. and Habbach, H. (2019). "'If I went back, I would not survive': Asylum Seekers Fleeing Violence in Mexico and Central America," *Physicians for Human Rights*, 1–101. Retrieved from https://phr.org/our-work/resources/asylum-seekers-fleeing-violence-in-mexico-and-central-america/

Nivens, J. (2019). "Tories say There's no Magic Tree Until They Need it for Themselves," *The Daily Record*, August 4. Retrieved from: https://www.nytimes.com/2020/12/25/business/coronavirus-vaccines-global-economy.html https://www.dailyrecord.co.uk/news/politics/tories-say-theres-no-magic-18823902

Orellana, V., ed. (2018). *Entre el Mercado Gratuito y la Educación Pública: Dilemas de la educación chilena actual*. Santiago: LOM.

Oreopoulos, P., von Wachter, T., and Heisz, A. (2012). "The Short- and Long-Term Career Effects of Graduating in a Recession," *American Economic Journal: Applied Economics*, 4(1): 1–29.

Organización Internacional del Trabajo. (2020). *Panorama Laboral en tiempos de la COVID-19. Impactos en el mercado de trabajo y los ingresos en América Latina y el Caribe*. Available online: https://www.ilo.org/wcmsp5/groups/public/---americas/---ro-lima/documents/publication/wcms_749659.pdf (accessed October 31, 2020).

Organization for Economic Co-operation and Development (OECD) (2019). *OECD Future of Education and Skills 2030: OECD Learning Compass 2030*. Report number: 13. Available online: http://www.oecd.org/education/2030-project/contact/OECD_Learning_Compass_2030_Concept_Note_Series.pdf (accessed October 14, 2020).

Palmisano, L. (2017). *Mafia caporale*. Fandango: Roma.

Pegg, D. (2020). "What was Exercise Cygnus and What did It Find?" *The Guardian*, May 7. Retrieved from: https://www.theguardian.com/world/2020/may/07/what-was-exercise-cygnus-and-what-did-it-find

Petras, J. (2014). "Brasil: O capitalismo extrativo e o grande salto para trás," *Tensões Mundiais*, 10(18–19): 311–23.

Pfiffner, James P. (September 17, 2018). "The Lies of Donald Trump: A Taxonomy." Available at SSRN: https://ssrn.com/abstract=3286278 or http://dx.doi.org/10.2139/ssrn.3286278

Postone, M. (2014). *Tempo, trabalho e dominação social: Uma reinterpretação da teoria crítica de Marx*. São Paulo: Boitempo.

Poulantzas, N. (1981). "O Estado, o poder e nós," in E. Balibar et al. (eds.), *O Estado em discussão*. Lisboa: Edições 70.

Puiu, T. (2020). "The story of Poland's secret 'Flying Universities' that gave Men and Women Equal Chance, Marie Curie among them," *ZME Science*, May 5. Available online: https://www.zmescience.com/science/flying-universities-poland/ (accessed November 14, 2020).

Quiñonez, S. A. (2019). 'Rutas para perfilar elecogenoetnocidio afrocolombiano: hacia una conceptualización desde la justicia histórica', *Nómadas*, 50: 93–110.

Ramonet, I. (2020). "La pandemia está estableciendo la crisis del modelo neoliberal" [interview by M. Muñoz], *Attac España*, August 15. Available online: https://attac.es/ignacio-ramonet-la-pandemia-esta-estableciendo-la-crisis-del-modelo-neoliberal/ (accessed September 21, 2020).

Red Docente Feminista (2020). "Las profesoras somos la primera línea de la educación y la cuarentena," *Facebook Red Docente Feminista*, April. Available online: https://www.facebook.com/redofem/posts/3921932764513616?d=m

Rivera, L (2020). "SPLC: Trump's Racist Response to COVID-19 Endangers All Americans, Including Immigrants," *Southern Poverty Law Center*, March 20, 2020.

https://www.splcenter.org/presscenter/splc-trumps-racist-response-COVID-19-endangers-all-americans-including-immigrants

Robbins, C. G (2008). "'Emergency!' Or How to Learn to Live with Neoliberal Globalization," *Policy Futures in Education*, 6(3): 331–50.

Robinson, W. I. (2019). *Into the Tempest. Essays on the New Global Capitalism*. Chicago: Haymarket Books.

Rose, J. and Falk, M. (2020). "Ending 'Asylum As We Know It': Using Pandemic to Expel Migrants, Children At Border," *NPR*, August 6, 2020. https://www.npr.org/2020/08 /06/898937378/end-of-asylum-using-the-pandemic-to-turn-away-migrants-chil dren-seeking-refuge

Roy, A. (2020). "Arundhati Roy: The Pandemic Is a Portal," *FINANCIAL TIMES*, April 3, 2020. https://www.ft.com/content/10d8f5e8-74eb-11ea-95fe-fcd274e920ca

Saad Filho, A. and Moraes, L. (2018). *Brasil; Neoliberalismo versus democracia*. São Paulo: Boitempo.

Santos, B. S. (2016). "Epistemologies of the South and the Future," *The European South*, 1: 17–29.

Saramo, S. (2017). "The Meta-Violence of Trumpism," *European Journal of American Studies*, 12(2). https://doi.org/10.4000/ejas.12129

Sato, M., ed. (2020). *Os condenados da pandemia*. Cuiabá: GPEA-UFMT; Sustentável.

Schalatek, L. (2020). "The Invisible Coronavirus makes Systemic Gender Inequalities and Injustices Visible," *Heinrich-Böll-Stiftung*, April 30, 2020. https://us.boell.org/en/2020/0 4/30/invisible-coronavirus-makes-systemic-gender-inequalities-and-injustices-visible

Sides, J., Tesler, M., and Vavreck, L. (2018). *Identity Crisis: The 2016 Presidential Campaign and the Battle for the Meaning of America*, I–Vi. Princeton and Oxford: Princeton University Press. doi:10.2307/j.ctvc77mmb.1

Simet, L. (2020). "Fault Lines Laid Bare," *Human Rights Watch*, October 26, 2020. https:/ /www.hrw.org/news/2020/10/26/fault-lines-laid-bare#

Simon, R. I. (1992). *Teaching against the Grain: Texts for a Pedagogy of Possibility*. Toronto: OISE Press.

Simonsen, E. (2012). *La mala educación: Historia de la revolución escolar*. Santiago: Debate.

Slowey, K. (2020). "Border Wall Construction Continues with Additional Contract for $1.2B Project," *Construction Drive*, March 26, 2020. https://www.constructiondive .com/news/border-wall-construction-continues-with-additional-contract-for-12b -proje/574917/

Spathopoulou, A., Carastathis, A., and Tsilimpounidi, M. (2020). "'Vulnerable Refugees' and 'Voluntary Deportations': Performing the Hotspot, Embodying Its Violence," *Geopolitics*, 1–27. https://doi.org/10.1080/14650045.2020.1772237

Sullivan, H. (2021). "South Africa Paying more than Double EU Prices for Oxford Vaccine," *The Guardian*, January 22. Retrieved from: https://www.theguardian.com /world/2021/jan/22/south-africa-paying-more-than-double-eu-price-for-oxford-as trazeneca-vaccine

Surian, A. (2001). *L'educazione interculturale in Europa*. EMI: Bologna.

Tarlau, R. (2019). *Occupying Schools, Occupying Land: How the Landless Workers Movement Transformed Brazilian Education.* Oxford and New York: Oxford University Press.

Tarnoff, B. (2020). "As vozes do Vale do Silício além dos CEOs: Entrevista com Ben Tarnoff" [interview by DigiLabour], *DigiLabour*, September 27. Available online: https://digilabour.com.br/2020/09/27/organizacao-dos-trabalhadores-de-tecnologia -entrevista-com-ben-tarnoff/ (accessed September 29, 2020).

Thielemann, L. (2016). *La anomalía social de la transición: Movimiento estudiantil e izquierda universitaria en el Chile de los noventa (1987–2000).* Santiago: Editorial Tiempo Robado.

Thorsten, H., Schmidt, P., and Heller, S. M. (2019). *Social Justice in the EU and OECD: Index Report 2019.* Gütersloh: Bertelsmann Stiftung.

Tribunal de Contas da União. (2017). TC 010.471/2017-0. Available online: http:// www.semesb.com.br/wp-content/uploads/2018/06/010.4712017-0-MEC-INEP.pdf (accessed October 31, 2020).

Trilling, D. (2020). "Migrants Aren't Spreading Coronavirus—but Nationalists Are Blaming Them Anyway," *The Guardian*, February 20. Retrieved from: https://www .theguardian.com/commentisfree/2020/feb/28/coronavirus-outbreak-migrants-b lamed-italy-matteo-salvini-marine-le-pen

Tsiakalos, G., Malichudis, S., and Papangeli, I. (2021). "Xenophobic Europe: Racist Policy Towards Refugees," in *Education, Equality, and Justice in the New Normal: Global Responses to the Pandemic.* London: Bloomsbury.

U.N. Committee Against Torture. (2018). *General Comment No. 4 on the Implementation of Article 3 of the Convention in the Context of Article 22* (September 4, 2018). U.N. Doc. CAT/C/GC/4, ¶ 9.

U.N. Human Rights Committee. (2001). *General Comment No. 29: Article 4: Derogations during a State of Emergency* (August 31, 2001). U.N. Doc. CCPR/C/21/Rev.1/Add.11, ¶ 7.

U.N. Human Rights Committee. (1992). *General Comment No. 20: Article 7 on the Prohibition of Torture, or Other Cruel, Inhuman or Degrading Treatment or Punishment* (March 10, 1992). U.N. Doc. HRI/GEN/1/Rev.9 (Vol. I).

United Nations. (2020). *#LeadTheNewNormal.* Available online: https://www.un.org/y outhenvoy/2020/06/leadthenewnormal/ (accessed October 31, 2020).

U.N.T.S. (1990). Depositary, Status of Treaties – Convention on the Rights of the Child. https://treaties.un.org/Pages/ViewDetails.aspx?src=IND&mtdsg_no=IV-11&chapter =4&clang=_en.

Valente, R. (2020). "Ação sigilosa do governo mira professores e policiais antifascistas," *UOL*, July 24. Available online: https://noticias.uol.com.br/colunas/rubens-valente /2020/07/24/ministerio-justica-governo-bolsonaro-antifascistas.htm (accessed October 14, 2020).

Valezuela, X. (2020). "Vacaciones en claustro y futura vuelta a clases: cómo facilitar el proceso a los niños," *Diario Concepción*, April. Available online: https://www.dia

rioconcepcion.cl/ciudad/2020/04/04/vacaciones-en-claustro-y-futura-vuelta-a-clas
es-como-facilitar-el-proceso-a-los-ninos.html

Verger, A., Fontdevila, C., and Zancajo, A. (2016). *The Privatization of Education: A Political Economy of Global Education Reform*. New York: Teachers College Press.

Vittoria, P. and Muraca, M. (2021). "Neoliberal Recrudescence Versus Radical Transformation of the Reality in Italy: What and Why Must We Learn from the Coronavirus Pandemic?," in *Education, Equality and Justice in the New Normal: Global Responses to the Pandemic*. London: Bloomsbury.

Vittoria, P. (2020a). *Educare a distanza: tre conversazione su Radio, Tv e Web con Marino Sinibaldi, Roberto Farnè, Simone Pieranni*. Marietti Editore E-book.

Vittoria, P. (2020b). "La prossima sfida sarà la 'didattica a vicinanza,'" April 04, 2020. https://ilmanifesto.it/la-nuova-sfida-sara-la-didattica-a-vicinanza/

Vittoria, P. (2020c). "Scuola non è mai troppo tardi. Intervista a Roberto Farnè," September 14, 2020. https://ilmanifesto.it/scuola-non-e-mai-troppo-tardi/

Walcott, R. (2020). "During the Coronavirus, Academics have Found Themselves in a Crisis of their Work," *Macleans.ca*, April 15. Available online. https://www.macleans .ca/opinion/during-the-coronavirus-academics-have-found-themselves-in-a-crisis -of-their-work/?fbclid=IwAR3tTWzo41aA1cD87W0Ge-fP_ZnV4JVfbdSzQabT3L -P1xZNJr1sBLhFgDk (accessed November 14, 2020).

Walicek, T. (2021). "Cities are Razing Homeless Encampments despite Record Cold Weather and COVID," *Truthout*, February 20. Retrieved from: https://truthout.org/ articles/cities-are-razing-homeless-encampments-despite-record-cold-weather-and -Covid/?eType=EmailBlastContent&eId=07db2f91-2b7c-41c4-b913-e41b2096554f

Wallace, R., Liebman, A., Chaves, L. F., and Wallace, R. (2020). "COVID-19 and Circuits of Capital," *Monthly Review*, May. https://monthlyreview.org/2020/05/01/ Covid-19-and-circuits-of-capital/#en38backlink

World Health Organization. (2005). "International Health Regulations," *Arts*, 3(1), 3(4): 32, and 43.

Wright, E.O., Becker, U., Brenner, J., Burawoy, M., Burris,V., Carchedi, G., Marshall, G., Meiksins, P.F., Rose, D., Stinchcombe, A. and Van Parijs, P. (1989). *The Debate on Classes*. London: Verso.

Wysong, E. and Perrucci, R. (2017). *Deep Inequality: Understanding the New Normal and How to Challenge It*. Lanham: Rowman & Littlefield.

Zambrano, O. (2020). Personal correspondence, March 20.

Zerán, F. (2018). *Mayo Feminista. La rebelión contra el patriarcado*. Santiago: LOM.

Zheng, J. (2020). "Pandemic, Emergency Power, and Implications on the Right to Seek Asylum," *American Journal of International Law (AJIL)*, 24(13). https://www.asil.org /insights/volume/24/issue/13/pandemic-emergency-power-and-implications-right -seek-asylum#_edn36

Žižek, S. (2020). *PANDEMIC! Covid-19shakes the World*. New York: Or Books.

Index